The Transforming God

The Transforming God

An Interpretation of Suffering and Evil

TYRON INBODY

Westminster John Knox Press
Louisville, Kentucky

To my wife and sons,
Fran, Mark, and David

Scripture quotations from the New Revised Standard Version
of the Bible are copyright © 1989 by the Division of Christian Education
of the National Council of the Churches of Christ in the U.S.A.
and are used by permission.

Book design by Jennifer K. Cox
Cover design by Pamela Poll
Cover illustration: Michelangelo Buonarroti. Last Judgment.
Sistine Chapel, Vatican Palace, Vatican State.

First edition
Published by Westminster John Knox Press
Louisville, Kentucky

This book is printed on acid-free paper that meets the
American National Standards Institute Z39.48 standard. ∞

PRINTED IN THE UNITED STATES OF AMERICA
97 98 99 00 01 02 03 04 05 06 — 10 9 8 7 6 5 4 3 2 1

Library of Congress Cataloging-in-Publication Data

Inbody, Tyron.
   The transforming God : an interpretation of suffering and evil /
Tyron Inbody. — 1st ed.
      p.   cm.
   Includes bibliographical references and index.
   ISBN 0-664-25711-9 (alk. paper)
   1. Suffering—Religious aspects—Christianity.   2. Theodicy.
I. Title.
BT732.7.I55   1997
231′.8—dc21   96-37844

Contents

Introduction

≠ "Evil's Back," the editor of the *New York Times Magazine* announced on the cover of a June 1995 issue of the Sunday magazine, followed inside by a weighty article by contributing editor Ron Rosenbaum titled "Staring into the Heart of the Heart of Darkness." Four years earlier, during the same month, the editors of *Time* magazine printed on the cover in large five-inch letters the word "Evil," under which they posed the question: "Does it exist—or do bad things just happen?" About a month before Rosenbaum's article ran in the *New York Times Magazine,* the *New Yorker* magazine published another notable article of his titled "Explaining Hitler." Radical evil has reentered the consciousness of many thoughtful people at the end of the twentieth century, a century of violence which has unleashed not only extreme suffering but also confusion about how or whether one can explain radical evil in our postmodern world. Radical suffering, the suffering both of individuals and of groups, has become a major preoccupation of many sensitive people today.

Although I reject the sweeping claim that theology is nothing but autobiography, I equally insist that theology is never done apart from a particular context, for a particular situation, with a specific set of questions in mind. There is no timeless or universal theology. Theologians never write apart from the deep formations and formulations of their own life experience. Even though a reader cannot read biography out of a theology text, a reader, nevertheless, cannot understand the theology—what motivates the theologians and why they say what they do—apart from the social setting and personal experiences of the theologian. Agendas emerge out of social and personal realities. This is especially true for any project in theodicy.

Why am I interested in theodicy, and why do I offer a contribution to the increasing list of books on suffering and evil that have appeared in the last quarter of the century? To a significant extent my historical and personal experiences have been very "traditional," if that term can apply to anyone's experience at the end of the twentieth century. I grew up in an apparently "intact" two-parent, four-children, post–World War II family in northern Indiana. The movie that represents my childhood experience with un-canny insight is *A Christmas Story;* my adolescence and early adulthood are cap-tured in *The Graduate* and *American Graffiti.*

I have been among the most fortunate of those anywhere whose life spans the second half of the twentieth century. My life pattern has been the dream of many members of the dominant culture—a small-town grade school and high school education, a private liberal arts college degree, a Ph.D. from one of the world's greatest graduate schools, one marriage and two children, a rel-atively successful career as a white male professor in a small college and a de-nominational seminary, and no debilitating life losses even into middle age. I vividly recall near the beginning of my project attending a Christmas party at my wife's school. I was asked what I was working on now and answered that I was working on a book on suffering as a theological problem. No one could fathom why I would be interested in such a depressing topic, and I soon de-spaired in trying to explain myself.

In another sense, however, my life experiences, though not paradigmatic, are, I think, at least representative of an encounter with suffering and evil by many white, middle-class Americans in the twentieth century. My life spans more than half the century; I am a product of all the ambiguity of the role played by the United States in the world in the twentieth century. My earliest recollections of a world beyond my family are of the end of World War II—the car horns honking on the streets of Goshen, Indiana, the day the war ended. I am a pre–baby boomer, and so my view of history and the world is shaped as much by that war as by Vietnam. I was shaped more by the "agen-daless" generation of "Happy Days" than by World War II or Vietnam, although the latter shook me to my core. The promise of modernity, most especially of the dispassionate reason of the Enlightenment and its benefits, evaporated into the dust heap of history. My grade school and high school teachers had cele-brated the promises and achievements of science, technology, industry, and democracy. That optimism continued to be conveyed in the courses I took in college. But even then I knew in my bones there was a vast gulf between the promise of modernity and the reality of historical experience in the twentieth century. Increasingly I experienced the twentieth century as a century of vio-lence. From high school years when I discovered the Holocaust and Hiroshima to the present, I have developed an inordinate rage against the injustices of life in our century, originally growing out of my awareness of the violence of war, and then against the violence and abuses of racism and sexism as they have become more apparent to me.

A shadow has been cast not only over twentieth-century optimism but also over my belief in the all-good and all-powerful God I was taught to believe in in the churches of my childhood and adolescence. Although offense could arise within anyone with any moral sensitivities, such anger was exacerbated for me because of the great cognitive dissonance between the kind of God I was taught in church school and sermons and hymns and the overwhelming realities of injustice and suffering I saw in the world. To this day I occasionally have been tempted to hang a copy of Edvard Munch's "The Scream" in my office, but have consistently resisted the impulse. The closest I ever came was hanging a large copy of Picasso's "Guernica" in my office when I taught college, and it turned out to be an offense to several of my students. Something had to give in the face of the incongruity between my experience and my beliefs. I could neither overcome my moral outrage nor give up confidence in some kind of God in the midst of all this suffering and evil. A theologian was being born in those early years; the seeds of this book were planted many years ago.

At the same time my experiences included a significant personal encounter with a kind of suffering typical of many middle-class Americans in the twentieth century. My family of origin was not nearly as intact as I thought it was at the time and as outsiders thought it was. I know nothing of the abuse that so many families know and admit today. Nevertheless, my family was somewhat dysfunctional, to use a talk-show term. My three sisters and I (I was the eldest) were raised by an exceedingly depressive father and a silent mother. In order to make the family "work" in the 1940s and 1950s, she, for reasons that increasingly make sense to me, dealt with this fragile situation by a high-wire act of balancing her care for my father and her care for us children. My father managed to survive through a combination of prescription drugs, an ineffective psychiatrist, religion, friends, and a raw courage and determination that were awe-inspiring. We children managed our lives, as has become apparent in retrospect, by staying "at a distance." I have increasingly discovered over the years the degree to which I learned how fragile and vulnerable appearances and claims to normalcy and stability can be.

All of this began gradually to change for me when I broke away from it and left for college; I was "born again" in college, thanks to two unusual professors and in large part to the woman I met and married. I began to reconstruct my life. The earlier part of the story, I must report, came to a tragic end when in 1974 my father committed suicide. To this day, when I talk about the "web of life," as I do in the following text, I think as much about the fragility of the beautiful spider's web as I do about the strength of the web of a fishing net or my baseball glove.

In the midst of my overweening sense of the injustices of modern history and the fragility of my primary relationships, then, the beliefs of one raised in a family and a church with traditional notions of an all-loving and all-powerful God get deeply challenged. Within the context of such experiences issues of power, and especially of divine power, inevitably arise. The problem of divine power became not so much the threat of omnipotence that was experienced and interpreted as abusive power but rather the search for a sovereign or redeeming power amid the radical injustice and fragility of modern life. Unlike for many, for me the issue of divine power in the light of my own life experience is not how to escape abusive power but rather how to find, formulate, respond to, depend on, and celebrate a power of creation and redemption in the midst of injustice and vulnerability.

This book, then, deals most persistently with the question of the nature of power, and specifically the nature of divine power. Discussion of omnipotence recurs in several places in the text, as an idea both to analyze and to criticize. I discuss it primarily as a theological problem. At the very beginning of the discussion, however, I must admit that the idea is not simply an abstract concept to be understood and evaluated. There are cultural and personal dimensions to the discussion, as should be obvious from the above. Nothing is lost on the significance of my intellectual arguments and much is gained by acknowledging that my discussion is not merely academic but political and personal as well. I am enough a product of the modern world to recognize that power, especially unilateral and authoritarian power, is tied to repression (Feuerbach, Nietzsche, Freud, Marx). That political and personal awareness, however, led more to a sense of the fragility and vulnerability of human life than to a compelling need to rebel against authority. I am not so much concerned with power as something to resent or to defy as I am to understand and respond to the kind of power that makes life possible, persistent, resilient, and significant in a fragile and vulnerable world. I see no evidence in history, scripture, culture, or my personal experience that omnipotent power exists. The kind of power I see evidence for, in history, scripture, the cross and resurrection of Jesus Christ, and my own life experience, is the kind of power that works, sometimes awesomely, usually gently, as a persistent, dependable, promissory, and even sovereign grace to create and transform our lives.

Clearly, at the same time, the idea of omnipotence persists in the text as it does in the background of the version of the Christian tradition I was taught in my childhood and adolescent churches. I cannot expel the concept altogether, and I must admit, against my better judgment, or at least against my desire, that there are situations of extremity in which I wish such a benevolent and sovereign power could "make right" radical injustice, abusive violence, and unremitting suffering. But my resources all converge against such a longing to show me that it is perhaps immature or is at least unrealistic. The divine power I have come to worship and serve is not the omnipotent power of God represented in the theistic tradition, but the power of creation and redemption that makes life in the midst of suffering and evil more than "a tale told by an idiot, full of sound and fury, signifying nothing." Theodicy, like theology, indeed, like real life, is a mixture of raw experience and frameworks of language, story, and interpretation. As the reader will soon discover, for me a theology of suffering and evil is not so much a problem of resolving a formal intellectual puzzle as an effort to understand the resources of faith in a good and powerful God in the midst of our deepest human struggles with suffering and evil.

What follows, however, grows not only out of my life experiences but also out of a specific dissatisfaction of mine and my students. I have taught a course on theodicy at my school seven times since the spring quarter 1980; it is consistently a course with the largest enrollment and has involved well over two hundred students. Almost all my students will be professional leaders of the church, most as pastors of local congregations. Although their motivation for taking such a course of study, like mine for offering it, is significantly autobiographical, their agendas are also theological and pastoral. They must interpret the work and will of God weekly to their congregations through sermon, study, pastoral care, and community action. From the beginning the course has been directed toward suffering as a theological problem. The syllabus, lectures, and discussions encourage students to examine their concepts of God, the goodness and power of God, and the will of God which inform their own experience and their pastoral work, especially during times of crisis, tragedy, and despair.

My dissatisfaction is this: I have never found a book that was adequate for my course. Technical philosophical and theological treatises are available, and there are books that explore specific questions or perspectives, but there is no book that discusses a broad range of contemporary interpretations of suffering and evil within the theological literature. Consequently, this book is, first of all, my effort to survey a wide range of theological literature on theodicy in the last quarter of a century. It is written primarily for theological students, pastors, and a broad audience of Christian laypersons who have a personal stake in interpreting suffering as a theological problem and who desire a survey of recent interpretations.

I do not pretend, however, to be "objective," either in my selection of topics or in my descriptions and evaluations of the range of views in the contemporary Western, Christian, mostly Protestant literature. No descriptions, and especially no evaluations and proposals, are ever made from a neutral point of view. My book, therefore, carries some other explicit subagendas beyond description. Although I try to be evenhanded in my accounts of others' ideas and arguments, with special attention to the reasons they advocate the views they do, I bring to my criticisms of the literature and the proposals I offer the broad perspective of "process-relational" theology. I eschew, however, any scholastic devotion to that perspective, helpful as it has been in my own theological reconstructions. I include a discussion of the similarities between process theology and trinitarian theology in their conclusions about the relation between God and human suffering in part to show that my perspective is not without criticism and real alternatives.

There is, finally, a thesis which undergirds the book and its judgments; this is made explicit toward the end. My premise is that there is a genuine "bias" in a Christian understanding of the problem of suffering as a theological problem and the resources that Christian faith offers for responding to suffering. This supposition differs from most forms of theism and from what most defenders of theodicy offer as a solution to the technical theological problem. I contend that Christians should thoroughly redefine the meaning of power, including divine power, when interpreting and responding to suffering in all its forms. Although process theology has made that claim central to its theological perspective, growing out of its Whiteheadian metaphysics, my contention is that this conclusion about the nature of divine power is not an exceptional point of view within a process perspective alone. Most everyone in the contemporary discussion who takes seriously the Christian dogma of the Trinity, including contemporary immanent doctrines of the Trinity as well as economic versions, also radically reconceives the concept of divine power. Consequently, the proposal to rethink the meaning of God's power is not an idiosyncratic theme of process-relational theology, but has its roots in the tradition of Christian liturgy and dogma as well. Trinitarianism, not theism, is the distinctively Christian identification of God, and that doctrine offers a distinctly different idea of God and God's power than Western theism, in its classical forms, has advocated.

If suffering and evil were primarily philosophical or theological problems, they would be of passing interest to most theological school students, clergy, or lay people. Few of them have any interest in speculative questions. A few sophisticated students believe such speculative questions are unanswerable or ideological, while the majority are simply uninterested in giving any time to such questions. But the issue is deeper than speculation. The religious response of most Western Christians to suffering has been far more deeply shaped by philosophical theism than by either trinitarian or process theologies of divine power. Clearly, most pastors or laypersons are not explicit philosophical theists, but their piety, especially as it is expressed in their understanding of the concept of "the will of God" in the midst of their suffering, is deeply underwritten and formed by the assumptions and implications of Western theism, not Christian trinitarian or process thought.

The framework for the book is supplied by traditional theodicies in the West. By that I mean the book is written by a Western, Christian, Protestant, white, male theologian; it is a book on theology; and I discuss the problem of suffering and evil within the framework of the Christian concepts of God's omnipotence and omnibenevolence. The structure of the book follows the traditional Western trilemma; namely, the problem is how to hold together simultaneously the ideas of divine omnipotence, divine goodness, and the reality of evil. Consequently, the subject matter, the structure, and the dilemmas for discussion are set by the Western theological tradition.

But the book is at the same time not a traditional theodicy at all. By that I mean I refuse to accept the theological problem as the very narrow, highly technical assignment of showing how the affirmations of omnipotence, divine goodness, and real evil are logically compatible beliefs. Although I accept these ideas as the appropriate concepts for the theological discussion of suffering and God for Western Christians, I consider the meaning of these terms not to be settled at all but to be subject to intense scrutiny in the light of contemporary experience and reflection. The meaning of these concepts is liable to reconstruction in our day.

Chapter 1 describes our encounter with suffering and evil in our daily lives at the end of the twentieth century. The main theme of this chapter is our shocking awareness of evil in light of the depth of personal and historical violence throughout our century. The chapter also attempts to explain why suffering and evil are distinctive religious problems for Christians. I argue that evil is a peculiar problem for Christians because of the concept of God most Christians have inherited.

Chapter 2 is a description of the classical Christian concept of God as it relates to our experience of suffering and evil. The chapter describes the theistic concept of God and its roots in scripture and tradition, then focuses specifically on the concept of divine power that lies at the core of theism. Efforts at modifying the harshest implications of the theistic idea of God are described, concluding with a description of why some, if not most, Christians have found the theistic idea of God to be religiously defensible even in the face of its conceptual liabilities.

Chapter 3 is an application of the classical concept of God to the life of faith and practice in the midst of suffering. After giving an account of the the free-will defense, the chapter describes how this perspective is applied to five beliefs about why Christians should accept suffering as caused or permitted by God. The chapter concludes with the argument that this tradition is no longer acceptable at the end of the twentieth century, as each form of theistic theodicy is so riddled with problems that a radically new form of thinking about suffering and evil is required for Christians today.

Chapter 4 begins to explore a variety of efforts to reconsider the notion of the goodness of God. The chapter describes some biblical accounts of God that present God as less than "omnibenevolent." The chapter proceeds, then, to describe a variety of religious and theological accounts of our experience of God that challenge the notion that God is to be identified with the summum bonum. The discussion focuses on two types of challengers to omnibenevolence, namely, Christians who experience God as an abuser, and Christians who experience God as indifferent to suffering and evil. The chapter closes with the question of whether evaluation of this type of theodicy is legitimate, since it is unclear whether the language about the ambiguity of God is about God or only about our experience.

Chapter 5 picks up with accounts of God as less than all-loving, which seem to be more explicitly theological and so challenge directly the heart of theism. The chapter provides accounts of God that present God as morally ambiguous, characterized by a shadow side, or a dark side. Both psychological and historical forms of this kind of theodicy are described. A brief defense of such a theodicy focuses on the religious significance of the protest tradition. The chapter concludes, however, with a series of criticisms of such a theodicy and rejects it as religiously inadequate and even intolerable.

This is the transition point of the book, then, as I move to my constructive argument that no Christian can deny the reality of evil in the twentieth century (one term of the trilemma), that Christians should not abandon the total goodness of God (another term of the trilemma), and that Christians must consider the possibility of reconceiving the nature of God's power. The remainder of the book is devoted to a description and defense of this option in theodicy.

Chapter 6 explores some biblical and theological grounds for a reconception of divine power, and develops some of the implications for theodicy when divine power is understood not as omnipotence but as creative and transformative power. The chapter opens with a consideration of what the power of God means in scripture, arguing that divine creative power is not omnipotent power, as is implied in the doctrine of *creatio ex nihilo,* but is the kind of power that brings order (a world) out of chaos (no-thingness). Within this understanding of divine power, natural law, chance, luck, and tragedy are offered as important concepts for how Christians might understand divine power in the midst of suffering and evil. The chapter concludes with the claim that in scripture, tradition, experience, and reason Christians have grounds on which to radically reconceive divine power in relational instead of unilateral terms.

Chapter 7 is a description of efforts to systematize the suggestions introduced in the previous chapter as they relate to the problem of theodicy. This chapter argues for the compatibility of the God of the Bible and of process theology. The details of a process theodicy are then developed, followed by an evaluation of such theodicies. I argue that although there are significant liabilities for many Christians with this type of theodicy, it has fewer liabilities than classical theism or protest theodicies and much to say for it in terms of its compatibility with scripture and experience.

Chapter 8 concludes the book with the claim that the reconception of divine power is not unique to process theodicies. Christians who take contemporary trinitarian theologies seriously also radically reconceive divine power. The conclusion of my argument is that there is a distinctly Christian "bias" in theodicy, namely, a conception of divine power in which God identifies with and transforms human suffering and evil, a view quite distinct from classical theism and its theodicies. I argue that the Christian dogma of the Trinity, along with process neoclassical forms of theism, both reconceive the power of God as creating, suffering, and transforming power, not omnipotence. Although there are differences among trinitarian theologians, they all imply that the power of God is to be defined by the cross and the resurrection, not by the omnipotence of theism. Although I conclude there are assets and liabilities to trinitarian as well as process theologies, the book ends with the claim that both types of contemporary theology concur about the need and the possibility of Christians' offering a new concept of divine power in the midst of human suffering and evil.

No amount of effort could succeed in naming all the people to whom I owe a debt for their contribution to the formulation of these chapters. The list would begin with the master of divinity and master of arts in theological studies students in my seven courses over the last sixteen years who listened to the arguments, read the preliminary drafts, challenged and sometimes rejected my ideas in class discussion, and formulated in their final course papers their own conclusions. The most recent contributors to the discussion were my eight doctor of ministry students (David Beach, Deborah Campbell, Julie Carmean, Gil Fauber, Michael Havey, Carol Potterton, Keith Rhoden, and Nancy Westmeyer), who devoted parts of two-and-a-half years of their work as pastors to their own struggles with these ideas for their own theology and pastoral ministry.

Along the way, many colleagues have supported my work in this project by listening and critiquing some of the ideas. Special acknowledgment should be made of the time offered for discussion by Tom Dozeman, Marsha Foster Boyd, Jim Nelson, Kathy Farmer, Carolyn Bohler, and Renee Jennings. My school, United Theological Seminary, also supported some of my work on this project through a generous sabbatical program.

I want to offer a special word of appreciation to Julie Carmean, who as a student, a colleague, and a friend has spent many hours of discussion helping me formulate and reformulate many of the ideas in these chapters, although she bears no responsibility for my concluding arguments. I would also like to thank Richard E. Brown, director of Westminster John Knox Press/Geneva Press, and Esther Kolb, copyeditor, for their fine editorial work on this book.

Finally, I want to express my deepest gratitude for the support of my wife, Fran, who through our life together and through many years of listening and responding to these ideas—especially at TGI Friday's after the many movies we have seen—has made my project significant to me beyond the classroom. Her love and companionship, which have persisted from our early years together in college until today when our two sons, Mark and David, are grown and have completed their own graduate education, are both a source and a confirmation of my belief in the reality of grace—a good not our own—which operates as a transformative resource amid suffering and sorrow. Even my spouse and children, however, cannot know the depth to which their love and support have shaped my interpretation of the grace that works latently within an ambiguous world. If this book succeeds in conveying the depth of a goodness not our own amid our suffering, the people here named and unnamed may know that their contribution to a theological interpretation of suffering and grace has moved beyond the confines of my family and friendships, the classrooms, hallways, restaurants, and movie theaters I inhabit with them to an even larger world of Christians who also struggle for faith when faced with suffering and evil.

1

"When the Waves Turn the Minutes to Hours"

Suffering and Evil as Religious Problems

⊰ The year was 1947, two years after the war. Stingo, a twenty-two-year-old aspiring novelist from the south, had moved into an apartment in Brooklyn to begin his "voyage of discovery." On the next floor lived Sophie, a thirty-year-old Polish Roman Catholic from Cracow who had survived Auschwitz, and her lover, Nathan, a brilliant but mercurial American Jew, who had found her unconscious in a library in Brooklyn about a year and a half after the Russians had liberated the camp. She had survived scurvy, typhus, anemia, and scarlet fever, and Nathan had nursed her back to health so that she had begun to "bloom like a rose." Gradually, fitfully, painfully, deceitfully, bit by bit she unfolded her story.

Sophie informed Stingo that her father was a professor of law in Cracow, had written articles during the war warning Jews of the Nazi threat, and had gotten help for those who were persecuted. But one evening after Stingo came home early from a date, Sophie invited him to her apartment and began to unravel yet another thread of her story. She revealed that, in fact, she had been married to a disciple of her father, and that she had seen both of them taken by the Germans to Sachenhausen and shot. Her mother had contracted tuberculosis, and Sophie had been arrested for stealing some meat for her mother, meat that in Poland had been reserved only for Germans. As a result she had been sent to Auschwitz.

Stingo, however, subsequently learned from a professor at Brooklyn College that Sophie's father had, in fact, been a Nazi sympathizer and had gotten killed inadvertently in a general Nazi sweep of all intellectuals in Poland, even though he had written anti-Jewish tracts and authored the law making it illegal for Jews and Poles to sit on the same bench in Poland. When confronted the next day by Stingo about her deceit, Sophie replied, "I was afraid I'd be left alone." As she revealed even more of her relation to her father, Stingo learned she had discovered his call for the extermination of the Jews while typing one of his speeches.

Later, in Warsaw, Sophie had a lover who wanted her to become involved in the resistance, but she refused on the ground that she would endanger her children. Two weeks later, however, she was arrested for smuggling meat into Warsaw and sent to Auschwitz. She described how her son was sent to Kinderlage, while her daughter was sent directly to a crematorium. Because of her own Aryan features and her secretarial skills, she was made secretary to Rudolf Höss, commandant of the camp. She once had tried to seduce him, claiming a mistake had been made in her arrest and even arguing with Höss that she had helped her father author the anti-Jewish policy. Höss had promised to send her son to the Nazi program to Germanize Aryan-looking Poles, but the next day Sophie was sent back to her old Block 3 and Höss did nothing about the fate of her son.

Near the end of this story by novelist William Styron, Sophie and Stingo are together in a hotel room. They have learned that Nathan is mad, and Stingo wants Sophie to marry him and move back to the south. She finally tells Stingo the truth about what happened in Auschwitz: The night was warm as the train approached the camp. There were crowds standing in line outside the train as she and her children disembarked. Guards were roaming about. One guard noticed her and propositioned her. He thought she might be there because she was a communist. At first she didn't answer him, but then she turned to the guard and told him she was not a Jew but a Pole, a person of racially pure blood and a devout Polish Roman Catholic. The guard saw his opening. "You believe in Christ the Redeemer? . . . Did He not say, 'Suffer the little children to come unto Me'?" He paused. "You may keep one. . . . The other one will have to go." In frantic, desperate hysteria, she cried, "I have to choose?" The guard calmly replied, "You are a Polack, not a Yid. That gives you . . . a choice. . . . Choose, . . . or I'll send them both over there, then." An argument ensued, and the guard shouted to another, "Send them both!" In a timeless moment of desperation, Sophie shouted, "Take my little girl!" And a guard quickly whisked the little girl off to the crematorium.

Stingo's final scene with Sophie is back in the hotel. Sophie and Stingo are making plans to go down to the farm in the south to live for a while. They make passionate love, Stingo admitting that Sophie has satisfied his inexhaustible lust; Sophie admitting that her plunge into sensuality has been an effort to beat back death. That night Sophie leaves Stingo, without saying good-bye, and we discover that she has returned to Nathan, where they have been found dead together after having taken cyanide. Stingo says, as the scene fades, "And so ended my voyage of discovery." His own self-discovery had been occasioned by the story of these two casualties of the Holocaust, but

[they were] but a few of the beaten and butchered and betrayed and martyred . . . of the earth. I did not weep for the six million Jews or the two million Poles or the one million Serbs or the five million Russians—I was unprepared to weep for all humanity—but I did weep for these others who in one way or another had become dear to me, and my sobs made an unashamed racket across the abandoned beach.[1]

At the end of the twentieth century, Christians have to choose whether to face or to ignore the diabolical events of our century. As the *New York Times*

Magazine announced on its cover page at the base of a graphic of consuming flame, "Evil's Back."[2] The roster of ubiquitous evil in our century seems unending: racism, genocide, ethnic cleansing, drug addiction, random murder, atomic bombings, death squads, violent suppression of human rights, ridicule of lesbian and gay persons, ecological degradation, abuse of women and children, punishment of AIDS victims, indifference toward the poor and the elderly, sexism, rape, terrorism, torture, holy and unholy wars, the Holocaust, and unmitigated cruelty and hatred. Such evil is a given reality, ever before us while theologians and pastors spout naïvetés about human goodness and divine omnipotence and benevolence.

The victims and perpetrators of evil in our century—embodied in Sophie and the Nazi guard—stand before Christians to be unconditionally embraced and unequivocally condemned. They also require interpretation in the light of the claims of our faith. How can Christians account for "the intrusion into human history of an evil so enormous that historical determinism alone is inadequate to account for it"?[3] Is our outrage at the suffering of the victim so overwhelming and the depth of the malevolence in the perpetrator so terrifying that people of faith cannot bear to face the massive evils of our century full view? Can belief in the power and goodness of God remain unquestioned in the face of the horrors of the twentieth century?

Good and Evil

Life is full of pain and suffering and sorrow, and it is all over too quickly.
(Woody Allen)

A complex interconnection between good and evil lies at the heart of our experience as human beings. Life is a mysterious mixture of well-being and woe. The reciprocity between our interpretations of our experiences as good and as evil is one of the most fundamental intuitions of human experience, language, and religion.

On the one hand, human life is a tapestry woven of rich experiences of value. Brilliant sunrises and sunsets, majestic mountains and seashores, singing birds and towering trees, rolling grasslands and river valleys offer an awesome environment for our lives. The gift of life mediated through birth, sustained and developed by care and even sacrifice, establishes gratitude, respect, and love between parents and children. Families, clans, and communities provide safety, support, and a larger framework of meaning for the members. Values are sustained and enhanced by the rich inheritance from the past conveyed through story, mythology, song, art, architecture, and social institutions. Science expands our knowledge of the magnitude and intricacy of our world, and technology makes our life more secure and pleasant. Freedom and autonomy have been extended to many groups and individuals, providing a diversity which enriches the treasure human beings can create and enjoy.

Our most fundamental intuition as human beings, even more basic than our experience of suffering, is our experience of value. Our experience is not merely our sense perceptions; it is also "a still more elemental and organic togetherness of the experiencing subject and the experienced environment."[4] To the experience of our five senses we must also add other experiences, such as the sense of beauty, the sense of "a more" (William James), the sense of aversion and attraction, the senses of quality.[5] These elemental perceptions, to which our language applies terms such as "goodness" and "well-being," stand at the center of the religious awareness. These moments of love, joy, and peace reassure us of our communion with a creative good that nurtures the value of life. Mystical writings, especially, reflect this intuition with heightened awareness.

> I was alone upon the seashore as all these thoughts flowed over me, liberating and reconciling; and now again, as once before in distant days in the Alps of Dauphine, I was impelled to kneel down, this time before the illimitable ocean, symbol of the Infinite. I felt that I prayed as I had never prayed before, and knew now what prayer really is: to return from the solitude of individuation into the consciousness of unity with all that is, to kneel down as one that passes away, and to rise up as one imperishable. Earth, heaven, and sea resounded as in one vast world-encircling harmony. It was as if the chorus of all the great who had ever lived were about me. I felt myself one with them.[6]

Clearly not everyone has such profound mystical experiences. However, it is hard to imagine many human beings who have not had glimpses, even if subconscious and minimally articulated, of a holiness or goodness that simultaneously confronts us with dread and awe and comforts us with moments of peace and well-being. Apart from such a ubiquitous intuition, concealed or accessible, sophisticated or elemental, it is hard to imagine what would or could sustain and motivate most human beings.

Even those who argue that life is absurd and meaningless bear a strange witness to the goodness of life.[7] Although they may argue that there is no correlation between the demand of reason to explain everything and the ability of reason to meet this demand, they nevertheless live their lives of free revolt and decision as if that determination itself made some difference ultimately to someone or something. Even suicide can be interpreted as the desperate effort to assert in the face of contrary feelings the instinct that life is meaningful, even if the free decision to terminate one's own life is the only apparent option available to affirm that meaning.

Life in its most fundamental character is valued. While any realistic view must see it as a mixture of good and evil, life must be on balance (at least potentially) good or worthwhile to be lived. If one thinks it is not, one must ask how life could emerge as human life employing a language that includes value judgments without such an intuition of creativity and goodness, and whether once it has emerged it could be sustained without the confidence that value is

rooted in the givenness of existence as such. The fact that human life continues, and that it continues on toward an open and hopeful future, even (or especially!) among the most despised and disfranchised of the earth, is the most
compelling evidence of this conviction that meaning and hope are more than
mere ideology.

Women and men live in hope. People sing when forced to pick cotton or
to live in desperate circumstances. Hope persists because people continue to
sing. A newborn child is a sign, even a sacrament, of hope. Even if one gives
weight to sociobiological theory that roots the persistence of all species, including the human, in the reproductive "drive" of the genes to reproduce themselves, one has to give an account of an animal that has language, and so symbols, and so meanings and values. Most people most of the time, and all people
enough of the time, experience their lives and the life of their community as
good enough to assume some positive ground in the world for the emergence
and persistence of life and its valuing.

Our experience of our environment, natural and social, however, is Janus-
faced, full of well-being and of woe. For every thread of experienced good
that is woven into the tapestry of human experience, there is a discordant
thread that is also woven into that same tapestry. Every experience of positive
value noted above also has a dimension of corruption within it or counter to
it. Even though on the whole life is good, there are murky sides to nature, society, and individuals which counter and qualify that primordial intuition so
deeply as to call into question that experience itself. It is equiprimordial in the
religious consciousness.

Nature experienced as harmonious and beneficent can also be experienced
as terrorizing and devastating. Earthquake, hurricane, cyclone, volcanic erup-
tion, flood, drought, and famine indiscriminately inflict fear and destruction on
multitudes. Bacteria and viruses spread disease, epidemics, and plagues
throughout every human society.

In fourteenth-century Europe and England, at least one-third of the 4.2 million population died of the *Pasteurella pestis,* or bubonic plague, a bacillus that
found its home in the stomach of fleas that resided on the hairs of rats. Originating in the Lake Issyk-Koul area of Central Asia, the "Black Death" entered
Sicily on trading ships in October 1347 and moved by the main trade routes
onto the mainland by January 1348, decimating one-third of Europe and England within two-and-a-half years.[8]

Statistics alone, however, do not touch the psychological and spiritual significance of such a calamity. "Plague" has been and continues to be a metaphor
for a fateful element in the human condition. From Boccaccio's descriptions in
his *Decameron,* Albert Camus's descriptions in *The Plague,* to the contemporary panic about AIDS, "plague" remains a metaphor for the sense of helplessness and calamity visited on humanity by nature.

Our facing of such threats is made more arduous by our recognition that most
of the evil in our world is caused by human decision and deed. Even the evil

that is not caused solely by human resolution is frequently exacerbated by human actions or lack of them. It is worth noting that the "Black Death" of the fourteenth century came to the Continent as a strategy of warfare. In 1347 the Kipchak army, besieging a Genoese trading post in the Crimea, catapulted plague-infested corpses into the town as an act of war. The plague traveled with the traders to Genoa, Venice, and Messina by galleys from these Eastern ports.

People continue to build near floodplains and earthquake faults. They fail to build tornado shelters and ignore or defy hurricane warnings. Ethiopians face starvation for reasons of political policy as much as lack of rain. Population resettlement, mismanagement, and above all civil war between the government and rebel factions regularly threaten to extend the suffering of famine. Research into ways to control the spread of the AIDS virus has been slow in part because the predominant victims are despised by many citizens.

A primary source of our encounter with suffering and evil in the twentieth century, however, is the unbelievable horror and cruelty inflicted directly or indirectly by human beings on other human beings by conscious decision, policy, and practice. The strong often victimize the weak. Frequently, this aggression is open and direct, as in homicide and rape. More often, it is more subtle and circuitous, the by-product of psychological intimidation or economic and political manipulation and exploitation.

Suffering, Evil, and Religion

One of the major functions of religion has been to offer meaning to our experiences of disruption, pain, and suffering. That function remains the most basic and most troublesome problem with which religion has to deal at the end of the twentieth century.

The most deep-seated American misunderstanding of religion is the presumption that the purpose of religion is to produce happiness. The primary function of religion is not to generate happiness but to construct meaning.[9] Human beings can endure the most intense suffering with resolve and confidence as long as they believe their distress has a place in a larger context of meaning. The threat of meaninglessness is deeper than the threat of pain, suffering, and guilt. When a system of meaning is threatened, the problem of evil is not primarily how to fathom and thereby endure particular experiences of suffering with equanimity but whether understanding and meaning are possible at all in the face of the apparent irrationality of the suffering.

Thus, the most serious peril that confronts us today is not the presence of suffering as such or even its inevitability but the apparent purposelessness of it, all things considered. The reasons evil persists as the basic religious problem at the end of the twentieth century are that (1) the traditional Western theistic theories that explain the presence and meaning of suffering have become preposterous or ineffectual in the light of our experience of suffering in the twentieth century, and (2) more fundamentally, the traditional assumptions about the character of

God, which provided the foundation for the entire theistic superstructure of meaning, have become problematic in the light of other contemporary perceptions. Instead of the presence of evil as one of the basic problems religion must solve, the magnitude of evil has made religion itself problematic.

What is religion? Peter Berger contends that "every human society is an enterprise of world-building."[10] Religion occupies a distinctive place in this enterprise. It is not concerned primarily with understanding the details of the world; it is concerned with creating a meaningful order, or *nomos,* out of the chaos of experience. Religion is devoted to understanding how our individual lives, our society, nature, and the vast galaxies of the universe fit into a patterned, coherent world. It is based on the drive for meaning and aims at establishing a sacred cosmos.

In addition, Berger maintains, "all socially constructed worlds are inherently precarious."[11] The potential chaos of marginal situations must be kept at bay. So religion is also concerned with "world maintenance." How an individual and community maintain or reestablish the world order when it is disrupted by ignorance, stupidity, error, corruption, chance, evil, and death is one of the primary tasks of religion. Religion, then, maintains the socially defined reality by legitimating marginal situations in terms of an all-encompassing sacred reality. Berger defines religion in the light of this responsibility. It is "the establishment, through human activity, of an all-embracing sacred order, that is, of a sacred cosmos that will be capable of maintaining itself in the ever-present face of chaos."

This deep-seated function of religion is confirmed by Clifford Geertz, who stresses the distinctiveness of the human animal in its absolute need for symbol systems for survival and meaning. Given the generality and variability of our innate genetic endowment and response capacities (unlike other animals, we do not know how to build a dam without symbols), we are thrown back on a symbol system to be viable as human beings. Even the remotest hint that the symbol system may be unable to cope with some aspect of experience raises great anxiety. Humans can adapt themselves somehow to anything their imagination can cope with; but they cannot deal with chaos. When we are at the limits, not simply of interpretations but of interpretability, at the limits of chaos, we are at the most fundamental challenge to which religion must respond.

In Geertz's viewpoint, religion is a cultural system that seeks to synthesize ethos and worldview. It formulates a congruence between a style of life and a metaphysics. Specifically, religion is "a system of symbols which act to establish powerful, pervasive, and long-lasting moods and motivations in men by formulating conceptions of a general order of existence and clothing these conceptions with such an aura of facticity that the moods and motivations seem uniquely realistic."[12] What is important is that religion forms "conceptions of a general order of existence." The dispositions of the individual are shaped by general ideas of order. At those points where chaos threatens to break in (the tumult of events that lack not only interpretation but interpretability), it is religion that provides an answer.

The point where the meaningfulness of a particular pattern of life threatens finally to dissolve into chaos is meaningless suffering, namely, suffering that occurs at the limits of the human power to understand. Evil is like a pit bull. We assure ourselves it is domesticated in a safe house built of optimism and wit. Then, at some innocent provocation, evil surprises us by its viciousness: Susan Smith, Eric and Lyle Menendez, Jeffrey Dahmer, and Oklahoma City trespass into our innocent lives. Deep within the inner life of our culture lies an awareness of evil as a threatening, uncontrollable, harrowing, mysterious reality that encroaches, unexpected and uncontrollable. Evil is not merely a problem to be managed; it seems rooted in something deeper than abuse, co-dependency, or a poor self image. It appears as a mysterious reality of wicked-ness, malignant wickedness, to be encountered, interpreted, and endured.

For those who can embrace the story, religious symbols, Geertz says, pro-vide "a cosmic guarantee not only for their ability to comprehend the world, but also, comprehending it, to give a precision to their feeling, a definition to their emotions which enables them, morosely or joyfully, grimly or cavalierly, to endure the world." When the symbol system fails to provide a vocabulary by which to grasp the nature of the distress and relate it to a wider world, the experience of suffering passes into the problem of evil. Instead of being a problem of disciplining our emotions in light of the larger order, the problem of an order as such and of our ability to make judgments in light of such an order becomes a problem. "What is involved in the problem of evil is not the adequacy of our symbolic resources to govern our affective life, but the ade-quacy of those resources to provide a workable set of ethical criteria, norma-tive guides to govern our action."[13] Insight becomes inadequate to experience.

I do not want to be misunderstood here as claiming that interpretation of our experience of suffering is the only function of religion. Nor do I want to be misunderstood as implying that by interpreting our experience of suffering under a sacred canopy religion makes evil no longer evil. Rather, my argument is that one of the most distinctive functions of religion is to provide a way of building a world out of our suffering, and that the most serious challenge of radical evil to the theistic world is "the disturbing 'interruption' (Cohen) of all theological thinking and speaking about God and especially the providential role of God."[14]

The Case
of Suffering Children

Although I had originally thought of talking to you about human suffering in general, I have now decided to talk to you only about the suffering of chil-dren. . . . For the hundredth time I repeat, there are many questions that could be asked, but I ask you only one—about the children—because I be-lieve it conveys fully and clearly what I am trying to tell you. Listen, even if we assume that every person must suffer because his suffering is necessary to pay for eternal harmony, still do tell me, for God's sake, where the children come in.[15]

Our most immediate encounter with evil is the suffering of individuals. And our most acute experience with this kind of evil is the suffering of children. If anyone is innocent in our discussion, it is the children. If any suffering is meaningless in terms of deserved punishment or soul making, it is the suffering of children. Yet nearly all human beings know through firsthand experience the suffering endured by innocent children, whether that suffering be imposed by nature, by human error, or by malevolence. Stories succeed better than discourse in describing our encounter with the suffering of innocent children.

Frances Young, professor of theology at the University of Birmingham, England, is the mother of a profoundly handicapped son, Arthur, born in Cambridge on June 1, 1967, while she was completing her studies in theology. She and her husband, Bob, learned that Arthur was microcephalic, brain-damaged at birth because the placenta was too small and inefficient, thus depriving Arthur of sufficient oxygen during his development in the womb. Being new parents, they were unaware of how to interpret the first signs of the handicap during the early months, although the general practitioner who eventually sent them to a specialist after eight months knew from the beginning. When the full nature of the problems was revealed, she and her husband were shocked, puzzled, and angry, overcome by a dreadful sense of failure.

Professor Young began her book, written in 1984 (when Arthur was seventeen, a few years past the worst "middle years" from 1974 to 1979), by describing a day in their life of caring for and coping with Arthur. For seventeen years they had washed "nappies," changed leg splints, dressed him, carried him downstairs, and fed him. Arthur will never talk. In development he was not even a toddler at seventeen. He overreacted physically and emotionally to anything that disturbed him. Although at one stage in his development he could stand for a few seconds by himself (by the time the book was rewritten in 1989, he had lost ground), he still cannot feed himself. Although she had done nothing wrong during her pregnancy, and was convinced that it was an accident and not her fault, she knew that no amount of effort could make Arthur normal. "These are the facts we have to face, and it is no good being sentimental about it. Arthur is lovable, a source of joy. But it is hard to see any satisfactory future in the long term. But then the past has not been all roses and we have survived so far. Who knows what the future holds? It is no good worrying about it."[16]

Frances and Bob had different interpretations of Arthur's handicap. Bob, who had the experience of a handicapped brother, accepted it from the beginning as just one of those things that happen, and he understood all of them simply to be unlucky. Frances, however, had more difficulty.

I thought I had accepted it. But at a deeper level I had not. I simply could not understand it. It was not just Arthur. He focussed my perception on the much bigger problem. If this world was created by the loving purposes of God, how could this sort of thing happen? If God intended people to grow to maturity in faith and love, what about those who were incapable of doing so?[17]

Arthur challenged all her assumptions and solutions. If God's purpose was soul-making, which she had learned from John Hick's theodicy, what was she to make of an individual without the potential to respond and grow and mature in faith and virtue? Arthur represented the cases where there is no potential, where the handicap does not produce greater love but the kind of desperate burden that causes marriages to crack and distorts the development of other children. Even if she could allow that there is something good in her relation with Arthur, he still represented these cases where there is no potential. Everything in her protested against it as cruel and unnecessary.

If every individual is important to God, she asked, how could even one of God's creatures be afflicted this way, let alone the 2 percent of humanity that is born with some handicap or other, denying them the possibility of fullness of life? God has set us in a world where accidents happen, and we have to bear the consequences, whether they are the results of blameworthy carelessness or just one of those things. Her faith in God was no easy answer to her dilemma.

> It is not true that Christians are better people. My husband [an agnostic] is one of the best people I know. Nor is it true that faith gives you the edge in coping with the problems of life. It may delude you into never facing reality, into false hopes, into a sentimental and unrealistic optimism about things. Or it may compound your problems by setting up a sharp dichotomy between an accepted idea of what the world is like and the awful reality you actually have to face. My experience has proved that religion is no escape. It led me into deeper and deeper agonies over the state of the world. It raised questions and difficulties which the non-believer never had to face.[18]

Suffering is always in one respect the suffering of persons. Although suffering never occurs in isolation and apart from social structures that inflict, support, and attempt to justify it, suffering finally occurs in individuals with real names and faces and feelings and stories. Camus says:

> But what are a hundred million deaths? When one has served in a war, one hardly knows what a dead man is, after a while. And since a dead man has no substance unless one has actually seen him dead, a hundred million corpses broadcast through history are no more than a puff of smoke in the imagination.[19]

In one of its dimensions, evil is always microevil, the suffering of flesh-and-blood persons with names and faces and stories. No event intensifies our encounter with evil more starkly than the innocent suffering of a single child. In that context, as Irving Greenburg has argued, "No statement should be made that could not be made in the presence of the burning children."[20] The problem of the suffering child (in Cabrini Green housing projects in Chicago, in

Ethiopia or Bosnia, yours, mine) is a spiritual problem that gnaws away at the souls of the people in congregations every Sunday, much deeper even than the problem of how to expel our sin or assuage our guilt.

Twentieth-Century Violence

> The best lack all conviction, while the worst
> Are full of passionate intensity.
> (William Butler Yeats, "The Second Coming")

> Where's the new world, now the fighting's done?
> ("Turning," from *Les Misérables*)

In the twentieth century the ascendant civilizations of Europe, North America, and Japan accomplished horrors that have amounted to the usurpation of the power of God over creation. The world throughout this century has gone about the work of de-creation. The twentieth century shattered the lenses and paradigms, the very mind, of reason itself. Any underlying assumption about proportion, continuity, and rationality in the world perished. A minuscule event, even an atom, could mushroom into vast obliteration.[21]

I want to be clear that I am not implying that macroevil is distinctive to our century. We do not live in an age that is any more evil than any other time of human history. There is no historical evidence that as a human race we are morally any better or any worse than we have been since we came down out of the trees and starting walking around. The Holocaust has become the paradigm for radical evil in our century, not because the twentieth century is the worst century of violence, but because we have come at the end of this century to live in a "postmodern" world. That is, we have discovered, or at least acknowledged, at the end of the modern era the depth of suffering and evil caused but ignored by the illusions and self-deceptions of three centuries of modern liberal optimism about inevitable progress.

The problem of evil has taken new directions at the end of the twentieth century. The massive suffering made possible by modern science and technology and enacted by the modern nation-state has heightened the problem of evil in its macrodimensions. Instead of the problem about how suffering is related to the seemingly impersonal workings of *nature,* as in the Lisbon earthquake of 1775 (which occasioned Leibnitz's *Theodicy*), the definitive form of the problem in its contemporary postmodern form is *history,* the relation of evil to modern politics, such as the concentration camp at Auschwitz, or the bomb over Hiroshima, or racism in North America.

It is noteworthy that since World War II, or at least since the late 1960s, we have begun to live in a postmodern era in which few think we might overcome evil largely through our own efforts to see the dawn of a new paradise based on science, technology, the market, and our own creativity. That dream (or illusion) is no longer alive.[22] We have had to learn to live with and interpret evil again, not because it has increased but because it has not disappeared, as moderns believed it would. Indeed, evil has taken on its own distinctive forms in the shape of our modern technologies.

> There are, in my view, two factors that, above all others, have shaped human history in this century. One is the development of the natural sciences and technology, certainly the greatest success story of our time. . . . The other, without doubt, consists in the great ideological storms that have altered the lives of virtually all mankind: the Russian Revolution and its aftermath—totalitarian tyrannies of both right and left and the explosions of nationalism, racism, and, in places, of religious bigotry, which . . . not one among the most perceptive social thinkers of the 19th century had ever predicted.[23]

In addition, plumbing the depths of our lives psychologically in the twentieth century has made us even more aware of our vast potential for evil.[24] As in old fairy tales and mythologies, we now recognize in our postmodern art and literature how pervasive is the expression of evil in our conscious and subconscious lives, even in our language. Our contemporary films and imaginative literature (our contemporary versions of old fairy tales and mythological themes) have not reassured us of a scientific elimination of evil. Macroevil appears as grotesque, pervasive, demonic, and despairing themes in our postmodern literature and movies.

During the first twenty years of this century, a civil war within Christendom engulfed Europe and North America and effectively ended the nineteenth century. Within twenty more years, Asia also became involved in interludes of savage mutual destruction, economic collapse and mass unemployment, and barbaric persecutions in the name of political ideologies and nationalism. The two great wars that dominated the history of Europe during this period differed from all their predecessors in two ways: They were virtually worldwide, and they were wars of unlimited liability, that is, peoples and entire national populations and their economies and their media were mobilized on both sides.

Wars and revolutions became one of the distinguishing marks of the twentieth century. Volume 12 of the *New Cambridge Modern History,* which covers the twentieth century, titles the volume on the twentieth century *The Era of Violence.*

> The phase of European history which is analyzed in this volume has, therefore, a character and an internal coherence which make it possible crudely to summarize it as "an era of violence." . . . The capacity of science, technology and mechanization to produce material wealth, the ability of administration and organization to produce greater welfare and social justice, result also in the enhanced power of modern societies to destroy one another and in a great facility for modern dictators to establish inhuman despotism. Perhaps, with so much power at man's disposal, the marvel is that its abuse has not been even more persistent.[25]

The twentieth century has been a century of "man-made deaths." The number of such deaths by mid-century was about 100 million. A more precise figure depends on the definition of the phrase, but in any reasonable meaning the number cannot be less than 80 million, and is unlikely to be more than 150 million.[26] Robert McNamara, in an interview on *Good Morning America,* offered the figure of 160 million in the twentieth century.[27]

The symbol for the extent and character of the violence of the twentieth century has become the Holocaust. The Third Reich's system of concentration camps, murder squadrons, and killing centers took more than 15 million lives. Of these, 5 to 6 million were Jews (3.8 million in 1941–1942 alone), which consisted of two-thirds of all European Jews and one-third of all world Jewry. That number more than doubles when one adds 3.3 million Soviet POWs who perished in Nazi captivity, 4 million Soviet citizens, 2.5 million Polish citizens, and 1.5 million Yugoslav civilians. Up to 500,000 of Europe's 700,000 Gypsies were slaughtered in the camps.[28]

Racism remains *the* unresolved dilemma of life in the United States, the deepest, the most widespread, and the most resistant of the macroevils of our nation.[29] Basil Davidson, in *The African Slave Trade,* traces European and North American participation in the four-hundred-year African slave trade from 1450 to 1850, and our intensive trading from 1650 to 1850. Before 1960, the time slave trade studies got into their stride, a generally accepted figure was that about 15 million Africans landed alive, which was a guess. Philip Curtin, in his 1969 *The Atlantic Slave Trade: A Census,* concluded that those who landed alive were 9.5 million between 1451 and 1870, with an upper number of some 12 million. The conclusion of most of those who followed him in the 1970s was that although he was substantially right in reducing the number previously accepted, his 9.5 million number was probably too small. Davidson finally estimates a total of 21 million Africans were deported during these two centuries; 12 million landed alive in the Americas, 2 million were lost on the ocean crossing, and 7 million died before embarkation.

The real history of blacks and whites in America, though, is far grimmer than either statistics or textbook accounts reveal. Even though suffering might be inevitable for all human beings, four hundred years of unrelieved suffering for an entire group of human beings introduces a qualitatively new dimension to the problem of evil.

Any fuller account of our encounter with microevil and macroevil would focus on the interrelation of these two dimensions of suffering and evil. The suffering of individuals never occurs without an environment that causes, shapes, exacerbates, or sustains the suffering through the natural, social, cultural, political, and economic systems within which suffering occurs. Likewise, macroevil is evil because it implicates persons with distinct names, experiences, stories, and interpretations of experiences of suffering. One of the reasons *Schindler's List* is so powerful as a movie is that it attaches real names and faces—

Schindler's list of names is read near the end of the movie—to the over-whelming though abstract numbers and social systems of the Holocaust.

From Paper Cuts to Genocide:
The Meaning of the Term "Evil"

"Does evil exist?" sounds like a rhetorical question that one mouse might ask another mouse in the forest after examining an owl pellet composed of bleached rodent bones and matted hair.[30]

Evil is a *concept,* not an experience. Experience happens to an organism through a mutual interaction between organism and environment. Experience is neither good nor bad intrinsically. To interpret an experience as suffering and to call that experience *evil* is to impose an evaluative interpretation on it. To the question, "Who knows what is good or evil?" one must reply, in part, "No one, until one can locate its place in a larger framework of interpretation."

Our encounter with evil is connected with our sense that there is a radical fault in ourselves, in society, in nature, and perhaps even the divine that goes beyond our everyday notions of mere negativity. Even though the idea of evil has a depth and range to it that surpasses any clear definition, it is neverthe-less a notion that interprets a specific range of our experiences.

The question of whether evil exists was posed by the editor of *Time* in a cover story.[31] He knows a man who does not believe in the existence of evil. The man knows about the horrors of the world, but he thinks that to describe these as evil gives too much power and status to the horrors. One must not, his friend believes, allow lower instincts and mere calamities to get dressed up as a big idea. In his friend's view, evil is a subjective response or a reification of experiences and responses to negativities in the world.

One of the readers of the essay expressed a similar sentiment in a later is-sue in a letter to the editor.

Good and evil are purely subjective. What we experience is either pleasant or unpleasant to a degree. As I see it, God does not exist; Hitler was a para-noid schizophrenic with political ambitions; AIDS is a disease; Saddam Hus-sein is a calm, intelligent man and a gangster.[32]

The concept of evil surely *means* more than that. Perhaps the greatest and fi-nal triumph of evil is its ability to convince us that it does not exist but is merely a subjective response. Still at times we must use the word *evil.* It is the word we use when we come to the limit of our comprehension. *Evil* is a destructive, over-powering menace, an enemy to be resisted. It seems to be qualitatively as well as quantitatively different from most of our negative experiences in life.

If *evil* is more than a rhetorical term used to express nothing more than the subjective feeling "I don't like that," then what, more specifically, does the term mean? Where does our experience of suffering appear in such a way as to sug-gest the use of the word evil?

One place to begin our discussion is with the experience most commonly associated with our everyday encounter with evil, that is to say, the loss incurred by death. Death remains one of our most enigmatic human experiences. Not only does it threaten the continuity of human relationships; it threatens the basic assumptions of order on which all societies depend.[33] Death certifies the ultimate precariousness of all human life, and as a result threatens the meaningfulness of existence itself.[34] As Peter Berger argues, "Every human society is, in the last resort, men banded together to face death."[35]

There is, as a result, an almost innate human compulsion to deny death. Ernest Becker has demonstrated our Western obsession with death and our heroic attempts to deny death's reality.[36] Regardless of whether one takes the "healthy minded argument" that "fear of death is not a natural thing for humans, that we are not born with it," or the "morbidly minded argument" that "the fear of death is natural and is present in everyone, that it is the basic fear that influences all others, a fear from which no one is immune, no matter how disguised it may be,"[37] the reality is that our culture is obsessed with denying "the terror of death"[38] in myriad ways, such as the obsession with youth, heroic defiance, camouflage, and finally denial through a belief in immortality.

Although death may remain as a question mark about the meaning of life, death does not, however, always introduce "an element of disturbance requiring explanation."[39] Death in its "proper" time and place and in its "proper" manner can be met not only with a judgment of inevitability but also with resignation, purposefulness, and even affirmation because it is "a good death." "Entirely different, however, were those instances when death came out of season and violently."[40] The "ugly side of death" has risen to ascendancy in our century, and it is this side of death which prompts us to identify evil with death. Millions endure pain, suffering, and the threat to existence quite apart from death as the inevitable but natural terminal point of a each person's life. It is the suffering, brutal, and violent deaths imposed by modern societies on countless individuals and groups that make the problem of evil deeper than simply the loss of death. The terror of death may be a factor in this experience of evil, but death itself cannot be the sufficient factor in identifying our use of the term evil with death. It is our grief about loss in death, and not death itself, that prompts us to think of death when we think of evil.[41]

If evil is to be identified not with death itself but rather with the losses of death, perhaps it is the pain and suffering that surround so much of death in our century that prompt us to associate evil with death. No one could deny the overwhelming pain and suffering in our century.

Although pain may be one condition for suffering, suffering cannot be equated with pain.[42] Suffering can be caused by pain, but pain itself is merely a physiological event, a sensory quality of specific pain-receptor nerves. In itself it is not evil, serving [inefficiently] as a warning system and serving self-preservation. Pain can be a cause of suffering, but it is not always and is not the predominant cause of suffering. Suffering is that state of mind in which we wish violently or obsessively that our situation were otherwise.

Even more dreadful suffering may result from fear, anxiety, shame, humiliation, estrangement, and injustice than from pain. Such suffering may have no connection with pain at all. Yet such experiences cause intense suffering; they are the most dreaded conditions of life to be avoided. The threat of having to undergo these mental states can cause as much suffering as the inability to terminate their duration. Being the victim of injustice may cause more suffering than sheer pain. Many people can endure pain without mental anguish, but few can endure injustice and shame without intense suffering. We come closer to identifying the meaning of the term evil when we connect it with suffering than with death or pain as such.

In our era, however, the dimension of suffering that is most enigmatic is *violence*. The suffering that generates the most distress is that inflicted by violence, the violation of the person. The heart of evil in our time seems to be the abuse of all kinds of creatures who can suffer.[43] Sometimes the abuse is physical, sometimes mental, and at times it is spiritual. Evil is experienced as wanton cruelty and destructiveness, hurt deliberately inflicted. "Evil is meaningless, senseless destruction. Evil destroys and does not build up; it rips and it does not mend; it cuts and it does not bind. It strives always and everywhere to annihilate, to turn to nothing. To take all being and render it nothing is the heart of evil."[44]

Although some of the discussion of modern violence has focused on superhuman demonic powers of annihilation,[45] the focus in our time is on the violence within the human frame. Some have estimated that between one-third and one-half of all girls have had an abusive sexual experience before the age of eighteen, and that 5 to 10 percent of all boys have been sexually abused.[46] Rosemary Ruether has shown how sexism, the strictly human social system of sexual hierarchy and repression, has worked the violence of subjugation and negation on women. James Cone has shown how racial violence has been inflicted on African Americans, both the violence of the lynch mob and the violence of dehumanization. Rebecca Chopp speaks of the "massive public suffering" of "history's victims," namely, those persons and groups who have lived outside of modernity and suffer the "nonidentity character" of "the nonsubjects of history."[47] Violence in her view refers primarily to the systematic and hidden destruction of human persons through ideology, exploitation, and repression.

The problem of evil in our era, then, is primarily the problem of how to interpret the meaning of violent, abusive suffering—what Wendy Farley calls "radical suffering,"[48]—within a framework of understanding that acknowledges both the reality of evil so contrived, the depth of it, and our defenses against it.

It seems to me, though, that there is another dimension to the meaning of evil which must be added to the suffering of violence and abuse. Such suffering is undeserved, and it has a menacing quality of malevolence to it.[49] In this context, the concept of evil points to the *meaninglessness* of suffering. Abusive violence is experienced as meaningless suffering inflicted by an "abuser," be it a virus, a parent, a spouse, an institution, bureaucracies, an economic or political system, an indifferent nature, the gods, God [Job and Jeremiah]. The problem of evil in our century is about the meaningless suffering of individuals and groups.[50] The overwhelming sense of meaninglessness makes such suffering intrinsically evil.

Meaningless suffering can be experienced by individuals, either in moments of *extremity* (terminal illness or premature death, most poignantly the death of innocent children), or in long periods of *despondency,* of unendurable or irremediable suffering of individuals (as in suicides of the terminally ill or depressed). Such suffering can also be experienced by groups and communities, either in moments of extremity (the holocaust of Native Americans or Jews or Russian peasants), or long periods of despondency (four hundred years of African-American slavery and dehumanization).[51]

When we are talking about evil as a religious and theological concept, then, I propose that we are not talking about the routine discomforts and even failures of daily life, for which the self-help advice of "grow up a bit" is perhaps the best theological advice to give. We are using a language that points to the abusive violence individuals and communities undergo, the kind of suffering that confronts mature individuals and communities with the threat of meaninglessness and hopelessness. *Evil* is the term we use to describe dimensions of our experience that threaten the meaning created and maintained by what Peter Berger calls the "sacred canopy" of religion. Our concept of radical evil is the deepest challenge to this function of religion.

The Theodicy Problem
Formally Formulated

Christian theology has consistently held in the midst of our experience of meaningless suffering that God is omnipotent and omnibenevolent, and that evil is real. The theological problem is whether or not one can hold all three of these affirmations simultaneously without contradiction. Theodicy [*theos* = God, *dike* = justice: Can one justify the ways of God?] *narrowly or strictly* conceived is the effort to show that Christians can hold all of these three beliefs simultaneously with logical consistency. "Theodicy is the attempt to *reconcile* belief in the goodness and power of God with the fact of evil in the world."[52] Theodicy *broadly or more loosely* conceived is the effort to *understand* the occurrence of, significance of, and response to suffering within the larger framework, under the "sacred canopy," of what one believes about God and the world.

William Blake's "The Tiger" asks in the most dramatic images the question that has troubled the human mind—both believing and unbelieving—for centuries:

> When the stars threw down their spears,
> And watered heaven with their tears,
> Did he smile his work to see?
> Did he who made the Lamb make thee?

Formulated in a simple syllogism, the logical problem can be stated in this syllogistic form:

> If God is omnipotent, God could prevent all evil.
> If God is perfectly good, God would want to prevent all evil.
> There is evil.
> Therefore, (an omnipotent, perfectly good) God does not exist.

Or more precisely formulated:

> God is a perfect reality.
> A perfect reality is an omnipotent being.
> An omnipotent being could unilaterally bring about an actual world
>   without any genuine evil.
> A perfect reality is a morally perfect being.
> A morally perfect being would want to bring about an actual world
>   without any genuine evil.
> If there is genuine evil in the world, then there is no God.
> There is genuine evil in the world.
> Therefore, there is no God.[53]

Is Theodicy a Modern Gender Issue?

In an era when we are increasingly aware of the contextual nature of all theological problems, it is necessary to ask whether theodicy is a distinctly modern European and North American male theological conundrum. This is an especially pressing question when we recognize that the term itself, *theodicy,* and the typical formulation of the philosophical and theological predicament, arose with Gottfried Leibniz during the eighteenth-century European Enlightenment. The confidence of his *Essais de théodicée sur la bonté de Dieu, la liberté de l'homme et l'origine du mal* (1710), was contested by the Lisbon earthquake in which thousands died on All Saints Day in 1755. This natural disaster had shaken the melioristic optimism of the European Enlightenment with its faith in the order and regularity of nature.[54] Insofar as the problem of theodicy is an Enlightenment problem, shaped by the presuppositions and agendas of the Enlightenment (order and melioristic optimism), the problem of theodicy as a technical problem might in the end be a distinctly European Enlightenment problem.

Furthermore, one must ask whether theodicy is a distinctly male question, that is, whether this formulation of the problem and effort to respond is peculiar to male experience and concerns. Nel Noddings, for example, has argued that theodicy is "thoroughly suffused with male interests and conditioned by masculine experience."[55] There is "a female morality of evil" which describes evil from the perspective of women's experience. By pursuing "the logic of thinking that arises in female experience," we can "avoid the distractions about God, sin, symbol, and medical science and remain fixed on human-to-human interaction."[56]

Noddings defines evil phenomenologically, preferring not to ask for definitions of evil and about some larger body of thought that defines the origin,
character, meaning, and ultimate resolution of evil. Her book *Women and Evil,*
rather, is devoted to a description of the way women experience and respond
to pain, to helplessness in poverty, to war and terrorism, and to psychological
abuse. Although she does not argue that theodicy is male ideology, she does
understand "the problem of evil" to be the problem of how to respond to suffering instead of being the problem of how to understand evil within a larger
framework of understanding. Her implication is that theodicy as such is a male
project in response to a male problem.

In an important sense, I think Noddings and the critics of theodicy proper
as ideology are correct. The word itself and its classical formulation have a specific social location. Furthermore, I know of no women who are engaged in
theodicy in its strictest sense, and I know of only one African-American theologian who has devoted serious attention to the theological problem in its
strict definition.[57]

I do not believe, however, that the theological problem can be dismissed
too easily by claiming theodicy is simply ideology. The only way one can do
that successfully, I think, is to define theodicy so narrowly and so contextually
that the problem does not exist outside a specific gender or racial or cultural
context. However, the religious and theological problems motivating theodicy
exist far beyond these contexts. And the task of *understanding,* of fitting one's
experience of suffering within a context of *interpretation,* is as common to religious life and practice as is the problem of *describing* and *responding* to our
experience of suffering.

Clearly there is no universal, even common, language of interpretation, description, or response to our suffering. But for many people in many contexts,
the religious life consists of interpretation as well as practice. For example,
Rosemary Ruether and Nel Noddings have a strong sense of the tragic sense
or dimension of life, as do Kathleen Sands[58] and Wendy Farley.[59] Womanist
theologians, likewise, have raised the theodicy question in their own context
and offered their own "answers."[60] According to my understanding, these
women are dealing with the questions of *adequate understanding* within their
religious perspective as well as accurate description and effective response to
suffering, and hence they are dealing with theodicy.

It is theodicy as understanding and interpretation as well as faith and practice as responses to suffering that together constitute the religious life. Unless
theodicy is defined in the narrowest sense possible, and is defined as a modern European male problem, I suggest that theodicy in the broad sense is an
intrinsic part of the religious life. There is no one, universal experience of our
suffering, and no transcendental perspective for interpretation and response;
hence every understanding of the problem as well as every response is socially
located. But the struggle to understand, to creating a context of interpretation
as well as practice, is a deep human quest, one that is at the center of the religious life itself.

Is Theodicy Possible?

The answer to this question, as above, depends on the definition of the term *theodicy*. In the *strict, formal* sense, the term has a very precise meaning: Specifically, can a person justify holding a theistic concept of God (God as an omnipotent and omnibenevolent being) while at the same time acknowledging the reality of evil in the world, without being involved in a contradiction? "Theodicy is the attempt to *reconcile* belief in the goodness and power of God with the fact of evil in the world."[61] Theodicy in this sense succeeds when one has proved that there is no self-contradiction involved in holding these three affirmations simultaneously.[62] In the strict sense of the term, then, *theodicy* is primarily a logical problem, a problem of how to hold apparently contradictory propositions simultaneously without contradiction.

There is, however, a less formal, less technical problem of theodicy, and that is the concept of theodicy that underlies my project. Theodicy *broadly* conceived is the effort to *understand* the occurrence and the place of evil within one's larger theological framework which defines and describes what one believes about God and the world. Specifically, how does one understand the reality and character of God in the face of real evil? Theodicy in this broader sense does not presuppose the necessity of the theistic God. In this broader meaning, theodicy is the search for a larger perspective on the divine reality and the reality of evil. Specifically, it is an effort to understand the nature of God in the face of the evidence of real evil. In this sense, any effort to address the reality of evil as an interpretive problem within the framework of an ultimate, or larger, or inclusive framework is a theodicy. Theodicy in this sense succeeds when it shows how a concept of God and the reality of evil "fit" within a believable and religiously workable framework.

Given this reconception of theodicy, we nonetheless must face two significant charges that are made against *any* effort to formulate *any* kind of theodicy. One objection is a political one, and the other is a theological one.

1. The political objection to theodicy is that every theodicy is in fact an ideology. That is, any attempt to interpret the nature of God in a world of real evil inevitably serves to defend and preserve the status quo, since theodicy serves to justify evil as inevitable, necessary, and hence ultimately good. Theodicy, specifically, is justification, and "the radicality of human suffering is such than any *justification* of it must inevitably trivialize evil."[63]

Theodicy is done by white, male, European and North American academics, who do it in order to preserve and defend their views of the world and their current interests as inevitable, necessary, right or good, and hence just. Theodicies seldom come to terms with the incommensurability and magnitude of evil by disallowing the screams of our society or any suffering people to be heard above their rationalizations. Formulas are substituted for reality. If one explains through a theodicy why the evils of the world are inevitable or necessary, one has cut the nerve of changing the world in any fundamental way.

This issue is a complex one, and anyone willing to devote any time to theodicy as an interpretation of any divine reality in a world of real evil must face the charge squarely. Every theodicy is based on the experiences as well as interpretive framework of the theodicist. For example, when I claim, as I did above, that human life is possible only on the basis of the conviction that life on balance is meaningful, I have to examine carefully the degree to which this claim is merely North American middle-class assertion reflecting my place in life. Because gender, class, and race inevitably play roles in anyone's thinking, it is essential that there be a variety of theodicies and that any proponent of one be prepared to engage in discussion and to hear counterarguments from other experiences and perspectives.

At the same time, I am unable to accept as decisive the charge that every theodicy is merely an ideology. First, *every* religious perspective, with its mythology, rituals, symbols, and rhetoric is implicitly a theodicy in the broad sense of the term. It not only provides means by which to accommodate or transform meaningless suffering; it provides a framework in which to *understand* it, to *explain* its origins, to *offer* resolutions, and to *recommend* responses. What critics might appropriately mean is that any specific theodicy is too class or gender specific, but they cannot mean that the effort to understand is itself class or gender or race specific, for every religious or semireligious or quasireligious or antireligious rhetoric offers a perspective through which to overcome suffering and evil by interpreting it within a framework of understanding and response. Even to interpret suffering as meaningless, random, arbitrary, or fate is to interpret the significance and meaning of it.

2. Theodicy also has been challenged on theological grounds. Kenneth Surin, for example, contends that any attempt to formulate a theodicy is likely to fail because in our era the historical conditions of secularization no longer permit the problem of evil to be answered by an essentially theological undertaking. The intellectual burden of the problem of evil has shifted from theodicy to anthropodicy, from God to humankind. Furthermore, theodicy by its very nature involves the application of the principles of reason to a problem that essentially defies the application of rational principles. The purpose of theodicy is to slot evil and suffering into a scheme of things compatible with the working of divine providence, thus taking on the role of Job's comforters who seek to render the intractable tractable.

Kenneth Surin's counterproposal is that the problem of evil can be reconciled with the existence of a loving God only if God becomes the God of salvation. The questions of suffering and evil can be approached only from the point of view of soteriology. The question of the coherence of theistic claims is secondary to the acknowledgment of the God of salvation. Interpretations of evil should be done only in such a way that the theologian can find out what God reveals through salvation about the suffering that exists in God's creation.

> The answer to the problem lies in a praxis, involving the very being of God. . . . The God who shares our suffering is a God who justifies himself, and the God who disengages himself from our afflictions cannot be justified, either by man or himself—the God who is a mere onlooker when confronted with gratuitous suffering is a demon and not a God.[64]

Terrence Tilly put forward a similar argument by distinguishing between a defense and a theodicy.[65] In a defense the believer is trying to show that the reality of evil does not conflict with the belief in God; in a theodicy, the believer is trying to show what God's reason is for causing or permitting evil. Theodicy cannot be used for the purpose for which it is constructed, namely, to explain evil. Christian theists cannot and should not try to explain evil. Rather the believers' task is to defend the plausibility of their faith in God in the light of the fact of evil. This search for plausibility is possible only by setting the fact of evil within the *wide range* of beliefs the Christian holds. In short, the problem of evil can be dealt with only within the context of a larger dogmatic theology.

Stanley Hauerwas claims even more directly that theodicy is a theological error.[66] There is no "problem of evil" in Christian faith. Theodicy is strictly a modern question created by seventeenth- and eighteenth-century Enlightenment philosophical theism. "The creation of 'the' problem of evil is a correlative of the creation of a god that, it was presumed, could be known separate from a community of people at worship."[67] Theodicy is a modern parasitic endeavor that draws its life from more positive modes of communal life. For the life of faith, suffering is real, but there is no such thing as suffering that challenged belief in the existence of God as such.

All theodicies explain too much; there is no explanation. In Hauerwas's view, suffering just happens.

> The problem of evil is not about rectifying our suffering with some general notion of God's nature as all-powerful and good; rather, it is about what we mean by God's goodness itself, which for Christians must be construed in terms of God as the Creator who has called into existence a people called Israel so that the world might know that God has not abandoned us. There is no problem of suffering in general; rather, the question of suffering can be raised only in the context of a God who creates to redeem.[68]

All three of these critics argue that our encounter with suffering can be understood only within the context of our larger community narrative of covenant and salvation, our presuppositional framework, or of our dogmatic theology, not in the context of philosophical theism which is abstracted from the life of faith and presented as an isolated conceptual problem to be answered by conceptual manipulation.

This argument is a quibbling over terms, not a disagreement about one of the tasks of the life of faith. Whether or not theodicy is possible and desirable depends primarily on *how one defines the term*. What should be obvious is that we have here a conflict over definitions of terms and whether one should use the term theodicy to describe one's theological work.

The strictest definition of theodicy is the only concept of theodicy these three critics accept. And there have been many theodicists, such as Alvin Plantinga, Michael Peterson, John Hick, and David Griffin, who accept this definition and work within its framework and goal, either by showing how the beliefs can be held simultaneously without contradiction (Plantinga and Peterson) or by refining the terms so that a coherent view of all three can be maintained (Hick and Griffin). That is, they attempt to explain how God works and why God works that way within the categories of classical or neoclassical theism. They claim to know what God's purposes and mode of operation in the world are and thereby offer a strict, formal theodicy.

There is, however, another kind of theological thinking about evil that is properly called theodicy, even though it restricts itself neither to the terms nor the goal of theodicy narrowly conceived. It, too, seeks to *understand* the nature and place of meaningless suffering within the context of belief in God. In this broader concept of theodicy, "it is not a question of whether the world of our compassion makes sense without God, but rather what kind of God it is Christians worship that makes intelligible our cry of rage against the suffering and death of our children."[69] The purpose of such a theodicy is not to defend theism, and the framework of understanding is not set by the traditional meaning of the terms goodness and power as defined by theism.

Surin, Tilley, and Hauerwas are as involved in theodicy as are the classical theistic theodicists. They claim to know the purposes of God and the divine economy about suffering and evil just as much as theistic theodicists. They simply disagree with modern theodicists about the goal, scope, and method used in exploring the questions. But they do not reject for one minute the effort to *understand suffering and evil within a theological framework.* Any Christian theologian who denies either the possibility or the necessity of theodicy in this broader sense, as the attempt to "make sense" or "fit" our suffering within a narrative or a theological perspective, within an understanding of the nature and activity of God, is more a clever sophist than a convincing theologian.

Indeed, I want to argue that anyone who has any interest in religion as an issue of life and death is inevitably involved in theodicy. Religion is not concerned primarily with understanding the details of the world; it is concerned to understand how the details fit together to make up "a world," whether that world be coherent, purposeful, illusory, fallen, or random happenings. *Rationalism* is one coherent theory about the world; *chaos* is another all-inclusive way of understanding what the world as a whole is like. Religion is devoted to understanding how our individual lives, our society, nature, and the galaxies fit together into a meaningful framework.

But all socially constructed worlds are inherently precarious. How one maintains or reestablishes a world order when it is disrupted by death, ignorance, stupidity, error, corruption, or evil is the other fundamental task of religion. One way to understand Christianity is to understand it as one grand theodicy, a constructed coherent account of what evil is, why it is evil, and how it can be overcome.[70] When we encounter the problem of evil and ask how to understand and overcome it, we stand at the heart of what Christian faith and life are about.

2

"Everything Is Beautiful in Its Own Way"

The Great Tradition

◄ As seventeen-year-old Joni Eareckson, attractive high-school honor society member of Young Life, dove into Chesapeake Bay in July 1967, she felt her head strike something hard. She sustained a diagonal fracture between the fourth and fifth cervical levels of her spine, and would be encased as a total quadriplegic in a Stryker Frame for several years. Because of her belief that the accident was part of "some cosmic plan," that it fit into the "overall purposes of God," that "God engineered circumstances" and "used them to prove himself as well as [her] loyalty," she concluded that her "injury was not a tragedy but a gift God was using to help [her] conform to the image of Christ." This belief enabled her to survive long periods of severe depression and to learn to draw by holding a pencil in her teeth. Joni has appeared on television and before mass audiences witnessing to her story of faith in Christ.[1]

Dave Dravecky nurtured the dream of many American boys of becoming a major-league baseball player. Graduating from college in 1978, he was drafted by the Pittsburgh Pirates and traded three years later to the San Diego Padres. After spending five years bouncing around the minor leagues playing AAA ball, he was finally called to the big leagues in 1982, appearing in the 1983 All Star game and the 1984 league championship and World Series games, pitching 10⅔ scoreless innings. In 1987, he was traded to the San Francisco Giants, the year they won the National League championship. During his time of striving to become a major league player, Dave had become a born-again evangelical Christian.

In 1988 he discovered a lump on his left pitching arm, which was said probably to be benign. Later that year, however, the lump was diagnosed by the Cleveland Clinic as cancerous, and surgery followed to remove one-half of the deltoid muscle; to kill the cancer cells, part of the humerus bone was frozen. The next year, 1989, after pitching some minor league games, he returned to the Giants' pitching rotation for his comeback game against the Reds. Five days later, as he was pitching against Montreal, his humerus bone snapped, and a couple of weeks later his arm was broken again in a postgame celebration. By the end of the month he was told that the

cancer had returned, and by the middle of the next month he announced his re-
tirement. His first book, titled *Comeback*,[2] ended in uncertainty about his future.

Dave's second book, titled *When You Can't Come Back,* describes the decision to amputate his left arm in order to deter the spread of the cancer. He is
clear that he never asked the question, Why? "Early on in my battle with cancer, I discovered the importance of asking the right questions. I decided not to
get mired in the question 'Why?' Instead I decided to ask, 'What good can come
out of this so that others might benefit.'"[3] Near the end of the book he describes
how his interpretation of the mystery of God enabled him and his wife, Jan, to
endure his disappointment and loss. "God willed a world that is as mysterious
as it is majestic. I believe God rules over that world, but I don't believe he gave
me cancer. He allowed it. Why? I don't know. I don't know the purpose of my
suffering. But I do know the results. When I compare the Dave Dravecky before cancer and the Dave Dravecky after, there's no comparison."[4]

These two stories are among countless other stories of Christians who have
located the confidence, security, and meaning of their lives and their interpretation of their suffering in their belief that God caused, intended, or permitted all the suffering that happened in their lives according to God's eternal,
mysterious, and perfect purpose. "Everything is beautiful in its own way," they
have affirmed. "Nothing happens outside the will of God."

What I intend to do in this chapter and the next is to describe as accurately
as I can what many Christians implicitly believe about the character and activity of God but do not articulate explicitly. The theistic idea of God is a subtle, translucent thread woven into the language of Christian liturgies, sermons,
and hymns, and deeply shapes our response to suffering. I will try to describe
as accurately as I can the concept of God that lies behind much Christian interpretation of suffering. I will also give reasons why many Christians continue
to hold to this view of God. At the same time I will criticize this viewpoint and
offer alternative views throughout the remainder of the book.

Classical Theism

There is no Christian concept of God. There are concepts of God held by
Christians. The center of theological debate today is not about whether we can
believe *the* Christian idea of God or not, but is rather about what concepts of
God are and are not usable by Christians. Many biblical scholars and theologians have stressed the diversity of the images of God in scripture and tradition, and others have argued that the biblical and trinitarian God is significantly
different from the theistic God of the philosophers and theologians of the
Western tradition. Our challenge in this book is to engage this discussion in
the context of theodicy.

Nevertheless, there are three initial observations to make.

1. There is a concept of God that has been typical of the philosophical and
theological discussion about God in the West. It exists alongside the trinitar-

ian formula of the creeds and liturgies of the churches. Shaped by the intuitions and assumptions of Greek philosophy as much as by biblical images and liturgical practice, the doctrine of God that informs our theology and philosophy is a distinctly Western creation. Pascal referred to it as "the God of the philosophers, not the God of Abraham, Isaac, and Jacob." This concept that exists alongside the trinitarian God of the creeds and liturgies is usually referred to as "monotheism" or "theism," sometimes as "supernaturalism." I will refer to it from here on as "classical theism."[5]

2. The theistic concept of God has determined the way most Western Christians understand their experience of suffering, and it has shaped the way most Christians in the West respond to the suffering in their lives. Although the vast majority of Christians are neither interested in nor able to formulate the theistic concept of God, their interpretation of suffering and their response to it are determined by this classical theistic concept of God. Behind the question, "Why did God take my baby?" or the claim that the death of my baby was the will of God lies a theistic concept of God.

3. Therefore, suffering and evil are the *kinds* of problems they are for Christians for a very simple reason. The classical theistic concept of God creates a trilemma which Christians cannot escape. At least on first view, it appears as though one cannot hold three fundamental claims simultaneously (God is omnipotent, God is omnibenevolent, and evil is real) without contradiction. If one could easily eliminate one of the terms or even make a significant modification of the meaning of one of them, the dilemma would evaporate. Such an accomplishment would not mean that Christians would cease to suffer. But the way they understand their suffering in relation to God would be radically altered. The "problem of evil" is created and shaped for Christians by the theistic concept of God they have inherited.

Who or what is God in the Western theological tradition?[6] Theism refers to the concept of God developed by medieval and modern theology in conversation with classical metaphysics.[7] One of the most succinct definitions has been provided by Richard Swinburne in his *The Coherence of Theism*. God is

> a person without a body (I. e., a spirit), present everywhere, the creator and sustainer of the universe, a free agent, able to do everything (I. e., omnipotent), knowing all things, perfectly good, a source of moral obligation, immutable, eternal, a necessary being, holy, and worthy of worship.[8]

For theists, God is the supreme being who is infinite (unlimited), *a se* (self-existent), and eternal. God is creator of the world *ex nihilo*. All these claims imply that God is not dependent for God's existence or for fullness of God's being, knowledge, and power on anyone else or anything else whatsoever. God is *essentially* unrelated to the world and hence unaffected by what happens in the world. These characteristics together imply that God is simple, perfect, immutable, omnipresent, omniscient, *omnibenevolent,* and *omnipoten* Nothing happens in the world that is beyond the sovereign power of God achieve.

Without violating the nature of all things, and without at any stage infring-
ing upon the human free will, God acts in, with, and through his creatures
to do everything that he wishes to do exactly as he wishes to do it. By his
sovereign, overruling action he achieves his goals.[9]

The Great Tradition in Scripture

There is no biblical theodicy. In the scriptures, "various solutions are
proffered" to our question about God and human suffering.[10] At least five
interpretations are offered in the Old Testament: retributive justice, or punishment for sin; pedagogy, or testing and cleansing; rebellion or submission;
resignation; and apocalyptic, or endurance or passive resistance.[11] However, to one of the most difficult questions asked in ancient Israel, Why do
the innocent suffer and the wicked prosper? (Jer.12:1), the most common
explanation given was human sinfulness. Suffering is the punishment for
sin. An entire "Deuteronomic theology of history" derived from this intuition
of divine retribution; it pervades the Yahwistic narrative and the work of the
Chronicler.

> This history of Israel from the conquest to the Exile was written in the shad-
> ows of the tragic events of 721 and 586 B.C. One might say that it was com-
> posed amid the ashes of the Holy City of Jerusalem. . . . The course of Is-
> rael's history had been the result of the covenant curse upon covenant
> disobedience. . . . According to the Deuteronomic historian, Yahweh's peo-
> ple were confronted at every important junction in their history with the sum-
> mons to obey the law and with the promise of blessing for obedience and
> with the threat of the curse for disobedience.[12]

This explanation achieved at least the status of the commonly held theology
of suffering in Israel, if not of orthodoxy. The three cycles of speeches of the
three counselors to Job all convey this dominant theology of suffering. The
protests against God and alternative suggestions were a response to this "official" theodicy. Divine pedagogy, a theophany of the divine presence, an eschatology of a messianic age, the unjust God, redemption or vicarious suffering, and antitheodicy, also themes in the Bible, arise in response to this
"orthodox" theodicy.

Walter Brueggemann develops a thesis about a primary theodicy and the
emergence of various alternative theodicies in the Old Testament.[13] Old Testament theology, and so Old Testament theodicy, he argues, must be understood in bipolar fashion. On the one hand, Old Testament faith serves to legitimate the structures and happenings of the world. It does this by sharing the
"common theology" of its Near Eastern environment. On the other hand, there
's a "minority report" offered by some sages in Israel who are skeptical about
 e truth of this shared theology.

 "Common theology" centered on a scheme of law, justice, and retribution.
  entire design served to give order and meaning to the world by ascribing

each to the rule of God. This theology carried with it a ground for social structure and moral coherence. Specifically, the common theology: (1) includes the
Sinai covenant, a tight system of sanctions, of punishments and rewards articulated as blessings and curses. (2) It includes also the Deuteronomic theology,
the sustained portrayal of Israel's royal history from the perspective of Torah
obedience and disobedience. It commits to the rigors of Mosaic sanctions, and
that includes a tight system of payoffs. (3) Even the prophets remain within
the domain of the common theology. The lawsuit genre is the basic form of
prophetic speech, namely, the indictment asserts Israel's disobedience and the
curse for Israel's disobedience. (4) Finally, some of the wisdom literature holds
a quite similar understanding of reality. Punishment and reward, deeds and
consequences dominate this material as well.

"There is a basic commitment to contractual theology, and if that is foundational to the Mosaic traditions, deuteronomic theology, the prophets, and
the wisdom materials, then we may say that it is the foundational construct of
Israel's faith."[14] The entire scheme created a *nomos,* a structure of order and
meaning, for there is a moral rationality and coherence to a life of suffering
that is ordered by God. "These are orders, limits, and boundaries within which
humanness is possible and beyond which there can only be trouble. This creation theology, a theology of coherence and rationality, this theology of God's
sovereignty and providence, is basic to the religion of the Old Testament. All
questions, doubts, complaints, and refusals depart from this common understanding of good and evil."[15]

The Great Tradition in Theology

To Thee there is no such thing as evil.
(Augustine, *Confessions,* 8.13)

There is not much in the history of Western Christian thought apart from
the doctrines of the Trinity and Christology that one can claim with some assurance are "orthodox" because they are creeds affirmed by almost all Christians. There is, however, a line of common teaching on the question of the
cause and nature of suffering and evil from at least the early fifth century
through the nineteenth century that is so deeply rooted in the language and
unconscious assumptions of Christians that this perspective might be called
"functionally orthodox" (an unusual phrase, to be sure).

This mainstream tradition, which I will designate as "Augustinian theodicy,"
has shaped not only the intellectual answers given to the questions of the origin and nature of evil but the piety and existential confidences and practices
of most Western Christians as well. From the time of Augustine's repudiation
of the Manichaeans through Thomas, Anselm, the Protestant Reformers, and
Leibniz (the originator of the term theodicy), up to and including Schleiermacher[16] in the nineteenth century, there has been a clear and unbroken line of
orthodox Christian thinking and piety on the problem of suffering and evil.

The fountainhead of this tradition unquestionably is Augustine. His writings on the origin, nature, and solution(s) to the problem of suffering and evil are scattered throughout his writings. John Hick has provided us with the clearest systematic statement of Augustine's theodicy that is available today.[17] Hick detects four major themes that are found in the writings of Augustine.

1. Evil is a *privation of the good*. "And I inquired what iniquity was, and ascertained it not to be a substance, but a perversion of the will, bent aside from Thee, O God, the Supreme Substance, towards these lower things, and casting out its bowels, and swelling outwardly. . . . For what is that which we call evil but the absence of good?"[18] In order to uphold God's absolute power and absolute goodness, Augustine rejects any notion of evil as having an ontological status and character over against or even apart from God. Hence, he thought of God's creation as inherently good,[19] and of evil as simply the corruption of a mutable good, a malfunctioning of something that is intrinsically good. Evil is a lack, a loss, a privation, parasitic rather than primary and essential.

For example, disease is simply a loss of normal bodily functioning. Although empirically evil is not merely the absence of something else but a reality with its own distinctive and often terrifying quality and power, evil cannot be anything substantial, a positive constituent of the universe, but can only be a loss of natural form and order, a malfunctioning of something that is in itself good. Otherwise, there is something inherently wrong with the creation as such from the very beginning. Evil would therefore be intrinsic to creation and not contingent, and that would impugn the holiness of God. This notion that evil is only a privation of the good is one of the primary meanings of the claim below that evil is "only apparent."

2. In order to account for how something could go wrong with an inherently good (perfect) creation, Augustine appeals to the *"free will defense."*[20] He attributes all evil, both natural and moral, directly or indirectly to the wrong choices of free rational creatures. All suffering and evil are attributable in their origin to sin and its penalty. The angels, and then Adam and Eve, freely and willfully turned away from their good. This disobedience of Adam and Eve was a free act of the will; that is, it was not coerced by anyone else, including God. Its origin, then, is finally hidden in the mystery of finite freedom. The corruption of the good creation comes wholly from a finite corrupt will, and all suffering and evil are the just judgment and punishment of God on the corrupt choices of the will. Therefore, every creature finally deserves all the punishment for sin that all must endure, if not for their own sin, then for the unspeakable sin of the primeval parents, Adam and Eve. In short, *all* the groaning of the whole of the creation, including human suffering, is just punishment for someone's sin.

God, however, ultimately controls the will of free creatures. "The wills of men are so much in the power of God, that he can turn them whithersoever it pleases him."[21] Therefore, God foreknew and foreordained the sin of the angels and then of Adam and Eve.

But because God foreknew all things, and was therefore not ignorant that man also would fall, we ought to consider this holy city in connection with what God foresaw and ordained, and not according to our own ideas, which do not embrace God's ordination. For man, by his sin, could not disturb the divine counsel, nor compel God to change what He had decreed; for God's foreknowledge had anticipated both—that is to say, both how evil the man whom he had created good should become, and what good He himself should even thus derive from him.[22]

3. But why did God make so imperfect a creature as human beings who could sin? Why did God not restrict God's creation to a perfect contingent being (free but *always* choosing right)? Augustine's answer came from the Neoplatonic *principle of plenitude,* namely, that belief that a universe containing every possible variety of creatures, from the highest to the lowest, is a richer and better universe than would be one consisting solely of the highest possible kinds of created beings. In creating the world, God is guided by the principle of plenitude, considering it better to produce all possible forms of being, each and all contributing to a wonderful harmony and beauty of the creation, than to produce only a society of blessed angels.[23]

This should not seem to be a strange idea at all to modern Westerners who have been influenced by Enlightenment liberalism, especially romanticism, or even by postmodern antifoundationalism, where variety, diversity, complexity, richness, difference, and plurality are taken to be intrinsically more valuable (or more "real," as in plural*ism*) than similarity and uniformity. If anything, the intrinsic value of plenitude is even more deeply admired today than in Augustine's day, at least by moderns and postmoderns, for today it is not simply an aesthetic principle but is a moral and even ontological principle as well (philosophical pluralists and pluralism).

This viewpoint did not originate with postmodernity, or the ecological movement, or romanticism, or medieval theology, or the classical theology of Augustine. It is the argument of God in the God-speeches at the end of Job. God does not create the world for human benefit alone. It is created in all its variety and enrichment for God's enjoyment. "Where were you when I laid the foundation of the earth?" asks God, the lover of carnivorous tigers as much as small birds. In the list of wondrous and unconquerable creatures God has created, the celebrated animal kingdom consists primarily of nondomesticated animals, animals that were not for direct human benefit: peacocks, lions, wild goats, oxen, asses, ostriches, cliff eagles, all recited joyously in front of the abused Job. They were creatures of sheer delight to God.

4. Directly related to the principle of plenitude is Augustine's *aesthetic* theme, his affirmation that, seen in its totality from the infinite standpoint of the Creator, the universe is wholly good. The apparent evil within it is determined by God to contribute to the complex perfection of the whole. God's creation is like a work of art, and like any beautiful work of art, such as a mosaic, it must contain purple as well as pink colors, jagged as well as smooth

chunks, dark areas as well as light. Alas, by analogy, the world as God's work of art must contain evil, including animal pain, human suffering, and even hell in order that God's creation may be aesthetically balanced. Thus, suffering and evil are essential to God's aesthetic sensibilities.

What this theme means is that even though we may not see the necessary place that pain, suffering, sin, and hell play in God's creation, we would know that all suffering and evil in every form and proportion is both necessary and good if we saw it from God's point of view. They contribute to the aesthetic cosmic harmony. Thus, *I* may not know *why* God caused or permitted my sorority sister to die in a weekend accident or *why* God caused or permitted the Holocaust, but I know *that* from God's point of view it has its place, purpose, and meaning in the harmonious whole of God's creation.

Regardless of whether one formulates this principle in a premodern formulation, that is, that God from the foundations of the world willed all that happens for *aesthetic* purposes, or in a modern formulation, namely, that God's omnipotent will makes all things good either now or in the next life for *personalistic* purposes, the assumption of this perspective nevertheless is that evil has its necessary place to play within the perfect purposes of God. Whatever happens is finally not evil but good, specifically in the sense that the world (from God's point of view and for God's purposes) would not have been better off without any event that happens in the world. This is the second meaning of my conjunction, below, of the two words "only apparent" in discussing the classical tradition.

Divine Omnipotence and Evil

I am convinced the problem of theodicy in the late modern West focuses primarily on the question of the nature of God's power. The concept of God's omnipotence is located at the center of classical theism. Without that notion theism falls apart. But the notion of omnipotent power has become problematic for many postmoderns for a variety of reasons, including not only philosophical and religious but political and moral ones as well. Thus, the theological problem of suffering and evil must face head-on the problem of the meaning and implications of the theistic notion of omnipotence in a postmodern world.

I am equally convinced, at the same time, of the contextual nature of this theological problem. Different communities give different meanings to the term omnipotence. I refer not so much to different definitions of the word, as to different uses in the religious life of the community. Sometimes the terms omnipotence, sovereignty, and Lordship are used interchangeably both in pious and theological interpretations of suffering. Also, in some communities the use of the word omnipotence functions in a religious sense without any intended commitment to what is implied theologically and philosophically by the word.

For example, in experience, intuition, tone, and implication, omnipotence seems to mean something significantly different for many African Americans (and many white Christians as well) than for other Christians whose ideas and sensibilities are shaped by the European theological traditions. The term *functions* in different ways in these different communities. For the latter, especially those influenced, through either education or popular culture, by the liberal and postliberal traditions of Feuerbach, Nietzsche, Marx, and Freud, omnipotence carries such connotations as hierarchy, threat to autonomy, repression, diminishment of freedom, dehumanization, and fate, whereas in the former communities the term conveys, instead, dependability, faithfulness, endurance, and life affirmation in the midst of suffering and evil.[24]

Many African-American Christians use the term very freely, indeed insist on retaining the term in common usage as essential to their religious faith. In their experience and their hope there is a transcendent, omnipotent power that is trustworthy, universal, and everlasting, a power of creation and transformation that is the ground of resilience, resistance, and hope, and the word omnipotence expresses this faith. Since the social location of many African Americans (as well as many white Christians) and of most liberal white Christians is so different, the word *functions* differently and therefore *means* something different within each community. For many who use the term, the word is used in the context of worship to express ultimate confidence in the divine power. For others, the word serves to sustain and justify the oppressive and abusive functions of theism in the Western world. Because of a certain kind of logic and piety, then, the idea is freely used in one community; and for reasons of another kind of logic and piety, the idea is problematic in another community.

If we use a pragmatic criterion of meaning and truth, in which the meaning and truth of the idea of an omnipotent God rest in usage and its consequence in the lives of its users, we must conclude that omnipotence means significantly different things and functions in significantly different ways in the lives of these communities. As Cheryl A. Kirk-Duggan describes the use of the term, then,

> African-American spirituals . . . celebrate an *omni*-God, champion of freedom, and hold human choice responsible for personal and institutional evil. . . . The spirituals are committed to a theodicy where God and human beings freely participate together in a society that demands the exorcism of the evils of slavery and racism. These chants cry out for justice and call for accountability, but avoid reductionism at the point of blame and asking *why*. My analysis has as its premise the concept of a liberating *omni-God* and a society made up of individuals who freely make either good, neutral, or evil choices.[25]

I do not intend to deny or even ignore such religious usages of the term omnipotence. People use words in the ways they choose to use them, and such uses have perfectly good meaning for the users. My intent, rather, is to analyze the term omnipotence as it has been used in the theological tradition from Augustine through the modern liberal period in the West. My own experience indicates that this is not first and foremost a difference is usage between black and white Christians. I know white Christians who use the term in the way Kirk-Duggan formulates it, and I know African-American Christians who intend to claim in their sermons and teachings all that is claimed in the classical theistic tradition. My concern is to critique the meaning of the term in the dominant Western theological tradition which has shaped the theology and piety of many contemporary African-American as well as European Christians.

In classical theism God is characterized, both philosophically and theologically, as transcendent, creative, omnipresent, eternal, omnipotent, limitless, omnibenevolent, and holy. The list of terms varies, but regarding the issue of theodicy all forms of theism have taught that God is *all loving* (I will discuss this concept in chapters 4 and 5) and *all powerful* (chapters 2 and 3).The question here is what omnipotence *means* in the classical theological tradition, and how that bears on the problem of suffering and evil.

Omnipotence means one of two things in classical Western theism. In one notion of divine power, *omnipotence* means "omnicausality." God is the only subject with power—the active, immediate, and originative cause of all things and of all events. Luther says, "By the omnipotent God . . . I do not mean the potentiality by which he could do many things which he does not, but the active power by which he potently works all in all. . . . This omnipotence and foreknowledge of God, I say, completely abolish the dogma of free choice."[26] The idea is more than the idea of immense power, maximal power, or even potential power to do things God does not do. This kind of omnipotence claims that *all* power and the *free exercise* of all power belongs to God alone. God is the sole originative cause of the world and all the events in the world; any other power would be a limitation on the power of God.

In a second meaning of omnipotence, the tradition of the "free will defense," omnipotence means that although God *could* exercise all power, God instead chooses to delegate power to a self-regulating nature and self-determining moral agents. God has the power to bring about any logically possible state of affairs. Furthermore, God possesses "overpower" or "veto power" or "coercive power." God has potentially the kind of power conceived in the first meaning, for God has the power to perform miracles, to harden hearts, to make God-self incarnate, and to bring history and nature to an end. If God does not actually exercise all power all the time, God can exercise all power at any time, did exercise all power in an absolute beginning, and will exercise all power in a determinate end. Natural processes in the world and free choices by agents are causes only in a secondary and derivative sense. They are not creative or originative but are *contingent* powers derived from a more ultimate power. They are dependent powers which ultimately carry out the will of God programmed into them in the beginning or effectively determining them from the future.

From John Calvin's point of view, although the true cause of all events is hidden from us, that cause nevertheless is God. "Therefore the Christian heart, since it has been thoroughly persuaded that all things happen by God's plan, and that nothing takes place by chance, will ever look to him as the principle cause of things, yet will give attention to the secondary causes in their proper place."[27] Again, "For his will is, and rightly ought to be, the cause of all things that are. For if it has any cause, something must precede it, to which it is, as it were, bound; this is unlawful to imagine."[28] Calvin does not mean simply that God permits something to happen or even that God has foreknowledge of it; he means that God wills it and causes it to happen. "All events are governed by God's secret plan; nothing happens except what is knowingly and willingly decreed by God." God governs the course of nature and history down to the smallest details, so that God "directs everything by his incomprehensible wisdom and disposes it to its own end."[29]

God's power is omnipotent also in the sense that it is infinite; it knows no limits because it is not dependent on any other source. Nor can it be affected by other creatures. "Since God is pure causality, pure actuality in relation to the world, and since the world is pure effect, pure potentiality in relation to him, God is the originative, initiating cause of, and is thus responsible for, everything that happens in the world."[30] The causal relation between God and the world is completely one-sided; God acts on and within the world, but not vice versa. Thomas Oden put the claim in a less stark but nevertheless clear way by saying, "God can do all that God wills to do. . . . God is not limited in any of his attributes by anything external to himself. No power has any other source than God. . . . Nothing that God conceives and wills is beyond God's ability and power to accomplish."[31]

There are, then, two distinguishable but closely related ideas entailed in the concept of omnipotence. (1) God is the only or primary cause of every event in the world, and (2) nothing happens in the world that God does not cause within God's all-powerful rule. Even though classical theism, from Augustine through Schleiermacher, has tried to mute the implications of this hard teaching by saying that God "permits" the "free will" to operate in the world, Calvin recognized in his *Institutes of the Christian Religion,* book 3, chapter 23, section 8, and in his *Commentary on Genesis,* that the "free will defense" is for the Christian but a verbal qualification with no real significance. It is a distinction with no difference.

> [There can be] no distinction between God's will and God's permission!. . . But why shall we say "permission" unless it is because God so wills?. . . As if God did not establish the condition in which he wills the chief of his creatures to be! I shall not hesitate, then, simply to confess with Augustine that "the will of God is the necessity of things," and that what he has willed will of necessity come to pass, as those things which he has foreseen will truly come to pass.[32]

Also, in his commentary on Genesis:

> Adam did not fall without the ordination and will of God. It offends the ears of some when it is said that God *willed* this fall; but what else, I pray, is the *permission* of Him, who has the power of preventing, and in whose hand the whole matter is placed, but his will?[33]

This claim is wider than the opinion of an idiosyncratic theologian. It also has had an explicit dogmatic formulation. Chapter III, "Of God's Eternal Decrees," in the Westminster Confession of Faith, says in article 1, "God from all eternity did by the most wise and holy counsel *of his own will, freely and unchangeably ordain whatsoever comes to pass*" (italics added). The confession follows out the logic of this affirmation of faith:

> By the decree of God, for the manifestation of his glory, some men and angels are predestined unto everlasting life, and others fore-ordained to everlasting death. These angels and men, thus predestined and fore-ordained, are particularly and unchangeably designed; and their number is so certain and definite that it cannot be either increased or decreased.[34]

This understanding of omnipotence has implications for piety as well as doctrine. Although many, indeed most, modern Christians do not advocate intellectually (or even permit themselves to say aloud) the philosophical, theological, or dogmatic implications of the idea of omnipotence, they nevertheless hold the notion as the heart of their Christian piety. "What happened to me was God's will," many Christians say in moments of suffering. "God wills everything that happens," they say at times of loss. "Nothing happens that is not the will of God," they confess in moments of ultimate threat.

Acknowledging criticisms of this theological claim, classical theists might ask, rhetorically, How do you know this happening is not the will of God, this is not the best of all possible worlds within the scope of the purposes, foreknowledge, and will of God, this world does not know the bounds of human freedom within the omnipotent power and omnibenevolent purposes of God?

Even from the human point of view, we can imagine, for instance, that World War II and the Holocaust were exhibitions of divine omniscience, omnipotence, and omnibenevolence. If God has an ultimate perfect plan for the people of Israel, how do we know that God did not create or permit the Holocaust to bring forth that plan? If God's plan included the formation of Israel as a state, and if it had been nearly two thousand years since Israel was a state by any common definition of that term, then perhaps the Holocaust was the only possible way that divine power could establish the State of Israel within the parameters of human freedom. And if so, perhaps God unilaterally protected Hitler from assassination or permitted Hitler's life story and the political bureaucracies of the twentieth century because, like Cyrus of old, Hitler played his necessary part, willy-nilly, in the creation of the State of Israel.

Furthermore, God may have used Hitler in another way. Perhaps God unilaterally set the boundaries of what could and couldn't happen in World War II, knowing that if another leader, less megalomaniac and more rational than Hitler, would have been in power, the situation would have gotten so far out of control and so far beyond what was permissible or necessary within the perfect divine plan that that person must be prevented from assuming power, so God protected Hitler to keep the carnage within the boundaries of the perfect divine plan. So God is the "bounds of providence" in the sense that the divine plan moves inexorably toward its completion and no one has any power what-soever to move short of or beyond the limited boundaries of that plan. In that sense, World War II and the Holocaust would have been permitted within the boundaries of finite human freedom and divine omnipotence. Although I may find such an "explanation" to be a psychological, political, moral, and religious outrage, I can find reassurance in the midst of our finite, limited perspective in my belief that, from the point of view of faith in the omnipotent God, "Every-thing is beautiful in its own way."

Strategies of Modification

The implications of this interpretation of divine power have been too diffi-cult, even horrendous, for most Christians to abide. Thus, there have been sev-eral ways Christians have tried to soften the offense of the claim.

The first way is simply to *assert* that the teaching about omnipotence does not conflict with other cherished beliefs. Thus, the Westminster Confession, Chapter III, article 1, after affirming divine omnipotence continues to assert, not to explain, the claim: "yet so as thereby neither is God the author of sin; nor is violence offered to the will of the creatures, nor is the liberty or contin-gency of second causes taken away, but rather established."[35]

So offended are modern Reformed Christians by the monstrous implications of the doctrine of omnipotence and predestination that, in 1903, authors of the *Book of Order* added a "Declaratory Statement," saying,

> While the ordination vow of ministers, ruling elders, and deacons, as set forth in the Form of Government, requires the reception and adoption of the Con-fession of Faith only as containing the system of doctrine taught in the Holy Scriptures, nevertheless . . . the United Presbyterian Church in the United States of America does *authoritatively declare* as follows: First, with refer-ence to Chapter III of the Confession of Faith: that concerning those who are saved in Christ, the doctrine of God's eternal decrees *is held in harmony* with the doctrine of his love to all mankind, his gift of his Son to be the pro-pitiation for the sins of the whole world, and his readiness to bestow his sav-ing grace on all who seek it (italics added).[36]

Another effort to interpret the teaching is offered through the Aristotelian distinction between primary and secondary causes. Thomas Aquinas was one to employ this strategy.

> There is a difference between universal and particular causes. A thing can escape the order of a particular cause, but not the order of a universal cause. For nothing escapes the order of a particular, except through the interven-tion and hindrance of some particular cause. . . . Since, then, all particular causes are included under the universal cause, it is impossible that any ef-fect should escape the range of the universal cause. So far then as an effect escapes the order of a particular cause, it is said to be by chance or fortuitous

in respect to that cause; but if we regard the universal cause, outside whose range no effect can happen, it is said to be foreseen.[37]

The natural world operates according to secondary causes. Principles of cause and effect and human freedom explain at one level of explanation what happens in the world and why it happens. However, the primary cause of all that happens is the will and power of God. Primary causes are not visible or evident to the observer or agent, but the "real cause" or "hidden cause" or "ultimate cause" of all that happens in the world is God. God works *through* secondary causes to accomplish God's will and express God's power. Hence, we explain through science the everyday things that happen according to the secondary causes of events, but the primary cause is God working hiddenly *through* these natural causes and freedom to accomplish God's eternal will.

The religious version of this distinction is the claim that we may freely decide, may will, and may try to enact our decision, but we can do nothing to frustrate the will of God. God will do whatever God wills to do, regardless of how we will, what we decide, and what we do. God will accomplish God's purposes regardless of the laws of nature or human decisions.

Thomas Oden expresses this distinction in terms of a straightforward supernaturalism rather than the Aristotelian distinction between primary and secondary causes. He distinguishes between *absolute* power and ordinate power, that is, power that is without limit and can be exercised without mediating causes in the creation and that power which works through the order of nature. He wants to assert both, without denial (or any effort to relate the one to the other).[38] In a less supernaturalistic way, Langdon Gilkey formulates the distinction not between supernatural and natural power but between the invisible or ultimate cause of any and all events and the visible or proximate causes of any and all events, both operating simultaneously. The point is that one can formulate either a natural or supernatural version of the notion of divine omnipotence as compatible with secondary causes.

Another modification proposes a *provisional* substantial, "real" revision of the doctrine of omnipotence by offering the "free will argument," that is, that God in God's freedom decided to limit God's omnipotent power, to distribute some of that freedom *provisionally* to creatures, and to bind Godself to that free decision, at least until the eschaton.[39] The argument for a creatural free will was made by Augustine, Aquinas, and Calvin. One might even say that Augustine was preoccupied with the problem of human freedom because of his argument with Pelagius. The problem for all three, however, was how to define human freedom in such a way as to maintain the classical notion of omnipotence and still be able to affirm some kind of freedom.

The way to hold both of these ideas together was to define freedom as the absence of external causality. As long as one is not forced by some external reality to do what one in fact wills, one is free, even if the ultimate, hidden will of God is the final or ultimate cause of what one wills. This freedom, however, is only *provisional* in the sense that *ultimately now and especially as will be apparent in the end* all must fulfill the ultimate purposes of the omnipotent God, destined everlastingly by divine decision and power. Hence, the classical notion of freedom must be distinguished from what we have come to mean by the word in the modern world. In the modern world, freedom is thought of as genuine freedom in the sense that human decision and action is one of the real causal factors that determine whatever happens in the world.[40]

This interpretation of freedom is provisional in another sense. Because God is eternally omnipotent, past and *present* as well as future, God *could* at any time for any good reason *modify* or *restrict* or *withdraw* any or all of the freedom of creatures. The common idea of miracle as a "supernatural suspension" or "contradiction" of the natural law makes no sense apart from this possibility. Presumably God is also bound by other divine qualities in addition to omnipotence, such as rational or moral principles or purposes. But divine power in principle both is unlimited by any other power and is the ultimate source and destiny of all the power there is.

Another attempt at revision is to hold that God's will and power may not be omnipotent with respect to *individual* autonomy or with respect to particular events. God's purposes for individuals can fail if individuals repudiate God's purposes for them. God does not will that any should suffer or perish, but that does not mean these will not happen in particular cases. For individuals or for specific events, God's aims and power are not omnipotent. There is real freedom at the microlevel of creation.

However, our individual liberty is not complete autonomy but is exercised under the directing and controlling hand of God. Omnipotence is understood to mean providence. Providence is

> the almighty and ever present power of God whereby he still upholds, as it were by his own hand, heaven and earth together with all creatures, and rules in such a way that leaves and grass, rain and drought, fruitful and unfruitful years, food and drink, health and sickness, riches and poverty, and everything else, come to us not by chance but by his fatherly hand.[41]

The circle of our personal freedom exists within the larger circle of God's freedom and controlling power, over each individual life and over history. God does not lose God's "grip" on our lives and the world, their general direction and final outcome. Although God's micropurposes may be limited, God's macropurposes for the world as a whole cannot be restrained. God's will for specific things can ultimately fail, but God's will for the social-historical realm cannot be frustrated. God's knowledge of the contingencies of the process and the power of our decisions to thwart God's will is "perfect," like a master chess player who will "inevitably," even "infallibly" win the chess game.

There is one final effort to revise the classical notion of omnipotence. Leslie Weatherhead tells this story.

> During the first world war, as a young officer, my duties took me to Persia and I had the privilege of watching the weaving of the famous Persian carpets.

With a medical student who knew the language, I saw a rug set up vertically. Facing the side on which people would tread was the artist. On the reverse side, planks were placed, on which quite young boys sat ready for work. Work went forward, the artist directing the boys who put in the stitches.

I was made to understand that if a worker made a mistake, either in color or in design, the artist would not necessarily interfere but would weave the mistake into the pattern. The latter might be different, but, my interpreter explained, not necessarily less beautiful, if the artist were a great artist.

When the workers have finished their work on the wrong side of the carpet, where, admittedly, there is little sign of pattern or plan, the artist calls them down from their plank and brings them round to the right side, to see what he has achieved through their labours, including their mistakes.

The experience became a parable for me. Working, as we do, in positions from which we can see little plan or pattern or purpose in human life, the Great Artist nevertheless is weaving all into meaningfulness, and at the end of the day will take us to a point from which we can see all He has done with our sorrows, our frustrations and our pain, whether caused by our own mistakes and sins, or by those of others.[42]

There are two observations I want to make about this analogy and its implications for the concept of omnipotence. First, this is a significantly different concept of omnipotence than one finds in most premodern ideas of divine power. Weatherhead's analogy does not directly state unilateral causality, predestination, or fate. The weavers seem to have something to do, if not to say, about the outcome of the process of weaving. Second, this is a concept of omnipotence, in the sense that the final product *is* beautiful and therefore presumably good, assuring us that God's will is infallible and inevitable. Although perfection in the analogy is aesthetic instead of cognitive or moral perfection, the outcome seems to be perfect.

However, there are two questions I want to raise about the analogy before I can accept it as a satisfactory interpretation of divine omnipotence in the context of real evil. First, this is not omnipotence in the classical meaning of the term. God is not the sole or even the primary cause of all (or anything) that happens. Hence, one cannot say that everything that is done by the weavers is the will of God. The analogy implies that there are other real centers of freedom, power, decision, and causality in whatever happens in the process of weaving a carpet. Second, the analogy claims that at the end all will be beautiful (and therefore good, since we are using an aesthetic concept of goodness in the analogy).

But then we are left with the most basic claim of all classical theisms, namely, that there is no genuine evil (in terms of the analogy, no genuine ugliness). But that denies my claim in chapter 1 about the reality of evil. There *are* some things in the world that are genuinely evil, that are genuinely ugly, and that do not simply fit into a beautiful, coherent, patterned, meaningful whole. In terms of the analogy, the carpet has *real* blemishes in it, blemishes that cannot be made to look beautiful, even if the carpet overall is functional and aesthetically appealing.

Hence, I am left with the question of whether this analogy implies an interpretation of omnipotence or a total reconception of divine power, as I will propose in chapter 7. At this stage of the discussion, I simply leave that question hanging until I have explored alternative views of divine power.

Why Some Christians
Hold This View

We ought so reasonably to understand these as that we may not seem to impugn his dignity.[43]

Those who ascribe just praise to God's omnipotence . . . benefit thereby. . . . They may safely rest in the protection of him to whose will are subject all the harmful things which, whatever their source, we may fear; whose authority curbs Satan with all his furies, and his whole equipage; and upon whose nod depends whatever opposes our welfare.[44]

There are very good reasons most Christians, past and present, have held to the classical theistic understanding of the nature, origin, and solution to the problem of suffering and evil.

Logical Possibility

Assertion of all three claims simultaneously (omnibenevolence, omnipotence, and real evil) is not logically contradictory—so the claim goes. The major defender and proponent of this argument today is Alvin Plantinga. Does the theist contradict herself? No, Plantinga answers. By distinguishing between a "free will theodicy" (showing what God's purposes *are*) and a "free will defense" (showing what God's reasons *might possibly be*), he proceeds to show (in superb technical logic) that the reality of evil does not make a strictly logical disproof of the theistic God possible. He sets about to establish the logical possibility of holding the theistic view. His is not a theodicy, or an effort to explain the existence of evil, but a defense of a certain concept of God as compatible with the reality of evil. As another defender of Plantinga's position, Michael Peterson, claims,

> To defend the consistency of these propositions, the theist simply needs to show that it is possible for them both to be true. However, the theistic defender does not have to show that they are true, or even probably true. What the theist must do is to show why repeated atheistic attempts to demonstrate inconsistency fail and why God could have some legitimate purposes for evil. This same strategy applies to the rebuttal of all of the different formulations of the logical argument from evil.[45]

Although the argument is put forward in detailed logical form, the argument is really quite simple. It has not been and cannot be shown to be logically impossible that God allows evil for a good and justifying purpose. To claim this conclusion, one does not have to know what the divine purpose is, but one has only to be able to conceive one possible good, long-term aim in relation to which evil is temporarily permitted. Plantinga spends his time showing how, given God's purposes, it is *possible* that God could not have created any other kind of world than a world in which creatures freely go wrong. It is *possible* that it is *not possible* for God to have created a world containing free beings of whom none ever goes wrong. It is *possible* that God cannot create a world that both contains free beings and is devoid of evil.[46]

Stephen Davis adopts from Plantinga the same strategy in his free will defense. The logical problem of evil is misconceived, he argues.

> Now what is the proposition that the free will defender can use to show that evil and omnipotence and omnibenevolence are consistent? Let me suggest the following: All the evil that exists in the world is due to the choices of free moral agents whom God created, and no other world which God could have created would have had a better balance of good over evil than the actual world we have. What this says is that God's policy decision to create free moral agents will turn out to be wise and that it was not within God's power to have created a better world. This certainly seems *possibly true;* I can detect no contradiction or incoherence in it.[47]

When asked whether some other kind of world would have been possible given the purposes of God, whether the kind and amount of freedom is cost-effective for God's goal, what is the purpose of hell, or why God could not have foreseen moral monsters, Davis consistently says, "I just don't know." But it is logically possible, he claims, to believe in the kind of God he does. He knows that God is the kind of God consistent with these beliefs on the basis of divine revelation.

Religious Necessity

The classical theistic concept of God is the only concept of God that makes God *God*. Any concept of God that does not include the classical attributes is not a Christian concept of God. The issue in theodicy finally is not conceptual but religious. God is worshipful and worthy of our devotion and loyalty because God is *holy,* and the holiness of God can be expressed conceptually only through the omni-qualities of classical theism. Any concept of God that modifies these qualities does not make God worthy of our worship. All other concepts of God proffer a minigod or a pseudogod, an idol who is too much like us.

Even though there may appear to be, or even are, conceptual inconsistencies in holding this concept of God, the Christian faithfully *must* maintain theism in order to remain true to the one God. Intellectual effort might be expended on trying to show that there are no real contradictions in holding such a concept of God or why one can or must hold the apparent contradictions in the concept. But success in the effort is no final criterion for holding the theistic concept of God. Nor is moral offense a decisive criterion for rejecting the idea either. The final issue is *religious,* that is, it is what makes God *God.* And the answer that is religiously adequate is the idea of *power,* divine power, which means omnipotent power.

What is at stake in theodicy is not simply a philosophical or theological concept of God. Genuine Christian faith is at stake. The affirmations of omnipotence and omnibenevolence are not first of all intellectual issues in theology; they are first and foremost issues of genuine religious faith. Any willingness to redefine the divine power is evidence of willingness to abandon the one, true, perfect, and worshipful God in the name of some lesser god than genuine faith demands. Christians today must hold to the classical theistic idea of God, not only because it is biblical and traditional, but because that is the only one true God of genuine faith. One may choose between the Christian God and some other god, but one may not choose between Christian Gods. "Christian Gods" is at least an oxymoron, if not a blasphemy. It is God's omni-power that makes God *God.* Any "lesser" concept is at best children playing with building blocks trying to build a god, and at worst prideful adults offended by one of the definitive components in any concept of the true God.

Ultimate Meaning

Although the implications for classical theism may be an offense to the moral and religious sensibilities of some modern Christians, these implications are *the* source of comfort, security, and meaning for countless millions of Christians yesterday and today. Former Governor of New York Mario Cuomo, in speaking about the meaning of his brother's son freezing to death at age five, says,

> What my brother, my sister-in-law, my whole family concluded then is that either it is some explanation that eludes me at the moment, or there is none. If there is no explanation, if there is utterly no rationale, then I'm not sure I can deal with the rest of my life. I'm not sure I can make myself sufficiently comfortable in this environment to go forward in it. Therefore, I must accept the thesis that there is some justification.[48]

Offensive as it may be to me that many Christians believe that God killed or caused or willed or permitted the death of the boy for some reason, that belief is exactly what assures the ultimate meaning of the birth *and death* of the boy, not only for Cuomo, but also for millions of other Christians.

Even though I may not know *what* God's *reason* may be for taking a child, and consequently may suffer all of the psychological and spiritual anguish of the loss of her, I nevertheless know *that* God had a perfect reason for taking her in childhood instead of old age. Therefore, her life *and her death* are meaningful. I can endure the suffering and the loss of a child's early death, but the one thing I *cannot* endure is the possible meaninglessness or purposelessness of it. Knowledge that her death was God's will, that God took her for God's own secret but perfect purpose, ensures and reassures me that her death was not meaningless. Indeed, it was meaningful in the most meaningful sense of the term, that is, it had its necessary place in the plan of the One whose plan is all-powerful and all-loving. As Calvin said, "Then the heart will not doubt that God's singular providence keeps watch to preserve it, and will not suffer anything to happen but what may turn out to its good and salvation."[49]

The purpose of religion is to establish and maintain a *cosmos* and a *nomos*. There is no stronger challenge to that *cosmos* and *nomos* than our experience of suffering and radical evil. Belief that all that happens is the will of God, that God secretly but infallibly works God's perfect will, reassures millions of Christians that their world is finally safe, secure, coherent, meaningful, and perfect because of the infallible purposes and power of God. No defense of the finality of human freedom and no potential for ultimate purposelessness implied in that defense is worth the threat to meaning implied by radical evil. Consequently, many Christians have good reasons for holding to the classical theistic concept of God. Belief in such a God at both the intellectual and emotional levels is how security and meaning are established and maintained in the life of many sufferers. No religious person will relinquish that function of religion, whatever the intellectual costs. If it is possible to maintain that function of religion only by holding conceptually contradictory beliefs, so be it.

Critics, who come with different experiences of their world and different assumptions about what establishes their world as meaningful, may not understand the coherent and religiously satisfying world of classical theism. But theism for many is "coherent" in the sense that it provides a worldview that assures meaning and purpose for them. Millions of Christians find it to be not only a plausible but a compelling view of God and human suffering. They have good reasons, compelling reasons, decisive reasons for holding to classical theism and all its implications for our understanding and response to the suffering and evil in our lives.

Some Significant Implications

Sin is a dangerous toy in the hands of the virtuous. It should be left to the congenitally sinful, who know when to play with it and when to let it alone.[50]

One of the problems with theism is that it has never been able to offer a lavish interpretation of God's omnipotence without lapsing into systematic ambiguity or downright inconsistency. God is finally responsible for the evil as well as the good in the world, because God is the originative cause and/or ultimate determiner of everything that is. Hoping to escape the trilemma simply by asserting we can have it both ways at once—divine omnicausality and creatural freedom—we are finally stuck with a contradiction. Unfortunately, there is no difference between asserting two logically incompatible propositions

(God is omnipotent; God is not responsible for the evil that happens in the world) and not asserting anything at all.

Even if one wants to argue, as Plantinga, Davis, and Peterson do, that there is nothing logically inconsistent with holding these claims simultaneously, I think the problem finally is not logical possibility but plausibility.[51] The problem of suffering and evil does not exist simply within a logical vacuum. Is it *plausible* to hold to the theistic ideas of omnipotence and omnibenevolence and to the reality of evil all at the same time? "Surely the philosophical task is not merely to construct a logically possible hypothesis, but to construct one which also accounts for the data of human experience and is consistent with our existing knowledge."[52]

The way most theists have tried to avoid the contradiction in the trilemma is to imply that in the end there is no real evil in the world. Evil is ultimately only apparent. It is, in the first place, merely a privation of the good. It is, in addition, a term referring primarily to the problem of our finite perspective, not to anything the world would genuinely be better off without. We understand things as evil only because of the limitations of our finite perspective. If we had a "God's eye view" of things, we would recognize that evil is good in disguise, or at least it is an element of God's more inclusive good, and therefore the world would not genuinely have been better off without it.

My interpretation of classical theism, then, is that God is responsible for the evil as well as the good in the world in the sense that nothing happens that God did not cause or will or permit but could have prevented, even though the reason for it cannot be comprehended by our finite minds. Though I may not know *why* God killed or permitted the death of my baby, I know *that* God willed or permitted it within the inscrutable divine will. Hoping to escape the dilemma by simply asserting that we can have it both ways at once, divine omnipotence and real evil, the theist is finally stuck with an inconsistency.

My conclusion is that, finally, the only way theists have been able to avoid contradiction is to assert there really is no evil in the world after all. Evil is only on the face of things because finally it is the result of our finite perspective. I want to be clear that I am describing here the implication of a belief system, not the experience of most Christians. No Augustinian theologian I know anything about ever denied the existential reality of suffering, loss, and evil. It is the metaphysical reality of these that is denied within the theistic understanding of the good and sovereignty of God.

Divine power must be the highest conceivable form of power, so say theists. So far so good. Every form of theism I know, including process and trinitarian theism, claims this. But what is the highest conceivable form of power? That is the question we must reconsider. Supernaturalism assumes it must be the power strictly to decide and to determine every (or at least any) detail of what happens in the world. The forms of theism we will consider in subsequent chapters propose a radically different concept of the divine power.

3

"Why Did God Take My Baby?"

Theism in the Life of Faith

◁ Father Paneloux, the Jesuit priest in Albert Camus's *The Plague,* preached a sermon at the end of the first month of the plague in Oran. The ecclesiastical authorities of the city had organized a "Week of Prayer," during which the cathedral was consistently filled with worshipers. A person of passionate, fiery temperament, Father Paneloux proclaimed, "Calamity has come on you, my brethren, and, my brethren, you deserve it." Recalling the plague in Egypt, he said,

> The first time this scourge appears in history, it was wielded to strike down the enemies of God. Pharaoh set himself up against the divine will, and the plague beat him to his knees. Thus from the dawn of recorded history the scourge of God has humbled the proud of heart and laid low those who hardened themselves against Him. Ponder this well, my friends, and fall on your knees.[1]

He continued,

> If today the plague is in your midst, that is because the hour has struck for taking thought. The just man need have no fear, but the evildoer has good cause to tremble. For plague is the flail of God and the world his threshing-floor, and implacably He will thresh out His harvest until the wheat is separated from the chaff.[2]

Describing the flail as a huge wooden bar whirling around, striking at random, he assured his congregation that

> God is not mocked. These brief encounters could not stay the fierce anger of his love . . . unfailingly transforming evil into good. . . . This, my friends, is the vast consolation I would hold out to you, so that when you leave this house of God you will carry away with you not only words of wrath, but a message, too, of comfort for your hearts.[3]

Suffering Is the Result
of the Misuse of Freedom

Father Paneloux is a representative of Western theology and piety. Suffering, he claims, is the result of the misuse of creatural free will and its consequences. Theism is not only a theology (a doctrine of God); it entails, also, a theodicy (an explanation of *why* God causes or permits evil things to happen in the world). The theistic explanation of the purpose of God for inflicting or permitting our suffering is not only a component of pastoral advice about how we can respond to suffering with confidence, but also a theodicy in the broad sense of the term. It offers *reasons* and a comprehensive *explanation* of why we suffer, and so attempts to make sense of the presence of suffering and evil in the world.

The core of most contemporary theistic theodicies is the "free will defense." God has freely, willfully, and bindingly limited God's absolute freedom and power and given a free will to humans so that free human agents now freely decide, at least within the parameters of an overarching providence, what happens in the world. All suffering and evil are related to the misuse of this freedom; they are the result of the sin of finite creatures. The free will defense, then, provides a theodicy in the sense that it offers the explanation of the misuse of freedom as the reason for every form of suffering and evil in an originally perfect creation. Suffering and evil are the consequences of sin, the punishment by a just God for the disobedience of the free creature.

In chapter 2, I discussed the idea of free will in classical theology, namely, the belief that freedom is simply the absence of external coercion. The more modern version of the free will defense is the claim that God has put a real limit on God's power so that God in principle cannot be, at least provisionally, the only or the unilateral cause of events connected with finite but free creatures. Freedom is now operative in the world at both the primary and secondary levels, so that there is genuine freedom in the sense that there is not some other agent, either finite or infinite, who is the only real, hidden cause behind all that finite creatures in their freedom choose.[4] Most versions of the modern free will defense still retain a concept of miracle, and almost all claim that in the eschaton God will complete God's perfect will with unilateral power. But in this world God has genuinely limited God's power in nature and history (unless God decides to exercise, on occasion, God's omnipotent power through miracles), so that creatures freely decide.

For modern and postmodern Westerners freedom is not so much the idea that we will an event (psychologically) as it is the belief that we are a *creative* agent of an event, that is to say, that through our willing and decision, we help to originate an event. Every event is unknown and unknowable by anyone, including God, before it occurs. "Whereas for us, therefore, God's foreknowledge and a fortiori his 'foreordination' deny real freedom as creative of the genuinely new, for Augustine neither one poses any such threat to a freedom defined merely as a voluntary willing that is independent of external compulsion."[5]

In the modern free will defense, all suffering and evil are explained as the result of the misuse of the freedom of finite creatures and its consequences. Even if God is in some ultimate sense the sovereign Lord of the creation and history, God is not responsible for evil because free will is the cause of sin, suffering, and evil. All suffering is the consequence of the free will gone bad.

Four Interpretations
of Suffering within Theistic Faith

The free will doctrine has been the foundation for the theistic answer to the question of why the powerful, good, and loving God allows suffering. This doctrine has also provided the basis for additional themes in Western theodicies. In addition to the argument that God is good and powerful, cannot force humans to be good because that would deprive us of our free will, and that suffering and evil are our fault and not God's, there are four accompanying themes that "fill out" the explanation of the role of suffering in the overall purposes of God. These accompany the free will defense and provide more elaborate elements of traditional theodicy in the strict sense.

Punishment:
"We Deserve What We Get!"

We are not innocent but are sinful creatures, in thought and intent if not in actual deed; therefore, we deserve punishment because God is just. Suffering represents the judgment of God on human sinfulness. Suffering is connected with the *retributive justice* of God directed against our sin and guilt. In the Western moral and legal tradition, retributive justice is the use of punishment (or reward) as a specific device for giving persons what is "due" them in the light of their past acts.[6] It is important to recognize that defenders of suffering as retributive punishment do not think punishment is simply an expression of anger or vengeance of God. It is an act of requital demanded by a good and just God to balance out or set right a past wrong. It is a matter of justice.[7]

Joel Freeman, pastor of Stillmeadow Community Church in Columbia, Maryland, contends that in coming to terms with life's raw deals we ought to recognize that God is not "fair" in our modern sense of the term.[8] Our "misfortunes" come to us as punishment for sin, either for our sins, or the sins of our fathers and mothers, or the sins of the race, or the sins of Adam and Eve. God gives people what they deserve. Indeed, because of the outrage of our sin, we deserve far more punishment than we get. It is only because of the mercy and grace of God that we do not continually receive more just punishment than we in fact do receive.

In fact, if we want to magnify the "fairness" issue and demand our rights, we'd better be thankful that He doesn't take us up on our requests. Let's face it— we all deserve hell and damnation. There's not an obedient bone or tissue in

our bodies. Our hearts are deceitful and desperately wicked. We couldn't ob-
jectively determine the proper standard for our rights, even if we tried.[9]

Freeman even titles one of his chapters "The Cosmic Killjoy." God is just,
not fair. The source of our complaint about injustice is the power of the devil,
who uses us in trying to get even with God. God is into justice, not fairness,
and God's justice is beyond our comprehension. Therefore our task is to adjust to the justice of God, not complain about God's lack of fairness.

> Before continuing, we must understand a fundamental principle: *God is in
> control.* Absolutely nothing can happen to us or to anyone else without his
> consent. Even the devil has to check with God before he can cause disease,
> separation, or destruction.[10]

Our criterion of fairness reduces God's standards to a human point of view.
God's eternal viewpoint is the meaning of real justice, and "nothing escapes
the ultimate justice of God."

Our goal as Christians is to adjust to God's justice, to accept what happens
to us as the justice of God. "Hey, God's Got Rights, Too!" Freeman assures us
in the title of one of his chapters. There are human rights and God's rights, and
human rights play no role in divine justice.

> If God's rights were honored and guarded, almost every other human right
> that demands attention would be non-existent. "Fairness" would no longer
> be the issue that energizes so many causes. Wounded individuals would sub-
> mit to God's word instead of wallowing in self-pity. . . . He will exercise His
> right to challenge wounded crybabies with "unfair" circumstances, hoping
> that they'll stop griping and start growing.[11]

From God's point of view, then, there are no righteous or good or just people. The question posed by Rabbi Kushner in his book *Why Do Bad Things
Happen to Good People?* is a theological and spiritual oxymoron. *Good* and *people* are ideas that do not go together to make a sensible concept east of Eden.
Misdeeds cause misfortune. We may not get what we deserve immediately; the
so-called innocent may suffer, and the seemingly more wicked may prosper
in the short run, but over the course of time, or at least in the next life and for
all eternity, we all will get what we deserve, except for those who have been
chosen by God (the elect) or those who have chosen God (the born again).[12]

There is a more sophisticated version of retributive justice in which the tone
of revenge is replaced by a reassurance of the rational character of the creation. "The retributive scheme is undergirded by a worldview which believes
that a moral order in the world is the only foundation for a sensible and tolerable life."[13] The notion of retributive justice, then, is part of a rational and
harmonious view of the world in which all parts work together to contribute
to an orderly cosmos. Because of the "laws of nature," justice triumphs
notwithstanding. This notion is deeply ingrained in human nature and culture,
in our innate sense that unless retributive justice is honored, our world col-

lapses into chaos, and good and evil deeds are no longer recognized for what they are. "The law of retribution represents an egalitarian principle and enables society to move away from punishment and suffering as irrational fate or as demonic possession, toward a standard of equitable justice and order."[14]

Retributive justice in the end is directly related to our hope for the future. It expresses our belief that our suffering is not an irrational blow, by chance. At the very least, the doctrine of just suffering helps mute the offense of tragic suffering or the suffering imposed by fate.

Pedagogy: "Our Suffering Is Education for Our Growth and Maturity"

Our experience of suffering is necessary in order to develop our virtues, strengthen our character, and shape us into mature, loving, and complete persons. Suffering is part of our education for maturity, for "personhood." Suffering can make us better persons, and that is why God permits our suffering. Indeed, without suffering we cannot be mature, loving, virtuous persons.

> They who feel less, certainly, suffer less; but the more we suffer, the more we may improve; the more obedience, the more holiness we may learn by the things we suffer. So that, upon the whole, I do not know if the insensible ones have the advantage over us.[15]

Suffering purges us of our impatience, selfishness, superficiality, and egotism. It teaches us such virtues as strength and endurance. It can make us noble creatures who can love and even exhibit sacrificial love for the greater good of others. Just as a parent may permit, or plan, or cause unpleasant or even potentially dangerous things to happen to a child for the child's own development into a mature adult, so God permits or causes the suffering of God's children for their own perfecting or maturing.

Everything and anything that happens to us can serve the purpose of enhancing our growth. God is trying to teach us something through everything that happens to us. God may be teaching us how to change, to grow, to grow up, to learn more, to learn more about God, the world, and ourselves, to grow into the perfect love of God. Through these educative experiences we may become more human, more humane, even more spiritual.

John Hick is the primary advocate of this kind of theodicy in contemporary theology.[16] He agrees that the task of theodicy is to offer a picture of God, the world, and the suffering of the world as a coherent whole. That task, however, is not simply to examine the logical possibility of classical theism. The task is to seek a plausible, comprehensive picture of the relation of God and the world. From his point of view, Augustine's and Plantinga's views of God and evil are possibly true but are implausible because of the depth of suffering and evil.

The solution, for him, is to pursue an "Irenaean" instead of an Augustinian theodicy. In Hick's interpretation, Irenaeus viewed God's purpose for the human being as a two-stage development toward "soul making." Humanity was not created perfect in the beginning, after which it fell and thereby introduced suffering and evil into the world. Humanity was created with the potential for perfect love, but is still in the process of being brought by the Holy Spirit to that mature and complete relationship. Homo sapiens emerged from the later stages of the creation as a free and rational creature capable of relationship with God (the image of God); it is still to be made perfect (the likeness of God).

Since the purpose of God is to bring this creature to a mature relationship with God, God had to create an environment in which the creatures could be brought to a free, conscious, spiritual relationship with God. Adam and Eve were put in a kindergarten, not a paradise. God's goal and mode of operation, then, precludes omnipotence in the classical theistic sense of the term. The creature must be free, and must have an environment in which the creature can develop freely into a spiritual relationship. Perfection is not a stage at the beginning; it is a potentiality toward which the creature moves through the work of God the Spirit.

God created the world in such a way, then, that the creature could be brought freely to such a relationship. The environment, therefore, must be one that includes freedom, finitude, death, temptation, sin, and evil. This is the kind of environment created by God, and necessarily so if the creature was to be brought freely to the love of God. Otherwise there would be no freedom through which the creature could come to fulfillment. The world is not and was not perfect in the beginning. It is, rather, an environment in which perfection can happen at the end.

Goodness, then, for Hick, is human development toward moral and spiritual maturity at the end, not something already real at the beginning which we lost and need to recover. God is "responsible" for evil in the sense that suffering and evil are a necessary part of this environment for soul making. Nevertheless, God is not indictable, for such an environment is necessary for God's purpose. What "justifies" the suffering of the world is not that God wills it to be in a condition of sin and evil, but that sin and evil are necessary parts of the only kind of environment in which God could bring the creature freely to perfection. Given Hick's concepts of divine love and of omnipotent power in the next world, this world and its suffering and evil are "justified" because they will result in the fulfillment of the purpose of God in the eschaton. God will use all that happens within this environment ultimately to bring all creatures to full vision and love of God.

Eschatology:
"All's Well That Ends Well"

The final part of Hick's theodicy is a component of many theodicies in the West. Finally eschatology "justifies" the pain, suffering, and evil of the world. The eschaton for Hick, however, is not compensation for the suffering of this life, as in most forms of eschatology. Rather, because God is omnipotent in the end, all creatures will ultimately fulfill God's purpose of relationship. Suffering will be made right in the end in the sense that God will use suffering as instrumental to the sovereign purpose of God in the eschaton. All's well that ends well, and the world will end well because God's sovereign power and love will bring all creatures to a full relationship with God.

Central to Hick's eschatological solution is his distinction between eschatology as compensation and eschatology as fulfillment. Most eschatological solutions hold that the sufferers in this life will be compensated for their suffering in the next life. What the sufferer endures in this life will be reversed, negated, and the loss compensated for through a reward for enduring the suffering. The suffering, the loss, the terror will be negated, rendered nonreal through a reversal and compensation in the next life. Hick's eschatology does not negate the reality of suffering and evil, even in the next life. The suffering of the sufferer was and will be real. The loss was a real loss, never to be recovered or made to be unreal. No compensation can turn real evil into something other than what it was. Hick's view is, rather, that the sufferer will be moved in the suffering through the work of God the Spirit into closer relationship with God and therefore toward the ultimate fulfillment God intended for the creature.

Christiaan Beker represents with power the more apocalyptic version of traditional eschatological theodicies. The New Testament does not celebrate suffering, even the suffering of Christ, he argues, as good. Rather, the New Testament asserts that the present power of God's love in Christ is an anticipation of the triumph of a love that will defeat the power of death and its attendant suffering in God's world. The gospel of the suffering love of Christ is inseparable from the gospel of hope. "It anticipates that at the time of the resurrection of the dead all God's people together will celebrate the defeat of the power of death and its suffering in the kingdom of God."[17] Paul's answer to suffering at the hands of the power of death is anchored in his theology of hope, a hope lodged in the coming apocalyptic triumph of God. "And thus Paul's thought compels us to speak about hope in terms of the triumph of God; without the beckoning horizon of that final triumph, hope degenerates from a gift of God into a purely human disposition, if not a utopian ideology, an idle wish, or another form of 'false hope.'"[18] Beker has such an overwhelming sense of the suffering and absurdity of so much of the world that anything short of apocalyptic promise and hope that negates and reverses the power of suffering and death will leave us with only death and loss as the final word.

Mystery:
"All Is Finally Consumed in Mystery"

That God causes or permits suffering is not doubted by many Christians, and *that* God causes or permits it for an ultimate good reason is not doubted. God has God's own reasons for causing or permitting evil. Finite creatures, however, are in no position to know *what* God's reasons are or to judge them. Nevertheless, we know that hidden in the divine will, foreknowledge, and wisdom is a good, indeed perfect, reason for willing or permitting anything that happens. We can know not only *that* everything that happens happens for a reason, but that it happens for a *good* reason. The reason simply is lost in the divine mystery that surpasses human knowing and perhaps even human imagining.

If an innocent child dies young, it was the appropriate time in God's scheme for the person to die. Their time was up in the divine plan. God has a plan, a pattern, and a providential rule under which every life must develop, and that pattern includes "twisted" lives and "premature" death as much as "good" lives and "the good death." The tapestry may look ugly to us in spots (or even as a whole), but through faith we know that to God the work as a whole is beautiful. Why the evil that occurs in our lives is meaningful or how it is meaningful is neither possible nor important to know. What is important is to know *that* it is meaningful in the inscrutable will of the divine mystery. In some cases, especially in the "extreme" cases, the other three "explanations" may fall short of plausibility. But the suffering is not meaningless. Instead, its meaning is lost in an ultimate mystery of the ways and means of God.

Defense of Traditional Theodicies for the Life of Faith

The are two commanding reasons many Christians affirm these teachings of the tradition which explain the reasons for our suffering.

1. The most powerful reason for affirming the traditional teaching about the omnipotence and omnibenevolence of God is that it answers for many the most important problem of religion, namely, the establishment and maintenance of security and meaning in the midst of suffering.

Corrie ten Boom, a Dutch woman whose family hid Jews during the Nazi Holocaust, was eventually betrayed by Jan Vogal, one of the hired workers in the household. As a result, she spent several months in the concentration camps in Ravensbruck and Scheveningen. She asked, "Was it possible that this—all of this that seemed so wasteful and so needless—this war, Scheveningen prison, this very cell, none of it was unforeseen or accidental?" She concluded, unlike Elie Wiesel after Auschwitz, that "life in Ravensbruck took place on two separate levels, mutually impossible. One, the observable, external life, grew every day more horrible. The other, the life we lived with God, grew daily better, truth upon truth, glory upon glory."[19]

A person can endure and survive *anything* if that person believes there is a purpose (or Purpose) for that thing happening. The final threat is not the threat of death, loss, pain, suffering, or any form of radical evil, but is the threat of meaninglessness and despair over suffering. If I can believe that God took my baby for some reason (or Reason), I can overcome the final threat that my baby died for no good reason at all.

Offensive as a traditional theodicy is for many modern people, because of the idea of power portrayed in it, such theodicies assure people of an ultimate meaning to their suffering and the suffering of any other person or group. Most religious people will not sacrifice that assurance, *no matter what ideas are required to maintain it*. That is precisely what classical theodicies offer many Christians. Few Christians will sacrifice this classical teaching about the character of God, even if it contradicts other experiences, sensibilities, and beliefs, unless they can be assured that a *better* theodicy will maintain adequate meaning for them to go on loving and serving God in the face of radical evil and the threat of meaninglessness.

2. There is *some truth in each of the four "explanations"* of the tradition, and much truth in all of them together. *Up to a point* each of them helps to explain why the things that happen to us happen, and what God's purposes are or at least might be in causing or allowing them. There is a distinction to be made between *an explanation* and *the comprehensive explanation*,[20] between *a* truth and *the* whole truth. To conclude there is no final answer is not the same thing as to conclude that there are not some good answers.

Even though I reject the adequacy of the theistic tradition as a strict theodicy, I think it is important to acknowledge some truth in each of these traditional answers to the question of why human beings suffer.

How any theodicy could make sense apart from some concept of creatural freedom is nearly impossible for any modern person to imagine. Every Christian theodicy of whatever type has made freedom important to its explanation. Whether or not that freedom is "genuine" is part of the debate between various theistic theodicies. But giving an essential role to some concept of freedom is hardly in doubt. Even strong doctrines of predestination include some concept of freedom. Most non-Calvinist or non-Lutheran forms of Christianity, whether Catholic or Protestant, conservative or moderate, evangelical or liberal, have made freedom a decisive part of their theodicy. The question of whether the concept of freedom alone is adequate to account for the presence of evil in the world, and how that is correlated to a concept of a sovereign God, remains to be answered. But its importance in theistic theodicy is nearly self-evident.

In addition, much if not most of the suffering in the world is directly related to, if not the result of, sin. This is simply empirically true. The Augustinian tradition offers significant insight into the role of sin, guilt, and its consequences for human suffering. Corrupted freedom and its consequences for our relationships with God, nature, community, and ourselves are deeply implicated in most suffering.

Indeed, again it is hard to name, even to imagine, cases of genuine evil, especially radical evil, in which human transgression, complicity, pride, sloth, perversity, or passivity are not directly involved. Much suffering is caused by the deliberate or compliant infliction of abuse and violence on a victim by a victimizer.[21]

Sometimes the suffering of sinners is the direct consequence of their sin. Sometimes suffering is visited not only on the victim of sin but also on the sinner as well, as judgment on their sin. Abusers sometimes "do themselves in"; extortionists sometimes are brought to justice through their own stupidity; empires sometimes fall of their own overreaching; victimizers sometimes become victims of their own fears; groups sometimes swagger toward their own fall.

That judgment and punishment and justice do not happen to all or even to most sinners does not negate the evidence that some suffering is caused by sin and that sin sometimes is punished either for reasons of retributive or distributive justice. Regardless of whether one interprets this judgment as the *wrath of God* directly inflicted by God, or nature, or society, or the group on sinners, or as *retribution* on the sinner, or as the inevitable *consequences* of our own sin or the sin of groups in a world of consequences that God has created, it is clear that much suffering is tied up with human sin, both in the sense that sin causes suffering and that sin can be punished through suffering.

However, this is a very *dangerous* theodicy. Used in the hands of a sinner, which is each of us, these explanations of suffering can themselves become instruments of abuse; they can function to "blame the victim," thereby becoming ideologies of victimization. The absence of justice (victims always suffer the consequences of abuse far more than abusers) shows how limited this understanding of suffering can be if it is offered as a comprehensive theodicy.

Still further, any modern or postmodern person who has a personalistic view of God and an evolutionary view of human nature can identify immediately with major themes of any educative theodicy. Evangelical Christians who have a strong doctrine of sanctification along with justification can find truth in this kind of theodicy. That a personal God who loves free creatures created an ambiguous, even dangerous, environment in which that love is achieved through a long process of developing relationships and maturation seems not only apparent but necessary from these points of view. Although this theme does not dominate classical Western theodicy, it is present in the Eastern church as early as Irenaeus, and has been reintroduced to Western Christian theology since Schleiermacher and the entire liberal tradition in nineteenth- and twentieth-century theology.

Finally, no one knows so much about God as to be able to know the *fullness* of the divine being, character, and mode of operation. There is always a deep mystery to what we mean by God. That mystery is at least a mystery about why God is my God, the God of this particular contingent being.

This point cannot be taken too far. Even the person who claims that God is wholly mystery is telling me something about the character, and even being, of God. Nevertheless, at least in the theistic tradition, mystery is one of the primary characteristics of God. Any theodicy needs a strong sense of the ultimate mystery that lies behind our talk about the being, character, and operations of the divine reality.

My own conviction, then, is that each of these themes in traditional theodicies, properly interpreted as playing *a* role in understanding our lives with and in God, are factors among a multiplicity of factors in explaining theologically within the Christian story, or metanarrative, or perspective why suffering occurs in our world and how God is related to that suffering.

But there are so many problems with each of these theodicies, which I find so onerous, that I am finally forced to rethink the tradition's teaching both about the omnipotence and the omnibenevolence of God. In the remainder of this chapter I provide some of the reasons I find it necessary to reject the theistic solution to the problem of suffering and evil before I begin to reconstruct the ideas of divine goodness and divine power in the remainder of my discussion.

Problems with the
Free Will Defense

Freedom is a presupposition of genuine relationships, human and divine. Nevertheless, an omnipotent God who loves us can surely keep the extreme liabilities of genuine freedom in some check while maintaining genuine freedom. We can easily imagine an analogy. Many of us would say that society can legislate against murder and rape and even restrain the murderer and rapist without eliminating the freedom of either one. In light of the vast disproportions of unjust suffering in the world, one can imagine some kind of better balance between real freedom and real evil than we find throughout human history. In such contexts, the free will defense itself becomes part of the problem of evil. It *justifies too much* in a world in which omnipotence, or at least sovereign power, apply to God.

There are, in my view, two preliminary problems with the theistic version of the free will defense. The first is that most advocates of it hold that God *could* be the unilateral cause of any event. God could perform a miracle and unilaterally cause an "unnatural" occurrence or a different result than otherwise free agents might choose. God usually doesn't choose to intervene, but *can* at any time and *does* so on a *few* selected occasions. So most theistic versions of the free will defense qualify in principle the concept of freedom. Why God chooses to perform a miracle now and not then moves the discussion away from the nature of God's power to the goodness of God, to the question of why God would choose to perform no miracle when we really need one to establish, maintain, or reestablish even some minimal kind of justice in a world of intense suffering.

Second, there are some advocates who hold that God's self-limitation is so binding, so "ontological," that God in principle cannot (by God's own decision) override or qualify natural causes or the freedom of creatures. So God is *in fact* limited (though voluntarily), and *cannot* unilaterally establish justice. Many of the advocates of this free will defense hold, nevertheless, that at some point in time God *will* in fact unilaterally establish justice by way of punishment and rewards (Augustine and Calvin) or universal salvation (Hick and perhaps Barth) in the eschaton. So what is apparently (self-)binding on God in this world is not binding on God in the end.

However, if God is omnipotent either in principle or in fact in the next world, this eternally self-same God is omnipotent in this world as well, apparently choosing not to establish justice in this world. But why in the next world and not in this one? And why should we affirm with certainty that we know that God *will* establish absolute justice in the next world if there is no evidence of either the ability or willingness to do so in this world?

Furthermore, the promise of a resurrection in the next life is no answer to this question, for at least two reasons. First, as Dostoyevsky argues in Book 5 of *The Brothers Karamazov,* the eschatological answer is not worth it, at least in the case of the suffering of innocent children. Wendy Farley interprets this point. Eschatology may provide consolation, but it is not redemption. Future vindication does not erase the wrongness of radical evil. "If a time comes when every tear is wiped away, when death, mourning, and pain have all ended, there will be release from suffering; but even that cannot make the past as if it had never been."[22] Second, the power of resurrection in the next life does not require omnipotent power in either this world or the next. It requires the power to bring new life out of death. Furthermore, such a belief does not imply absolute justice. It implies only the continuation of "spiritual life" or "spiritual death" in the next life.

There is a way to interpret resurrection as a theodicy. That way is to interpret resurrection as a cosmological instead of an anthropological idea, that is to say, an eschatology in which resurrection means the reconstitution and fulfillment of the total cosmos into a state of perfect justice. Thereby it becomes primarily a cosmological or at least historical concept, not an individualistic one. The only link to divine justice in this world is through human justice, and the only divine link here is Jesus, who is now gone and will accomplish this cosmologically at the end of history.

With all these problems, however, I continue to acknowledge that the free will argument in its theistic forms remains a very powerful one for many Christians. Nevertheless, I know of no advocate of the free will defense as a theodicy, regardless of whether that person is the liberal John Hick or the conservatives Alvin Plantinga, Michael Peterson, and Stephen Davis, who relinquishes either the presupposition or the helpful reserve of omnipotence. The persistence of that belief mutes or, better, pushes up the ladder a rung or two the problems of how genuine is the freedom of creatures in the first place and how genuine or moral is the (self)-limitation of God's own power.

Other Problems
in the Main Traditions

The problem for theism arises when one takes these ideas, either the free will defense or the four derivative "explanations," as anything more than one partial factor in our interpretation of suffering and evil. When any one of them becomes *the* reason suffering occurs, it becomes inadequate, and in many cases a sheer outrage. Every "total solution" becomes dangerous. Each understanding is so partial or flawed as a comprehensive explanation that none can provide what they pretend to provide for theodicy, namely, the answer to the question of what God's purposes are in creating a world in which so much evil occurs.

In too many cases there is too much freedom, the punishment doesn't fit the crime, the person is overwhelmed or too much is lost in the process of growth, the eschaton does not negate or justify the abuse, or the mystery becomes irrelevant. Consider the following claims.

1. It is incredible to me that anyone can hold that there is even an approximate balance between sin and punishment, let alone a correlation between them. There is frequently (even usually?) little correspondence between the seriousness of sins, or even sin in the theological sense, and the degree of suffering endured by some groups or by some individuals. In Woody Allen's movie *Crimes and Misdemeanors,* Judah Rosenthal, a wealthy ophthalmologist and community pillar, engineers the murder of Delores Paley, his mistress, who has decided to take charge of her life and their relationship when she gets exploited even more by Judah. His "crimes" of murder, embezzlement, and adultery do not come to justice under the "eyes of God." He "gets away" with his crimes so thoroughly that no one who could do anything about it does, and in the end he experiences no guilt or even inner turmoil about this deed as he walks home affectionately and confidently with Miriam, his wife, at the conclusion of a wedding party. In the final scene his brother-in-law and patient, Ben, a rabbi, whose only crimes are "misdemeanors," is blind. The movie ends with him dancing with his daughter at her wedding.

Even if there is punishment, limited or eternal, in the next life, the punishment of sinners in the next life neither makes good nor justifies all that happens in this life. Nor does it justify the disproportion between sin and consequences in this life. "We must concede that there exists a crucial and mysterious 'dark residue' of evil and death in God's created order which cannot simply be attributed to human sin."[23] There is a much more complex relation between suffering and sin than is indicated in Paul's text in Romans 5:12–21 and in subsequent Western anthropology and theodicy.

2. Moral and spiritual education can establish genuine character and loving relationships. They may even be essential to the development of human and humane qualities. But testing and education, at least the kind we are talking about in real life outside the classroom, can crush persons or produce bizarre, distorted, or demolished character as often as they produce mature character. When so many people end up with such callous, distorted, destructive, and even demonic character as the result of the character-building experiences they undergo, one must ask what kind of God we are talking about if this environment for education produces as much evil as it produces good. As one student said in a paper for my theodicy class when reflecting on this problem:

> Answer me this question: Would you pour scalding water on your baby's hand, so that when he screams, you can attend to it? Reason and common sense say, "No!" Only a mentally-sick person would behave in such a manner—and I don't see God as treating us, his children, in that fashion.[24]

3. Finally, although mystery must be an important category in any concept of God, all these traditional theodicies in fact claim to know at least something, and in most cases quite a bit, about the purposes, character, and mode of God's activity. And they hold that this God is good and worthy of our worship and emulation. Most theologians, even the advocates of an apophatic theology, who claim that all is finally mystery, offer an amazing amount of knowledge about God, known either through philosophy, revelation, religious experience, narratives, or tradition.

An appeal to *total* mystery is finally an appeal to no God at all, at least to no God that we can know anything about or who makes any difference in human suffering. Such a belief can be asserted only on totally fidiestic grounds, and has no content of meaning that offers either any understanding or consolation in our encounter with suffering and evil.

Decisive Problems

It is not acceptance of suffering that gives life; it is commitment to life that gives life. The question is not, Am I willing to suffer? but Do I desire fully to live? This distinction is subtle and, to some, specious. But in the end the choice of which to affirm makes a great difference for how people interpret and respond to suffering.[25]

There are four problems with these traditional theodicies, which I find so compelling, that they must be rejected as plausible theodicies, or as complete or adequate understandings of God and the relation of God to the world.

Theistic theodicies for me are unacceptable, even intolerable, because (1) they justify or even celebrate abusive power, (2) they finally deny the reality of evil, (3) they cannot resolve the problem of proportionality, and (4) even though they are logically possible, the inherent problems with them make them implausible. Because I find these problems so compelling, I am forced to reconsider what Christians mean when on the basis of their scriptures, traditions, experiences, and reason they affirm the goodness and power of God in the face of evil.

1. Traditional theodicies lend themselves to underwriting abusive power. The concept of God offered by classical theism nourishes a kind of Christianity that justifies (if it does not glorify) suffering. It thereby tends to turn Christian theology into a justification of abuse. I think the understanding of divine power represented in theism lends itself to a justification of abusive power. Since suffering is explained to fit within the loving and all-powerful purposes of God, the suffering of humanity, of my group, and of myself is justified within God's power and way of working in the world. Christian theism has been a force in the West in our acceptance of abusive power.

For many if not most modern Christians, this seems like a wild, even absurd claim. Although there are plenty of examples of abusive violence in Christian scripture and traditions, most modern Christians interpret their scripture and traditions as a teaching against murder, abuse, exploitation, injustice, and oppression. The issue, however, goes deeper than interpretation of scripture. Christians have taught a concept of divine power and divine goodness that, when emulated, justifies a deeper compliance with violent abuse. Roots of that are in the theistic concept of God, and more specifically in the interpretation of Christology, and most especially in redemption theory, which is rooted in a concept of God's will to punish sinners. Specifically, God wills and causes the violent death of his son as retribution for sin in order that God's honor can be reestablished and God can forgive sinners. In this framework, we are not talking about the abuse of power; we are talking about abusive power as a kind of power that is sacralized.

Rita Brock claims that "the shadow of omnipotence" haunts Western atonement theory. The ghost of the punitive father lurks in the corners. He never disappears even as he is transformed into an image of forgiving grace. Hence the experience of grace is lodged, I believe, not so much in a clear sense of personal worth gained from an awareness of interdependence and the unconditional nature of love, as in a sense of relief from escaping punishment for one's failings.[26] The joint doctrines of divine omnipotence and atonement reflect by analogy, she argues, "neglect of children," or "child abuse," making the divine behavior "cosmic child abuse, as it were."[27]

Likewise, Joanne Carlson Brown and Rebecca Parker argue that in traditional Western theology God is responsible for the suffering and death of Jesus, and that suffering and death become the model which the followers of Jesus are to emulate in their relation to God and to each other, especially women in relation to men. Christianity is "the theology that says Christ suffered in obedience to his Father's will. Divine child abuse is paraded as salvific and the child who suffers 'without even raising a voice' is lauded as the hope of the world."[28] Suffering is redemptive; it is built into the very purposes of the all-loving and all-powerful God; we are to suffer as Christ suffered in complete obedience to this will of God. God is responsible for the life and destiny of Jesus. Just as God willed his suffering and death, and he was quietly obedient to follow that will, so God wills our suffering, and we are to accept it and be obedient to God's will. The life goal of the Christian is "to be like Jesus." Christology thereby becomes "divine child abuse," and we as followers of Jesus Christ become participants in that pattern of the divine life and will. "Our internalization of this theology traps us in an almost unbreakable cycle of abuse."[29]

The issue here is not whether Christianity has taught us to abuse each other, men to abuse women, parents to abuse children, whites to abuse blacks, rich to abuse poor. Very few Christians have taught that directly. Although there are teachings in scripture and traditions that might indulge such interpretation, most Christians with humane sensibilities interpret their scriptures in such a way as to reject any such teaching in them. The issue, rather, goes to the heart of the religious imagery itself and the sensibility about the nature of power conveyed. God is all-powerful. Christians desire to emulate God, especially God as revealed in Christ. Conformation to the character of God and Christ is the goal of the Christian life. Since God's omnipotent power can be interpreted as unilateral power, and since Christ is an obedient victim of both divine and human abuse, we, who are to be like God and Christ in our understanding and in our practice, get shaped in the deeper imagery and sensibilities of our story. Even more significant than the explicit teachings about our relationships with each other and with God is our notion of the divine character and will which we are called as Christians to worship, adore, strive toward, emulate. In the end, Christian behavior hinges more on our concept of the divine life, character, and will than on explicit teachings. If that character is abusive, we are part of that story or scheme too. If, however, the divine power is understood in some other way, then we are called to emulate a different perspective on power. As Elizabeth Cady Stanton said, "The first step in the elevation of women under all systems of religion is to convince them that the great Spirit of the Universe is in no way responsible for any of these absurdities."[30]

2. Traditional theodicies in the end deny the reality of evil. That claim, also, seems on the surface to be false and even patently absurd. I do not mean at all to claim that traditional theodicies do not take very seriously and talk at great lengths about our experience of suffering and our encounter with evil. I mean, rather, that finally they define evil as metaphysically or theologically "unreal," thereby attempting to exempt God from any direct involvement in the suffering and evil of the world.

Evil finally is unreal in the theistic tradition for two reasons. First, it is true that evil is experienced as an actual force in our encounter with our environment. Cruelty is not merely an extreme absence of kindness, it is something with a demonic power of its own. The traditional theodicies, however, say this is a statement about our finite, limited experience or perspective on the world, not a statement about what some things in the world are like in their fundamental character and structure within the mind and purposes of God. Thus, evil is *privatio boni,* a privation of the good. Augustine is finally led to say, "To Thee there is no such thing as evil." If evil is more than a privation or a departure from the good, then God is responsible for evil. That idea besmirches the "perfection" of God.

Second, traditional theodicies make a distinction between apparent and real evil. All Western theodicists I know about have granted that at first view the world is full of much suffering and evils. But we do not know with certainty that any one of these apparent evils is actually evil. We often can look at apparent evils a second or a third time and see that our initial interpretation of events we called evil was mistaken. They actually served a good or were shown to be good in the long run or in the larger picture. The picture would not be as good as it is without what appeared prima facie to be evil. How do we know that this is not the case with *all* evils, including the most horrendous evils in the world, such as genocide and even nuclear holocaust? We don't know because we don't and can't see things from God's point of view, knowing that God's perspective and purposes and plan for the world, if not in this life at least in the next, is perfectly good.

David Griffin makes the important distinction between "prima facie" and "genuine" evil.[31] The former includes all the experiences of suffering and evil we encounter; the latter, any behavior or event, from paper cuts to genocide, that the world would *genuinely* (that's the operative word) have been better off without. If we are willing to name one thing the world would genuinely have been better off without—metaphysically, all things considered from our point of view or God's point of view—we have named a "genuine" evil. But since we do not know and cannot know from God's point of view and within God's purposes that any event did not necessarily fit into God's perfect will and plan, we do not know that any event was genuinely evil. Any claim that we know of anything the world would genuinely have been better off without is an arrogant, even blasphemous, claim.

I find this teaching of classical theology intolerable to believe at the end of the twentieth century. It is obviously true we are not God, do not know the whole mystery of God's being or purposes, and do not see anything from God's point of view. I not only grant that claim, I affirm it as thoroughly as any apophatic theologian or any contemporary deconstructionist theologian! However, if God's judgments are the opposite of ours in all matters, and especially in the matters of good and evil, we have no grounds on which to be devoted to God at all (unless it is the adoration of sheer power and pure mystery alone that makes God worshipful). As C. S. Lewis says in *The Problem of Pain,*

> On the one hand, if God is wiser that we His judgment must differ from ours on many things, and not least on good and evil. . . . On the other hand, if God's moral judgment differs from ours so that our "black" may be his "white," we can mean nothing by calling Him good; for to say "God is good," while asserting that His goodness is wholly other than ours, is really only to say, "God is we know not what." And an utterly unknown quality in God cannot give us moral grounds for loving and obeying Him.[32]

If some events or qualities we call evil are not genuine evil, are not actually contrary to the will and purposes of God, then I see little grounds on which to worship and serve God as the source of human good. If from God's perspective everything that happens in the world is really beautiful within the divine scheme of things, then, from our point of view, God can only be seen as watching us from a distance and as indifferent to the suffering we experience within the messy details of everyday life.

But a God who only sees the beauty of the earth and the colors of life can be easily seen as indifferent to those in pain or who are suffering. Indeed, this picture of God is presented in the concluding chapters of the book of Job. There the most vivid, exuberant picture of life, far from the human-centered world we find in most of the rest of the Bible, is represented, which is akin, perhaps, to the American Walt Whitman's "Song of Myself." Stephen Mitchell says of the God-speeches at the end of the book of Job that

> the Voice now, in a series of gruff, most ironical questions, begins to speak explicitly about good and evil. *Do you really want this moral sense of yours projected onto the universe?* it asks, in effect. *Do you want a god who is only*

*a larger version of a righteous judge, rewarding those who don't realize that
virtue is its own reward and throwing the wicked into a physical hell? If that's
the only kind of justice you're looking for, you'll have to create it yourself. Because that is not* my *justice.33*

The interests of Job's God seem to be more aesthetic than personalistic, more
focused on the richness and beauty of the creation as such than on the strictly
moral concerns of justice. One sees a sort of righteous indifference in God to
the frustration and suffering the diverse and beautiful creation bestows upon
narrowly human interests.

Any theological interpretation of evil, to be sure, must understand God's notion of good as larger than human satisfaction. Yet the asymmetry between
God's good and our good can become so extreme as to make any relationship
between divine and human good and evil problematic. When this happens,
the nerve connecting God and humanity through worship is severed and the
purpose of the religious life is evacuated. Helpful as traditional theodicies are
in making a *partial* contribution to our complex understanding of the character and our response to evil, most especially in overcoming any Manichean dualism and in recognizing the extent to which evil is rooted in the privation of
goodness at the center of human selves, they, nevertheless, cannot be an adequate theodicy. To the extent that any theodicy denies the reality of evil, it
cannot be adequate to contemporary experience and understanding of suffering and redemption.

3. The problem of proportionality renders traditional theodicies inadequate. I refer to the problem of waste, of cost-effectiveness, of excess. Grant
that much in the traditional arguments is true. God has God's plans and reasons to will or to permit what happens in the world, evil as well as good,
and is powerful enough to make good out of what appears to be the evils in
the world, thereby making all evils only apparent because they have their
proper place in God's overall vision and purpose. I find this argument acceptable *to a point.* But "to a point" is crucial in my rejection of these arguments as a theodicy. There is a point beyond which it is no longer meaningful or tolerable to call God good if these arguments are attempting to provide
a comprehensive theodicy. A reason or a variety of reasons why bad things
happen is not a theodicy. A theodicy, in the stricter sense, calls for a larger
perspective, be it a metaphysics, a metanarrative, or a whole system of theological beliefs, which will inform and give coherence to these reasons which
are offered.

The breadth and depth of much of the evil in the world make it difficult, at
least at times, to believe that God is very "cost-efficient" in working toward
whatever God wills for the creation. I am talking about "the damn problem of
proportion." Granting the theist the claim that God may need or use evil to accomplish God's purposes, that that evil may be intense, widespread, and even
extreme, there nevertheless is a point beyond which it makes no sense any
longer. Everyone can think of examples in which the suffering of individuals

and groups is so intense, so enduring, so counterproductive, so asymmetrical in relation to any conceivable good whatsoever that it is a parody, and literally meaningless, to grant the use of the term good in relation to it.

4. The problem of plausibility persists after all the discussion about the logic of possibility. Although I am not knowledgable enough in modal logic (the formal logic of possibility and necessity) to draw a conclusion about the validity of the arguments of Plantinga, Peterson, and Davis, I see no obvious reason to conclude they are logically invalid. This strategy of the theistic defense of the omnipotent God cannot be proved to be invalid; there is no logical contradiction in the claim itself. It is logically possible that God allows this kind and this amount of evil for a good and justifying purpose. One does not have to show what that purpose is, only that there may conceivably be a good long-term purpose which justifies every kind of suffering and evil in the short run. Any claim that the theistic argument is logically contradictory is too rash.

However, the questions of possibility and plausibility are radically different questions. "For, granting that divine existence is logically possible, the question is whether it is reasonably believable in face of the appalling reality and extent of evil in its many forms."[34] This is my insurmountable problem with classical theism. There is, apparently, in principle, no amount of evil that can constitute evidence against the existence of the theistic God. No evidence could possibly, in principle, falsify such a belief.

For the Plantinga, Peterson, and Davis kind of theist, nothing short of logical disproof of a set of beliefs is allowed as evidence against the theistic concept of God. "But surely the notion of evidence, in distinction from proof, is precisely the notion of circumstances which 'count for' or 'count against' without amounting to logical certification."[35] I find this point a compelling, even decisive, argument against traditional theodicies, and have come to believe it is the line of demarcation between classical theism and the kind of neoclassical and trinitarian theisms defended in the last three chapters of this book.

From my point of view the question is more one of *evidence* than of modal logic. What is the *evidence* in nature, in history, in our own experience together and individually that counts for and against the existence of the kind of omnipotent and omnibenevolent God that classical theists propose in the face of evil? In the face of the evidence, the theistic God "is today almost totally lacking in plausibility."[36] The "logical" or "philosophical" problems cannot be so neatly separated from the "evidential" or "emotive" problems, as the theists want to do. "Surely the philosophical task is not merely to construct a logically possible hypothesis, but to construct one which also accounts for the data of human experience and is consistent with our existing knowledge."[37] As David Griffin argues, "He [Davis] does not consider what I would take to be the central meaning of the claim that the Christian view of reality should be plausible: it should be able to provide plausible answers to the various types of questions it arouses."[38] That problem increasingly has become the bottom line in my conclusion about theism as it attempts to provide a theodicy. It has simply become implausible at the end of the twentieth century in the light of the empirical evidence of our experience.

Retreating to appeals to logical possibility, ignorance ("I just don't know"), and mystery in the face of all the evidence of genuine evil in the world is, for me, at best counterproductive and at worst a demonic strategy in the midst of abused and burning children. As a strategy it renders the concept of God unusable in the midst of suffering, and for many is an idea that needs to be criticized, demolished, and reconstructed. From my point of view, no concept of God can be constructed apart from experience, apart from an appeal to all the evidence available in history and our own experience. So the problem for theodicy in our time is not to defend the classical theistic God as biblical, traditional, experiential, or reasonable. It is to use the evidence from these four sources to reconstruct a concept of God that can account for the reality of evil and can provide resources for understanding and resisting evil. In our era, "The problem of evil is not: Can the God of traditional theism be defended against the suspicion of being guilty of nonexistence beyond a reasonable doubt in the face of evil? It is instead: Which of the available views of God provides the most consistent, adequate, and illuminating account of reality in general, and of the relation between evil and the Holy Power in particular?"[39]

There are other concepts of God in the Western Christian tradition, especially in the modern world, besides the classical theistic doctrine.[40] In the following five chapters I will explore some of these concepts of God as they relate to our problem in this book. I will argue that every *concept* of God is a human construction, including classical theism, so that the question is which concept of God is most adequate to the "facts" of experience, which include scripture, tradition, and history as well as contemporary experience. That is, I am arguing for an empirical orientation to our question.

That orientation will lead many toward a concept of an ambiguous God, a notion I will explore in chapters 4 and 5. That empirical orientation will also lead to the "neoclassical theism" of process theology and the "trinitarian God" of much theology in the last quarter century. I will explore that concept of God in chapters 6 through 8. Thus, at this stage in the discussion, I consider the problem of the relation of God to evil to be reopened, not settled, in the light of my conclusions about classical theism. My conclusion is not the conclusions of most modern skeptics: the loss of the theistic God is the loss of any God whatsoever. That conclusion does not follow at all from the evidence. Some may find the problems with theism so deep, so offensive, so decisive that no concept of the divine at all can be recovered. They may return to anthropodicy. I can understand that response to the loss of the theistic God. Some of us, though, on the basis of experience, the experience of our Christian community and our own experience, are left with evidence and a confidence in an ultimate source of human good that goes beyond our own human resources. The theological problem today is how to conceive of this source of human good in such a way as to adequately understand and respond to our experiences of good and evil in an ambiguous world.

4

"Fatal Attraction"

Is God Too Good to Be True?

Tiger! Tiger! burning bright
In the forest of the night,
What immortal hand or eye
Could frame thy fearful symmetry?

When the stars threw down their spears,
And watered heaven with their tears,
Did he smile his work to see?
Did he who made the Lamb make thee?[1]

⊰ The movie is *Agnes of God*. The scene opens in a convent. The sisters
are praying. Suddenly, a scream is heard, and several of the sisters rush
to the room of Agnes, where they discover she is bleeding. Sister Miriam,
Mother Superior, locates a dead fetus in the wastebasket in the corner of
the room. Sister Agnes is rushed to the hospital by ambulance. The next
day Dr. Martha Livingston, a court-appointed psychiatrist, drives to the
convent to interview both Mother Superior and Sister Agnes. Mother
Miriam claims no one, including her, knew of Agnes's pregnancy. Agnes
herself cannot remember either the pregnancy or the birth. When asked
by Dr. Livingston during her initial visit where she thinks babies come
from, Sister Agnes replies, "When an angel lights on your chest." At the
end of that visit, Mother Miriam tells Dr. Livingston that Agnes is just different, not crazy but innocent, untouched by anyone but God.

Throughout the investigation by Dr. Livingston, we learn about
Agnes's history of abuse by her mother, Agnes's apparent innocence
about her own sexuality, and her image of herself as an ugly and un-
worthy person. In a desperate effort finally to discover what had really
happened at the convent, Dr. Livingston hypnotizes Sister Agnes. She finally recalls the surprise, pain, and anguish of the birth of her child. During a subsequent encounter between Mother Miriam and Martha Livingston in Martha's office, Mother Miriam continues to maintain that
Agnes is "touched by God," that God has the power to "split a cell in her
womb," that "God produced it," and that Agnes is innocent of any wrong-

doing. Then, in one of the key scenes in the movie, Agnes is hypnotized a second time. We see Agnes in her empty room again, where she is seated near the whitewashed wall. At the end of an excruciating scene of anguish and terror, Sister Agnes is pressed against the wall in what appears to be a rape scene, where she is left crying and bleeding. "I hate him for what he did," Agnes says. "Who?" Martha inquires. "God," Agnes replies. The baby was "God's mistake," and Agnes has given the baby back to God.

At the end of the story, we are left to wonder: Is Agnes simply an innocent child fearful of her own sexuality? Is she a victim of abuse who is suffering from clinical hysteria? Has she, indeed, seduced someone or been seduced, now reconstructing her dilemma within her own mind? Or has she been raped by someone? If the latter is the case, who was the abuser? Was it someone from the outside ("a fieldhand"), or a priest who knew the secret passageway to the bell tower? Or was she abused by God, as the scene in the empty room could imply? Was her story one of innocence, ignorance, parental abuse, deception, or hysteria? Or, possibly, was Sister Agnes "blessed" by God? Was the whole incident "God's mistake"?

Film critic Roger Ebert says of John Pielmeier and Norman Jewison's movie version of *Agnes of God:*

> We learn that . . . we should not overlook the possibility that the baby, in fact, had no father. In other words, Sister Agnes had a virgin birth. Or, in case the point still seems obscure, the murdered infant was a child of God. . . . There is a certain amount of pressure on [Dr. Livingston], an agnostic, to accept the possibility that a miracle has occurred. She resists it, quite sensibly, since the implications of the miracle are horrifying: If God indeed conceived the child in Sister Agnes's womb, then why did he in his omnipotence allow her to kill it?[2]

What kind of God do we see portrayed in this story? My instinct as a theologian is to dismiss the story as a study in the psychology of abuse, guilt, and hysteria. The story of being "blessed by God" is not an unknown story in the New Testament. In that story, however, a positive interpretation is given to the relation between God and the subject. But can we dismiss this story as theologically insignificant simply because a negative interpretation is given to a "blessing by God"?

What Is Negotiable? On Deciding
What Check You Are Willing to Sign

"Mr. Wolterstorff, I must tell you, Eric is dead. Mr. Wolterstorff, are you there? You must come at once! Mr. Wolterstorff, Eric is dead."

The call came at 3:30 that Sunday afternoon from Austria, just as they had sent his younger brother off on the plane to spend the summer with Eric. He had died in a mountain-climbing accident in his twenty-fifth year. Quick and bright, a National Merit Scholar, an art historian and artist, intense, somewhat self-centered but gentle and loving, Eric was inclined to overestimate his physical skills and strength.

Facing from the beginning the parents' grief and anguish over the loss of their son, Nicholas Wolterstorff asks, "But the pain of the no more outweighs the gratitude of the once was. Will it always be so?"

His suffering never disappears, never even subsides, through the hundred pages of his lament for a son. The professor of philosophy at Calvin College finally says,

> I cannot fit it all together by saying, "He did it," but neither can I do so by saying, "There was nothing he could do about it." I cannot fit it all together at all. I can only with Job endure. I do not know why God did not prevent Eric's death. To live without the answer is precarious. It's hard to keep one's footing. . . . To the most agonized question I have ever asked I do not know the answer. . . . I am not angry but baffled and hurt. My wound is an unanswered question. The wounds of all humanity are an unanswered question.[3]

Woltersdorff acknowledges that the only thing that angered him in what people offered was a small book by a father whose son had been killed in a mountaineering accident and who claimed his son's foot did not slip but that God had shaken the mountain because it was time for him to come home. He admits that God as the agent of death is one way to fit it together in a rational pattern, and he cannot shake the idea.

Many theologians today assume the sovereignty of God in the midst of suffering and conclude that, in the light of the depth of the evils of our century, the concept of the goodness of God must be reconceived in a way that differs from omnibenevolence in the theistic tradition.

Most of the theologians in these chapters 4 and 5 assume that (1) for Jews and Christians the omnipotence of God is essential to what makes God *God,* and (2) since they cannot compromise the concept of omnipotence on religious grounds, and since they are so outraged at the horrendous evils of the twentieth century that they cannot accept the notion that evil is only apparent, they must pursue the startling conclusion that God, indeed, is in some way "the God of evil."

These theologians concede that a theology of divine sovereignty has its problems and discomforts. But they argue, finally, that the appearance of indifference or even cruelty in God is more tolerable than the appearance of any limitation on the power of God. Unwilling to consider a radical reconception of divine power, they conclude that in some sense the all-loving God is indeed "too good to be true." Finally one has to sign a check if one wants to purchase a resolution of the theodicy problem, at least if one accepts my criticisms of classical theism. When asked which check they are willing to sign, this group of theologians finally signs off on the divine goodness.

Most of the theologians in this chapter are theistic in their basic religious sensibilities. Yet they are dissatisfied with the way the omnipotence doctrine of theism seems to deny the seriousness of evil today. They find it outrageous to claim that someone else's suffering or their own is not genuinely evil. Furthermore, twentieth-century violence (symbolized by the Holocaust and Hiroshima and abuse of children) has become a peculiarly difficult problem for these theists. Thus they are willing to reconsider the common understanding of divine goodness.

Whether this solution patches a gaping hole in the sacred canopy of theism or makes the problem even worse remains to be seen. But the intention of this radical solution seems apparent. It seeks to maintain what is assumed to be the center of the Christian vision of God and at the same time to accept the utter seriousness of the reality of evil within the theistic vision.[4]

The God of the Bible

One cannot escape the conclusion that in the three major forms of tradition in the Hebrew Bible and the Christian Old Testament, namely, the Law, the Prophets, and the Writings, God is sometimes the intentional source of suffering and evil as well as the source of good.

The Law

In the Exodus tradition, a dark side of God is unleashed on the enemies of the Hebrews. God sends the ten plagues on the Egyptians in order to harden Pharaoh's and his officials' hearts so God can use the hardness of heart as a reason to display God's signs and to defeat Pharaoh in battle (Ex. 10:1–2). In Deuteronomy, Yahweh says, "See now that I, even I, am he; there is no god beside me. I kill and I make alive; I wound and I heal; and no one can deliver from my hand" (Deut. 32:39).

One of the most striking expressions of this theme, however, is found in the monarchy tradition, particularly the tradition of Saul.[5] Saul's experience of God at the end of his life is of an evil God; he is tormented by God with an evil spirit. In the beginning (1 Samuel 8) Saul is put in place by Samuel at the concession of Yahweh. "The Lord said to Samuel, 'Listen to their voice and set a king over them'" (v. 22).

Soon, however, Saul's life takes a turn downward. God becomes his tormenter.

> The LORD said to Samuel, "How long will you grieve over Saul? I have rejected him from being king over Israel." . . . Now the spirit of the Lord departed from Saul, and an evil spirit from the LORD tormented him. And Saul's servants said to him, "See now, an evil spirit from God is tormenting you. Let our lord now command the servants who attend you to look for someone who is skillful in playing the lyre; and when the evil spirit from God is upon you, he will play it, and you will feel better." (1 Sam. 16:1, 14–16)

Evil comes to Saul from God. Because God for him remains a tormentor, he goes to the medium at Endor to find a more satisfying experience of the divine (chap. 28). In the end Saul is simply left sitting there until his death when he becomes a tragic character at the hands of God (chap. 31).

Summarizing the Yahwistic claim, the writer of 1 Samuel says, "The Lord kills and brings to life; he brings down to Sheol and raises up. The Lord makes poor and makes rich; he brings low, he also exalts" (2:6–7). Commenting on these stories of the Pharaoh and of Saul, Walter Wink says,

> One possible translation of "Yahweh" is "He causes to happen what happens." If, then, everything that happens has been caused by God, evil must also be caused by God. Thus when Pharaoh resisted Israel's liberation, it was not ascribed to his free will or his self-interest or sin, but to God's hardening Pharaoh's heart. So also it was Yahweh who sent the evil spirit on Saul, and who commissioned a lying spirit to enter the mouths of the four hundred prophets of Ahab.[6]

Other stories abound. The story of Jacob and the "angel" is not about his wrestling with his guilty conscience because he deprived his brother of his inheritance. The story is about the nature of Israel's relationship with God, and suggests that God is our opponent. Israel is locked in a covenant relationship in which God both promises and threatens to be its God. Indeed, the story suggests that the religious life is a big wrestling match and the opponent may be God.

The Prophets

Some prophetic literature also pictures God as the source of evil as well as good. Isaiah reports God as saying to his anointed, to Cyrus, "I form light and create darkness, I make weal and create woe, I the Lord do all these things" (Isa. 45:7). Amos says, "Is a trumpet blown in a city, and the people are not afraid? Does [evil] befall a city, unless the Lord has done it?" (Amos 3:6).

One of the most dramatic pictures in all the prophets is Jeremiah's experience of his call as a divine rape. He says,

> O LORD, you have enticed me,
>   and I was enticed;
> you have overpowered me,
>   and you have prevailed.
> I have become a laughingstock all day long;
>   everyone mocks me.
> For whenever I speak, I must cry out,
>   I must shout, "Violence and destruction!"
> For the word of the Lord has become for me
>   a reproach and derision all day long. . . .
> Cursed be the day
>   on which I was born!
> The day when my mother bore me,
>   let it not be blessed!
>
>   (Jer. 20:7–8, 14)

Robert Carroll points out that the language in verses 7–10 is the familiar cry of outrage and suffering in the scriptures. But on this occasion "the deity is part of the problem." God has deceived the speaker (v. 7). The phrase sometimes translated as "you have deceived me" (from the Hebrew word *pth*) has connotations of deception, seduction, enticement, and persuasion. "The combination of *pth*, 'seduce,' and *hzq*, 'be strong, prevail,' in verse 7 has led some exegetes to understand the accusation to be one of 'rape.'"[7]

Regardless of whether or not this is the most proper understanding of the image that lies behind Jeremiah's complaint, the claim that Yahweh is a deceiver and a violent oppressor seems to be central to his experience of God. Later Jeremiah generalizes from this experience of his prophetic call to Yahweh's work in history.

> "Thus says the Lord: I am going to break down what I have built, and pluck up what I have planted—that is, the whole land. And you, do you seek great things for yourself? Do not seek them; for I am going to bring [evil] upon all flesh, says the Lord; but I will give you your life as a prize of war in every place to which you may go." (Jer. 45:4–5)

The Writings

Lamentations says, "Is it not from the mouth of the Most High that good and bad [evil] come?" (Lam. 3:38). Likewise, many of the psalms are an embarrassment to conventional faith. "How long, O Lord? Will you forget me forever? How long will you hide your face from me? How long must I bear pain in my soul, and have sorrow in my heart all day long? How long shall my enemy be exalted over me?" (Ps. 13:1–2). The most embarrassing scripture passage for conventional piety, however, must surely be Psalm 88.[8]

> You have put me in the depths of the Pit,
>   in the regions dark and deep.
> Your wrath lies heavy upon me,
>   and you overwhelm me with all your waves.
> You have caused my companions to shun me;
>   you have made me a thing of horror to them.
> I am shut in so that I cannot escape;
>   my eye grows dim through sorrow. . . .
> O Lord, why do you cast me off?
>   Why do you hide your face from me?
> Wretched and close to death from my youth up,
>   I suffer your terrors; I am desperate.
>   (Ps. 88:6–9a, 14–15)

Walter Brueggemann says of this psalm, "There is no playing up to God. There is only anger."[9] Not only does death come, but Yahweh causes it. The speaker is utterly helpless, and the cause for the death is firmly fixed. Although the psalmist may hope that the speech may provoke some response from God, it does not. The psalm ends in silence. The speaker is shunned and is left in darkness. "The last word in the Psalm is darkness. The last word is darkness."[10]

Consider also the case of Job. At one level of the story, Job is merely the third-party pawn in a wager between God and (the God–appointed) "satan." Job is used by God in a project far more cosmic in scope than concern about human justice. At one level of the story, God can be described only as essentially indifferent to Job. In the key chapters, the God-speeches in chapters 38—41, God's primary interests are in nature (the size and structure of the world, the sea's power and depth, the dawn and darkness, the snow and hail and rain, the order of the stars, the cloud's patterns, and in the wild, undomesticated animals and birds [the lion, raven, mountain goat, deer, wild donkey and ox, ostrich, horse, hawk and eagle]) (Job 38—39). There God's interests are not primarily in humanity at all. God is basically indifferent to "the pain that the elaborate interlocking teleologies of life involve," and God "does not share with his creatures . . . the virtue of sympathy with physical suffering."[11] Job is simply left shaking his fist in God's face and demanding that God respond to his need for justice. To say that God loves him in the personalistic way most modern Christians claim God loves us and that Job should respond to God in unfettered doxology can be seen as inappropriate and perhaps even ludicrous.

Earlier, in Job 12, God is the *gibbor,* the warrior, who seems to be the One who has gone berserk in the life of one hapless mortal. Not only is this the case in Job's own life, Job accuses God of heavy-handedness.

> With God are wisdom and strength, he has counsel and
> understanding. If he tears down, no one can rebuild; if he shuts
> someone in, no one can open up. If he withholds the waters, they
> dry up; if he sends them out, they overwhelm the land.
>
> (vv. 13–15)

Norman Habel comments, "This God promotes cosmic destruction and social disorder rather than peace, order, and stability. His *modus operandi* is an exercise in anarchy, his style fosters violence, and his governance seems to negate the very nature of wisdom as the ordering principle of the cosmos and society."[12] In the various speeches of Job, "we meet an understanding of God that amounts to nothing less than a nihilistic credo. . . . It is clear that Job speaks of a God who is not amoral but actively immoral."[13]

New Testament

Although the New Testament contains several passages that give biblical grounds for the various kinds of theodicies we explored in chapter 3, especially in Paul and in the Pastoral Epistles, the New Testament does not seem interested in the question of theodicy, at least as it has been formulated theologically, even in the broader sense. There is no theodicy question in the New

Testament, at least in the ways represented in the Old Testament. In another sense, however, the New Testament is a comprehensive theodicy in that the Christologies developed there function as an answer to the problem of suffering and evil. I will explore that dimension of New Testament Christology in chapter 8.

Nevertheless, there are some New Testament passages that raise questions about the goodness of God in the ways I have been considering here. For example, Paul says in Romans 9:18, "So then he has mercy on whomever he chooses, and he hardens the heart of whomever he chooses," and then continues in verse 22 even more strongly, saying, "What if God, desiring to show his wrath and to make known his power, has endured with much patience the objects of wrath that are made for destruction; and what if he has done so in order to make known the riches of his glory for the objects of mercy, which he has prepared beforehand for glory?"

Furthermore, the picture of God offered in the Apocalypse of John (Revelation) represents God as imposing unrestrained vengeance on those who are outside the merciful election of God (or outside those who mercifully have selected Christ and remained faithful to him). One of the most problematic passages in the New Testament, though, is the one in which God is portrayed by Jesus as the abandoner: "My God, my God, why have you forsaken me?" (Matt. 27:46 and parallels). If there is any New Testament passage in which the human experience of God as the divine abuser comes in profound conflict with traditional theistic and christological claims, this is surely the case in accounts of the final moments of Jesus' life.

Raymund Schwager points out that one thousand verses in the Old Testament describe God's own violent acts of punishment, a hundred passages where God expressly commands others to kill people, and several stories where God kills or tries to kill for no apparent reason at all (Ex. 4:24–26).[14] Likewise, numerous biblical texts, such as Daniel 13; Judges 19:11–30; Genesis 34; 2 Samuel 13; Deuteronomy 22:23–39; Leviticus 18:6–18; Genesis 6; Genesis 12—22; Genesis 39:1–23; and Hosea 11, lead James Poling to speak of "the violence of God in the Bible," "God's ambivalence," and God's "ambiguous" role in scripture. "On one hand, God is compassionate and just, protecting the vulnerable and seeking alternatives to the evil intentions of humans. But on the other hand, God is presented as insensitive to the vulnerable members of families and even destructive toward whole populations. In some ways this tension between love and hate in the image of God is unresolved."[15]

No interpretation of any passage of scripture is possible apart from hermeneutics. Interpreters of these biblical texts who bring theistic presuppositions to the texts will find ways of interpreting them that protect their theistic ideas of God. Similarly, if one does not bring theistic assumptions to these texts, one can be open to biblical concepts of God that are in conflict with more traditional assumptions about the nature of God's goodness. I am interested in what such texts might imply about nontraditional interpretations of the nature of God for the problem of theodicy.

The Problem
of Divine Goodness

The claim that God is "good" is usually interpreted to mean "perfectly good."[16] But "good," and especially "perfectly good," are systematically ambiguous concepts. The affirmation frequently identifies God with the summum bonum, the highest good, implying that such notions of evil as privation of the good, ambiguity, ambivalence, or willing evil do not apply in any way to God's character or will. In light of the equation of God with the concept of summum bonum, or God's goodness as identified as "perfect goodness," *perfect goodness* means:

1. God's intentions and actions always and only serve the highest good;
2. God's intentions and actions infallibly serve the highest good in every event;
3. God's character excludes all intentions and actions that do not serve the highest good; and
4. God is love, and though that love may be "tough love," it does not include anything the world would genuinely be better off without.

Some theologians today, on the basis of scripture and their own experience, have serious doubt about affirming this cluster of claims as the meaning of divine goodness.

It is important to be clear about what the counterproposal usually does not claim. To talk about God being "too good to be true," or "the dark side of God," or even the extreme reference to "the God of evil," does not in any of the discussions I am familiar with mean:

1. God is a devil;[17]
2. God is a divine demon;[18]
3. God wills and does only evil;
4. God's good is our evil, our evil is God's good; or
5. God is not good in any ultimate sense.

Those theologians who question omnibenevolence do not suggest that God is not good but that God is not "*perfect* goodness" in the summum bonum meaning of goodness, namely, a goodness that excludes all evil or ambivalence or ambiguity from the divine will and activity. Their viewpoint questions the assumption that if God is good, God would not cause and would want to prevent all suffering and evil.

In most of the cases I will describe, statements about the ambiguity of God are more pragmatic judgments than psychological or metaphysical verdicts. That is, their conclusions do not result from an attempt to psychoanalyze God to detect the presence of a conscious, malevolent intent within the "personality or "mind" of God. Rather, they are an inference about God's character and purposes based on a pragmatic judgment about the nature of God in the light of experience. Representatives of this theological viewpoint look at human experience and examine the consequences of the divine activity in human life. God is the sum of God's acts, this approach assumes, and the acts of God, from creation to Calvary to Coventry, can be interpreted as evidence of an ambiguous as well as an omnibenevolent deity.

Such an empirical or pragmatic approach to our problem does not assume the ability to know God is intrinsically good or evil in God's being. It assumes that one can judge the character and purposes of God from the sum of God's "acts."Assuming that the character of anyone is represented in the sum of his or her acts, this approach plays down knowledge of the inner life and motives of God and increases the weight placed on God's activity in our experience. We know character retrospectively. We cannot judge alleged character independent of the acts of the person, past and present. Thus an interpretation of the character of God from the evidence of history and experience is central in almost all this kind of literature in theodicy.

From this perspective, then, to talk about God as "too good to be true" means:

1. God is not perfectly good in the sense that God's activity and character include characteristics or actions that can be described as evil.
2. God's actions and character are more ambiguous or more ambivalent than the simple concept of omnibenevolence conveys.
3. God's goodness includes a complex of moral qualities that carry negative meanings for us, such as irrationality, indifference, arbitrariness, destruction, vengeance, wrath, and hatred, which, although not liable to moral condemnation, are nevertheless not appropriately included in what we mean by omnibenevolent.
4. God is beyond good and evil. God's goodness simply transcends any moral criteria whatsoever, so that moral judgments are inappropriate to apply to any activity or characteristic of God. A more common version of this idea is the claim that God is "permanently incomprehensible." God is infinite and unknowable, so our language of morality and love when applied to God cannot mean what it means when applied to human beings. So when the college sophomore says she can disprove the reality of God by saying, "If God is all good . . . ," the senior can (politely) interrupt with, "God is all perfect goodness, but nothing follows from this claim, since we don't know what infinite goodness would be or do."

All the theologians I examine in chapters 4 and 5 argue that the Judeo-ʾhristian theistic God is "too good to be true" to our experience. These theologians, however, are not all identical in what they argue. Those described in this chapter describe their *experience of God* as shadowy. Their language about "the evil God" is explicitly a description of their personal experience of God or a description of their experience of the God of history. They claim that they experience God in their own lives or in contemporary history as an abandoner, a sadist, an enemy, indifferent or even terrorizing. They do *not* a offer a description of the being or character of God.

The theologians in chapter 5, however, come closer to defending or critiquing *a concept of the being or character of God*. Although their concept obviously is tied to their experience, they begin to venture a reinterpretation of the God who emerges from their experience. Unlike those in this chapter who tend to ignore the question of the being of God by describing only their experience, the theologians in the next chapter plunge into the problem of what kind of God is implied in their experience.

Theological Challenges to the Idea of an Omnibenevolent God

The literature that rethinks the traditional Christian teaching about the omnibenevolence of God can be grouped into two basic types, namely, those whose experience and understanding of God include a kind of indifference to the human plight of suffering and evil, and those whose experience and understanding of God includes a kind of divine abuse of the human being.

The Experience of God the Abuser

When in crisis, people rely on their basic beliefs and values about the world and their place in it.[19] Many victims of sexual abuse try to make sense of their experience by seeking a religious explanation. Marie Fortune finds that victims of abuse frequently combine self-blame and God-blame.

> A 55-year-old woman was raped by a stranger who broke into her home during the night. Her explanation for why this had happened to her was that God was punishing her for having divorced her husband ten years earlier.[20]

To victims such as this, their question, Why did God send me this affliction? is answered by their traditional theodicy. The abuse is God's way to test their faith, or punish them for their sins, or strengthen their character. Each of these explanations implies that in some way or another God is responsible for their suffering. In this respect, the "good reason" or the "greater good" that is offered follows the mainstream of Western Christian theodicy to interpret and justify suffering.

What is typical for many victims of sexual abuse, however, which goes beyond traditional reasoning, is their experience of being abandoned by God.

Some victims of abuse talk about feeling alone in the midst of their suffering because they have been abandoned by God. In addition to the lack of support and involvement of their family, friends, and community, the victim often feels as if God also has turned away.

> A second source of the feeling of abandonment comes from the victim's experience and understanding of suffering. . . . If a person believes God to be omnipotent, loving, and rewarding of the righteousness of good Christians, then suffering is either a sign of God's disfavor or a realization that God does not play by the rules. Either interpretation can lead to the feeling of being abandoned by God. This feeling of abandonment occurs for the victim who expected God to protect her from all pain and suffering. When she encounters suffering, she feels betrayed.[21]

God's "maleness" makes God worthless to her in her suffering. She feels abandoned by a God who cannot understand.

If a person believes that the sign of God's presence and love is protection from suffering, then the experience of suffering logically implies God's absence. Even if God is not normally thought of as an abuser or one who sanctions abuse, God is nevertheless experienced as the one who could and does abuse, because God is the omnipotent and omnibenevolent one who protects victims from abuse. Because the sufferer has experienced the awful pain of abuse, that one can only conclude that God has abandoned this sufferer. God is simply the last one in a whole series of abusers or complicit onlookers. God is experienced as the ultimate and cosmic abandoner.

Not all experience of abandonment by God is directly related to violent abuse, however. That feeling can be occasioned by more "routine" suffering. On the basis of his personal experience, Robert McClelland is led to speak of God as "our loving enemy."[22] In using this phrase, he intends to say something both about how we experience certain events in our life and also about how we sometimes experience God. Our common idea of the goodness of God, he claims, is shaped by the good times in our lives. When things are going well, God is thought of as the Great Benefactor who loves us. But when circumstances go against us, we should believe that these too are from God, that the loving God acts as enemy as much as benefactor.

The occasion for his reconsideration of the goodness of God is a disaster in his own life. In 1972, his career as pastor of a United Presbyterian congregation in St. Louis seemed at an end. He had no voice for four-and-a-half years as a result of spastic dysphonia, an incurable disease. Whether the cause of this disease was psychosomatic or viral, no one knew. In the process of trying to come to terms with his disease, he discovered "the God whom many of us encounter as the enemy." God became the target of his rage and the one on whom he vented his frustrations. That experience is what it is really like to meet God, he believes. God is the enemy, the Divine Heavyweight. When we cannot escape anxiety, insecurity, worry, and imperfection, "we meet God— the disturber of our contentment, the invader of our lives—God, the enemy."

McClelland has no doubts that God is loving, but that love can be frighten-ing. Indeed, there is a terrifying aspect to divine love. God's love approves of crucifixions. "The good news is that in addition to all the obvious tokens of his goodness, life's crucifixions are as much a part of God's grace-full will as the sunshine." McClelland does not understand this to mean that God is a cos-mic sadist, an idea we will encounter later. For him the God who has sen-tenced us to death is not malevolent, but is the one who conveys to us a truth different from our own truth. "We want life on our terms, but we encounter the Enemy who has a different agenda than ours." God hounds us until we face up to the truth about ourselves, our limitations, our imperfections, and es-pecially our death, which is "God's idea."

God our loving enemy has a purpose in bringing our crucifixions. In com-ing to us through crucifixion and resurrection, God shows Godself to us as grace. And this grace brings us into relationship with God. Indeed, in com-ing to us as the no-sayer to our hope for immortality, God, and not the finite elements of our world, is to be raged against. "I submit that it is terribly important to identify the enemy correctly, and the enemy is God! How can you rage against a piece of metal such as a carburetor? How can you rage against a kidney? How do you work through those emotions of absurdity with a carburetor or a kidney? No! God is the one to be blamed." The rea-son that God's crucifixions are not sadistic or arbitrary is that they have a purpose, namely, to help us see God as our Creator and Savior through rage as well as praise.

What is clear when one examines closely the assumptions as well as such experiences of God is that the characteristic that makes God God is power. In one passage McClelland speaks of God as Life, but then clarifies more pre-cisely what he means. In examining the Hebrew verb form for Yahweh, he says, "It seems to suggest that whatever is caused to be is of God. Everything that happens in life is of God. *Life is the glove of God's hand*" (italics added). In commenting further on his analogy, he says, "Only when we understand Isaiah's assertion that God is in life as a hand is in a glove, can we hear the good news he proclaims for God." Unless one has some assurance that cruci-fixions have God's approval, life makes little sense and chaos threatens.

In the end McClelland does not use his experience as the basis for a radi-cal reconception of the goodness of God. Finally, all suffering is good because it serves the final good of God. By dismantling our illusions and teaching us the ultimate lesson about our true relation to God as one of pure grace, God the enemy in the end is really God our Father.

Such experience, however, has led some Christians to an even more thor-oughgoing reconsideration of the divine goodness. Some are led to describe God as the divine abuser. Belden Lane, in a series of articles in *Christian Cen-tury* from 1987 through 1989, depicts God as playful and rough in God's rela-tion to us. In the first in his series of articles, Lane portrays God as hidden and playful. Drawing his analogy from the childhood game of hide-and-seek, *Deus absconditus,* the hidden God, is not hidden in obscurity, inaccessibility, and remoteness, as if the divine inscrutability were an end in itself. God is hidden as *Deus ludens,* a God revealed in playfulness.

As the real point to the childhood game is not so much to hide well as to hide in order to be found, Lane sees God's hiddenness rooted not in the effort to protect the divine majesty or to protect us from the God's fierce grandeur. Rather, God's playfulness with us is rooted in the divine compassion that longs to draw us through that playfulness to love. God's hiddenness is a playful teasing, a divine seduction which will lead to a surprise encounter.[23]

In a subsequent article, Lane pushes his analogy even farther. God not only plays hide-and-seek, but in the game of hide-and-seek God's playfulness is rough. His analogy is a chilling story about T. H. White, the great English medievalist and raconteur. He cried at his sixth birthday party because he believed that he was going to be shot by his father as part of his birthday present, which was a wooden castle big enough for his father to inhabit and equipped with real pistol barrels beneath its battlements. Similar to White we also misunderstand our father's true intentions, for God often "plays rough before breaking into laughter." To misinterpret God's play as God's anger with us is tragic. Divine play is not syrupy compassion but entails risk, a dimension of menace, "assuming at times the very aspect of evil."

Throughout his second article, Lane insists that God plays rough for the sake of a deeper love, exhibiting the divine humor in order to elicit relationship and delighting in the same boldness on our part that works to establish the bonds of intimacy. We are bound together by our mutual acceptance of play. God's relation with us includes the hidden love of rough play.

> The laughter of being beaten by God—trumped by the high card always up God's sleeve—is a joy known only to those who have entered the game and discovered losing to be yet another form of being loved.[24]

However, the experience of the abusive God has led some to an even stronger language about the ambiguous nature of God. One evangelical Christian, C. S. Lewis, referred to God as a sadist. In *A Grief Observed,* Lewis tells of his anger at God, when his wife, Joy, dies from cancer. This story is also recounted in the movie *Shadowlands.* "Talk to me about the truth of religion," Lewis says, "and I'll gladly listen. Talk to me about the duty of religion and I'll listen submissively. But don't come talking to me about the consolations of religion or I shall suspect that you don't understand."[25]

On the verge of losing his faith in God as the result of Joy's death, Lewis recognized an even deeper spiritual problem than the possible loss of faith. "The real danger is of coming to believe such dreadful things about Him. The conclusion I dread is not, 'So there's no God after all,' but 'So this is what God's really like.' Deceive yourself no longer. . . . Sooner or later I must face the question in plain language. What reason have we, except our own desperate wishes, to believe that God is, by any standard we can conceive, 'good'? Doesn't all the *prima facie* evidence suggest exactly the opposite?"

What choked every hope for Lewis was the memory of all the prayers he and Joy had offered and all the false hopes they had sustained. These hopes were not merely wishful thinking; their hope had been encouraged by X-ray photographs, by strange remissions, by one temporary recovery that might have ranked as a miracle. Step-by-step they were led up the garden path. Time after time, when God seemed most gracious, God was really preparing them for the next torture. Lewis is led, then, to entertain the idea of "the bad God," or God as a sadist, like the man who sat by him at dinner telling him what he had done to cats that afternoon.

Finally, distinguishing between his feelings and his thoughts, Lewis concedes, "I wrote that last night. It was a yell rather than a thought. Let me try it again. Is it rational to believe in a bad God? Anyway, in a God so bad as all that? The Cosmic Sadist, the spiteful imbecile?" Lewis in horror quickly rejects this thought and returns to his more "rational" viewpoint, outlined in his *The Problem of Pain*.[26] He finally concludes that his entry was "the senseless writhings of a man who won't accept the fact that there is nothing we can do with suffering except to suffer it." He poses the question, "Who still thinks there is some device (if only he could find it) which will make pain not to be pain?" So Lewis rejects the idea of the sadistic God, though the God experienced in *A Grief Observed* is much more "ambiguous" than the God he had defined in his more "rational" *The Problem of Pain*.

The Experience
of the Indifference of God

Not all experiences of suffering have led Christians to interpret God as the abusive God. Some have interpreted suffering to be evidence of a God who has qualities and agendas larger than and beyond human happiness, who therefore is to some degree indifferent to human suffering. We have already explored a biblical version of this theme in the God-speeches in the book of Job. That experience of God, however, continues to be a part of modern experience as well, and has led some theologians to speak of indifference as one of the characteristics of God.

In the third in his series of articles in *Christian Century*, Belden Lane's "rough play" is supplemented by "indifference" as the best way to understand God's love. Mountains, deserts, and rough terrain which embrace the void express the grandeur of God's sovereignty more than the self-absorption and self-realization theology that grows out of garden-tending metaphors. What we have on our hands is a God of fierce indifference to the assorted hand-wringing anxieties of human life. God is indifferent to our pressing human concerns and ignores us. Lane's interpretation of this majestic indifference of the austere God, the unaccommodating God of divine *apatheia,* to the petty self-conscious desires that consume us is reminiscent of McClelland's argument that it is God's way of teaching us that we live by grace. Judaism and Christianity have a tendency to view

the divine *apatheia* as a rich and subtle way of teasing us out of ourselves into relationship with God. Indeed, the divine indifference turns out at last to be another form of God's insistent love. "When the self has been wholly abandoned, only then is there the possibility of seeing it restored in Christ. Having lost one's life, it comes rushing back as divine gift."[27]

One might dismiss McClelland's, Lane's, and Lewis's concepts of the goodness of God as just another masculine, patriarchal, Calvinist God of the biblical and Christian religions. Some feminist theologians have argued that if we shift from a God-centered patriarchal religion to a Goddess-centered religion, we could overcome this dilemma of the malevolent, ambivalent, or ambiguous God of masculine religion. If we change to better images of the Goddess to conceive of the divine—mother, nurturer, healer, caretaker or crone, peacemaker, personified wisdom, miraculous virgin—thereby reconceiving God's role and character in the light of traditional feminine virtues, we would get our concept of God straightened out and overcome this distorted and distorting masculine image of God as malevolent or ambivalent.

A significantly different interpretation of the experience of God the abusive enemy, however, is offered by several feminist theologians in another version of "divine indifference." Less controlled by the assumptions of omnipotence, transcendence, perfection, and other concerns that seem to be peculiarly male preoccupations in the description and interpretation of experience, some feminist theologians have described their experience of the divine and the relation of the divine to suffering in the world in a way that conceives God's "indifference" in a less sadistic way.

Judith Plaskow makes it clear that she does not experience and believe in a God who stands outside history and manipulates it and can therefore be charged with moral failures.[28] She supports much of the contemporary feminist work on a new God-language. However, that project has too often, in her view, focused on some particular aspects of God while neglecting other aspects. Feminist characterizations of the divine often focus on the nurturing powers of the natural world. God is depicted as source, wellspring, mother, and womb of life. Although this is legitimate and even central to feminist experience, she believes it is only a partial description of female experience of the divine.

Basing her concept of the character of God on the breadth of her experience of the world as a female, she argues, "Unless the God who speaks to the feminist experience of empowerment and connection can also speak to the frightening, destructive, and divisive aspects of our lives, a whole side of existence will be severed from the feminist account of the sacred."[29] She notes how both experience and scripture, as in the stories of Uzzah and Nadob and Abihu, confront us not so much with the injustice of God as with a "divine unpredictability." The choice is not between God as good or evil but with "the irrationality and ambiguity of the sacred." The God of women's experience and scripture is not as predictable, rational, and nice as much talk about the goodness of God implies.

The God of these stories is an ambiguous God—the Goddess as energy of the universe, responsible for life and death and rebirth. S/he is a God who creates forms of startling fragility and beauty and also brings forth monstrosities that frighten and overwhelm us. S/he is the God who makes dry land rise up out of the waters and then washes it away with tidal waves and volcanoes. Creativity by its very nature seems profoundly ambiguous.[30]

A similar theme appears in the work of feminist theologians Rosemary Radford Ruether and Susan Thistlethwaite. Although most feminist theology has tended to emphasize the interrelatedness between human beings and nature, instead of the conflict between them, as womanist theologians tend to do, Thistlethwaite interprets relationships as much more ambiguous than most feminists usually do. Both Christian and pagan spirituality, in their emphasis on connectedness, want to integrate imaginative self-transcendence and bodiliness. "Yet I believe that even in this impulse toward connectedness, to wholeness, they have equated culture with evil and nature with goodness, reinventing the dualism. Both nature and culture are more ambiguous than white feminism has allowed."[31] Creation and nature include destruction as well as creativity. Good and evil, creation and destruction, evil and good, destruction and creation are more intertwined than either Christian tradition or Christian feminism has allowed.

Similarly, Ruether argues that there have been two directions most feminist theology has taken—revisionary Christianity and the recovery of a matriarchal, Goddess-centered religion. Although she does not question the authenticity of a spiritual quest that focuses on the symbol of the Goddess, she argues that there are some significant disagreements between Goddess feminism and Christian feminism. One of the basic differences is her claim that there is "considerably greater ambiguity" in the relationship between Goddess-centered religion and patriarchal religion than some Goddess feminists, such as Carol Christ, want to find. Christ traces the repression of the Goddess in ancient Near Eastern religion back to the impulse to "kill the Goddess" in Christianity, especially in the fourth century when paganism was declared illegal.

Ruether, however, criticizes this assumption and some other forms of Goddess feminism on three grounds. First, on historical grounds, the movement from polytheism to monotheism did not equal a movement from Goddess to a patriarchal, exclusive God. Second, the evidence to support the claim that monotheism promotes class hierarchy while polytheism does not is ambiguous. Polytheism, at least as far back as we can trace its literary traditions, also reflects a world of class hierarchy. That is, the religion of monotheism is no more or no less entrenched in the problem of class hierarchy than polytheism. Furthermore, "I want to argue that it is from the God of the prophets and of Jesus, and not from Isis or Athena, that Christians and post-Christians alike have learned to protest great inequalities of wealth and poverty and to seek a more egalitarian society."[32] Finally, she finds little evidence that modern neopaganism necessarily promotes peaceful, egalitarian values. The revival of ancient gods and goddesses is intimately linked with European nationalism. Modern

neopaganism quickly moved throughout modern history toward fascist racism and militarism.

> Obviously, that sort of neopaganism is not what egalitarian, antimilitarist feminists seek when they go in quest of the ancient Goddess. Nonetheless, the historical record stands as a strong reminder that post-Christian revivals of the ancient gods have served a variety of impulses. Fascist, racist neopaganism cannot just be dismissed by feminists as irrelevant to their quest.[33]

Although the experience of the divine as antihumanist—repressive, abusive, sadistic—may be the primary experience of many in male monotheistic cultures, the experience of inhumanity is also characteristic of the divine in the cultures of the gods and goddesses, including the recovery of matriarchal, Goddess-centered religion. If Ruether is correct, the experience of the divine as ambiguous cuts across female as well as male experience and imaging of the sacred. Apparently, a wide range of human experiences of the divine is more ambivalent than the doctrine of God's omnibenevolence represents.

Catherine Madsen, also, argues that the concept of omnibenevolence of God has little or no affinity to women's experience of the divine.[34] An agenda to reconstitute omnibenevolence, indeed, is little more than a hangover of the orthodox Christian search for a God who is wholly good. Discovering that "he" is not good, we still hope that "she" may be. Some feminists hope they can still maintain a dependent and docile relationship to God by a change in gender, making dependency on God the Father intolerable but dependence on the benevolent Goddess permissible. This provides the assurance that God is still good and will never get out of hand.

> But why is it necessary (and how is it possible?) to have a God one trusts and approves of? I say this not as someone who has known only the Father God, but as someone who has known the world: its droughts and floods, its extreme climate, its strange combination of tender bounty and indifference, and the uneasiness of human society with its descents into savagery. However certain one may be that one is loved by some presence in the universe— and it is possible, at moments, to be very certain of that—that same presence will kill us all in turn, will visit our lovers with sudden devastating illness, will freeze our crops, will age our friends, and will never for one moment stand between us and any person who wishes to harm us.[35]

Madsen maintains that the image of a nurturing Goddess involves us in the same difficulty as the image of a perfectly good God. There is no escape route provided in female experience of the divine or goddess religion. We come face-to-face in goddess religion with the same dilemma the theist faces, namely, that we are capable of being more ethical than God. To establish a Goddess in place of the Father God accomplishes nothing if we try to make her wholly good. To substitute feminine virtues for masculine powers is impossible. In the world of actual experience, virtues and powers are entirely mixed, so that no wholly good act takes place, even nurturance and comfort,

without its undercurrent of danger. "If we are made in the divine image, that is what we are up against: the inseparability of good and evil."[36] It is not so empowering to have an image of God who nurtures us. It is, for Madsen, as it is for theodicists like John Roth and Frederick Sontag, far more empowering to have a God we can stand up to, fight against, argue with, even exhort. This leads us to one of the biblical responses to this experience of the ambiguity of God in the midst of suffering.

One Response:
The Lament Tradition

There is a strand of scripture that offers one response to this experience of God. It assumes that the experience of God as enemy is an authentic, profound religious experience. Although this tradition does not question the reality of God, it does admit that faithful believers experience God in threatening ways. Instead of denying or fleeing the abusive God, this tradition stands full-face before God in lament. Lament is not only an acceptable way to stand before God, it is, perhaps, the only way to be authentically religious in the midst of this kind of experience of God.

Kathleen Farmer argues that the biblical texts reflect a variety of different ways people have responded to adversity in their lives, and nothing in the Hebrew scriptures speaks against rage, anger, and complaint as possible modes of response to pain and suffering. The "passive, stoic, unprotesting mode of response to tragedy and pain is not the only model, and in fact in the Scriptures it is not even the most predominant model of how the faithful can or should react to tragic reversals in their lives."[37]

Farmer argues that more than one-third of the psalms consist of just such fully articulated cries of anger, anguish, humiliation, and pain. "Those of us who have been taught to tiptoe quietly and to whisper politely in the presence of God don't really know what to do with this large bulk of embarrassing material which has been preserved for us in the book of Psalms. In most Christian communities, the psalms of anger and pain have been virtually forgotten."[38] As she points out, this lament tradition is so little known in the American Protestant churches that most churchgoers do not know Jesus was quoting from Psalm 22 when he hung on the cross.

The psalmist does not spend any time trying to justify the suffering God has imposed or adjusting to it. The psalmist simply explodes in anger. "The individual who cries out for help in Psalm 13 is angry and hurt by what seems to be God's deliberate neglect and the psalmist is not afraid to show that anger and that hurt to God. This is protest speech, not passive acquiescence to the will of God."[39] From her point of view, however, this response is not only catharsis. Insofar as it is addressed to God, it is an expression of faith and a source of new depths of spirituality. Even Psalm 88, the most despairing of all

biblical literature, is still faith; it is not indifference to God. In the psalms we find "a large group of texts (perhaps 50 in number) which tacitly acknowledge that wounded hearts and bodies, bruised spirits, broken relationships and even depression of the darkest kind can exist side by side with a deep and genuine faith in God."

Although such psalms are usually described as "psalms of lament," they are more accurately described, Farmer thinks, as "psalms of anger and complaint." She finds in them an element of protest which the notion of lament does not necessarily convey. In the former (as in Job, for example, and perhaps Jeremiah), God is "taken on" through allegation, indictment, complaint, rage, or even rebellion. Criminal charges are filed; God is put in the dock. David Blumenthal goes even a step farther and argues that in "facing the abusing God," the scripture includes a tradition of rage expressed against God. "The text [Ps 44] contains no language of revolution, no talk of revolt. It contains no language of redemptive suffering, no talk of salvific oppression. There is the Word of anger, the Word of anguish, the Word of demand, even of command. . . . no letting go of God and self; no letting Him off the hook. . . . The emotion of this psalm is rage."[40]

Even if the distinction between lament and protest is too casuistic, the point is that the scripture includes a rich tradition of complaint against God experienced as the enemy, a tradition that most Protestant Christians have written out of the canon.

Is a Critique Legitimate?

In one sense no evaluation of the views described in this chapter is appropriate. To the extent that the viewpoints expressed are not intended to be speculative claims about God but are about that person's experience of God, the viewpoints are not liable to criticism. People experience what they experience; they feel what they feel. No one can or should say to another person, "You cannot feel that way!" or "You should not feel that way!" The hearer can only hear the complaint and receive it into his or her own data about the world and how others experience the world and God. So if the theologies here described are statements of certain experiences, they should be heard and received just as they are, descriptions of experiences of God. The hearer perhaps may be changed by the hearing. But even if that transformation does not occur, no one should say to another, "You are mistaken about how you experience the world and God."

There are, however, three points that I think any auditors should consider after they have heard these confessions of faith and taken them into their own expanded range of data about how people experience the world and God.

1. To what extent is this language about God an expression of the spiritual and social circumstances of the speaker alone, and to what extent does the language intend to give an account of a more inclusive human experience of

God? This is a difficult question even to ask, let alone to answer. Many post-moderns have come to the conclusion that *every* statement we make about *anything* is restricted to the context of the speaker. There is no universal or transcendent or even common point of view from which to speak about anything. The contextual nature of every statement about God, and the constructive character of every theological statement about God must always be kept in mind. There is no transcendent place from which to make any statement whatsoever about God beyond the speaker's point of view.

Still, some theological claims are more self-consciously and intentionally expression of the social location, the time, space, gender, race, and class of the speaker, than are others. Sometimes theologians and preachers intend to make statements *about God* and not merely about themselves or merely about only their experience of God. Their statements are about their intention to describe from the point of view of their experience something about God. The dilemma about the status of theological statements as either theology or anthropology is more apparent in the range of theologians we have examined in this chapter than in many others, although the quandary is present in our entire discussion throughout the book.

Belden Lane is a case in point. Although he does not explicitly constrict his theological statements about God to his autobiography, he is fully aware later in his writings of how events in his life have shaped his particular concept of God.

> The first death I faced was my father's, which came with sudden, frightening violence when I was 13. At that time, the dread beast, its wings flapping and its breath foul as hell, took by two shots in the chest the person whom I loved and feared most in the world. This death was the monster of chaos, intruding into life in a dramatic way. It left me locked in combat, teaching me to expect tragedy, prepare against sudden loss and endure pain by making myself numb.[41]

In this and in subsequent articles, Lane describes a different kind of experience with death, the slow and more "ordinary" death of his mother. He admits that "it has been even more difficult to discover grace in the prolonged redundancy of ordinariness."[42] But this "common grace" becomes a more typical theme of his articles in the *Christian Century* than the series described above.

2. In the next chapter I want to make a strong criticism of theologians who make *theological* statements about God on the basis of these kinds of experiences. But at this point in the discussion such criticism is more problematic. It will be appropriate there because those theologians offer statements that are more explicitly about who God is and what God is like. Here the language about God is more implicitly, and sometimes very explicitly, autobiographical in intent and character. In the present context, the primary question is, Can we hear and accept how other people experience and formulate their own experience of God?

Nevertheless, any author must be willing to hear how the author's experience and description of God is perceived and interpreted by others who do not have the same kind of life setting, once a writing has been made public. Again, Belden Lane will serve as a case in point. Many women (and men too) perceive his kind of language about God as male experience and male culture in its most terrorizing and abusive form. Such descriptions must be questioned and even condemned, not as accurate descriptions of the experience of the writer but as appropriate descriptions of God. Mary Pellauer, for example, conveys her perception of this kind of language in a letter to the editor of *Christian Century* following Lane's second essay.

> Lane's opening story about how T. H. White at the age of six cried because he believed he was to be shot by his father as part of his birthday present is chilling to someone who grew up in an abusive household and has counseled many abuse victims. Despite the sentence proclaiming "I understood the child's response painfully well," the following exposition belittles the child's perception. He comments, "How many times have I, too, misinterpreted the ambiguity of play, thinking myself to be shot when the parent all along had meant only deliberate delight." But the child did *not* "misinterpret" the parent's behavior. The father, *not* the child, showed "limited imagination." The inability to empathize with the child's normal age-related development is typical of abusing parents. To frighten a child and then laugh is not merely "ambiguous," it is emotional abuse. Survivors often do confuse love with abuse; and so does much of the Western theological tradition.[43]

Although Lane has every right to offer, explain, defend, and advocate his experience of God for theological discussion, I think he (and each of us) must take seriously the implications and consequences of our experience for other persons in different contexts whenever our experience is offered as part of the public discussion of religious experience and is offered as a contribution to the construction of any language about reality, character, and activity of God.

3. Although I want to maintain the distinction between statements that express my experience of God and those that also propose to describe something about God, the distinction between these two functions of religious language is not absolute. Statements about my experience and perception of the meaning of God, when they become part of the public discourse, also become statements about God, even if that is not my conscious agenda. When they become part of the public domain, I no longer own them and can no longer determine their meaning and use. The implication of this is that statements about the experience of God made in this chapter, insofar as they are offered for public discussion, are finally liable to the same kind of criticisms I made earlier about the abusive God.

5

"I Form Light and Create Darkness"
The Shadow Side of God

⊰ In Tennessee Williams's play *Suddenly Last Summer,* Sabastian's mother, Mrs. Venable, is talking to a psychiatrist after Sabastian has mysteriously died.

> We saw the Encantadas, but on the Encantadas we saw something Melville hadn't written about. We saw the great sea turtles crawl up out of the sea for annual egg-laying. . . . And when it's finished the exhausted female turtle crawls back to the sea half dead. She never sees her offspring but we did. . . . The narrow beach, the color of caviar, was all in motion! But the sky was in motion too! . . . Full of flesh-eating birds. . . . They were diving down on the hatched sea turtles, turning them over to expose their soft underside, tearing the underside open and rending and eating their flesh. Sabastian guessed that possibly only a hundredth of one percent of their number would escape to the sea. . . . My son was looking for God. I mean for a clear image of Him. He spent that whole blazing equatorial day in the crow's nest of the schooner watching this thing on the beach of the Encantadas till it was too dark to see it, and when he came down the rigging he says, "Well, now I've seen Him!" and he meant God. [And] for several days after that he had a fever, he was delirious with it.[1]

One of the presuppositions of this study is that concepts of God should be constructed from or at least shaped by the evidence of experience—individual, communal, historical, and biblical experience. Experience should not be forced to illustrate, to conform to, and to confirm our doctrine of God. This principle is operative in all the theologians we explored in chapter 4, and it will be operative throughout the remainder of the book.

In this chapter, we examine theologians whose experience of cold-blooded, malicious wickedness in the modern world has caused them to reexamine the traditional doctrine of the omnibenevolence of God. For each of them, our experience of unrelieved suffering and radical evil is so deep and broad that we must reconstruct the whole idea of God to include a murky side in God's intentions and activity in the world. Since our experience is a basis for any theological language about God, we must take into account our experience of a grim side of God as well as that of a benevolent one. God exhibits some characteristics that conflict with the omnibenevolence prescribed both by classical theism and by modern liberalism. Since these theologians are unwilling to tamper with the concept of sovereign divine power, they are forced to rethink the concept of divine goodness. Thus, they consider the possibility of a somber side of God which helps to account for some of the evil in the world.

Theological Advocates

The microbes were by far the most important part of the Ark's cargo, and the part the Creator was most anxious about and most infatuated with. They had to have good nourishment and pleasant accommodations. There were typhoid germs, and cholera germs, and hydrophobia germs, and lockjaw germs, and consumption germs, and black-plague germs, and some hundreds of other aristocrats, especially precious creations, golden bearers of God's love to man, blessed gifts of the infatuated Father to his children.[2]

Psychological Entries
on the Shadow Side of God

Carl Jung is a monotheist. Indeed, he is such a thoroughgoing monotheist that he asserts very bluntly, "If Christianity claims to be a monotheism, it becomes unavoidable to assume the opposites as being contained in God."[3] Early on, however, Christian theism, he claims, abandoned its monotheism. Monotheism claimed, according to Clement of Alexandria, that God rules with the right hand (Christ) and the left hand (Satan). Christianity, instead, became "dualistic" by splitting one-half of the opposites off from God, projecting them onto Satan. However, if Christianity is going to remain monotheistic, according to Jung, it has to answer the problem of Job. Job taught God an ethical lesson by making the shadow side of God apparent to God, and God responded by becoming human to redeem humankind from the evil into which God had led them. The Christian answer to Job is to describe the one God who integrates both good and evil in Godself through the incarnation.

For Jung the shadow is not in itself identified with evil; the shadow is simply a fact. When the shadow is integrated into a whole personality as a part of it, the problem of evil becomes the problem of integrating the shadow into the mature personality. Thereby the forces of chaos, negation, and destruction become a part of the wholeness of the self and of the world.

Jung's concept of God, as do all concepts of God, has its historical location. The concept of a paradox of both good and evil within God has been denied by Christians from the biblical Apocalypse to modern times by identifying God with the summum bonum. But, according to Jung, that identification can no longer be made, in the light of twentieth-century experience. "We have experienced things so unheard of and so staggering that the question of whether such things are in any way reconcilable with the idea of a good God has become burningly topical."[4]

It is impossible any more for a reflective consciousness to sustain the identification of God with the highest good. "A more differentiated consciousness must, sooner or later, find it difficult to love, as a kind father, a God whom on account of his unpredictable fits of wrath, his unreliability, injustice, and cruelty, it has every reason to fear."[5] Jung finds in scripture (especially in Job and the Apocalypse[6]), as well as in Christian consciousness, a "divine darkness" that the monotheistic idea of God represses. The encounter with the God known in the human psyche reveals something of the inner life of God. "Job is no more than the outward occasion for an inward process of dialectic in God."[7] God is at odds with Godself. God is not "split," but there is "an antinomy—the totality of inner opposites," a "coincidentia oppositorum"[8] within God. God has a shadow side within God's unconscious. "With brazen countenance he can project his shadow side and remain unconscious at man's expense,"[9] at least until God's encounter with Job.

God revealed this dual nature to Job in the testing of Job. "His readiness to deliver Job into Satan's murderous hands proves that he doubts Job precisely because he projects his own tendency to unfaithfulness upon a scapegoat."[10] However, in this encounter with Job, God learns to recognize, to acknowledge, and to accept the antinomies that so far have been hidden in God's own unconscious. In this moment of self-reflection God discovers that if Job gains knowledge of God, God must also learn to know Godself. What God discovers at the level of consciousness is God's own dual nature: "the intolerable contradiction in the nature of Deity . . . the antinomy within Deity itself."[11]

> In his omniscience, of course, this fact had been known from all eternity, and it is not unthinkable that the knowledge of it unconsciously brought him into the position of dealing so harshly with Job in order that he himself should become conscious of something through this conflict, and thus gain new insight.[12]

Once this differentiated consciousness is discovered and acknowledged by God, however, God has to "answer to Job." God has to make up for this failure, to make "reparation for a wrong done by God to man."[13] God's answer to Job is to change God's own nature.

> He raises himself above his earlier primitive level of consciousness by indirectly acknowledging that the man Job is morally superior to him and that therefore he has to catch up and become human himself. Had he not taken this decision he would have found himself in flagrant opposition to his omniscience. Yahweh must become man precisely because he has done man a wrong. He, the guardian of justice, knows that every wrong must be expiated, and Wisdom knows that moral law is above even him. Because his creature has surpassed him he must regenerate himself.[14]

In other words, God's answer to Job is the incarnation. The incarnation becomes a world-shaking transformation of God's self.[15] By becoming human, God differentiates God's own consciousness and reaches a new level of consciousness. By becoming incarnate, God makes reparations to humanity and at the same time becomes more whole Godself through the recognition and integration of the shadow side of the divine unconscious. The dark side, the shadow of the self, is as much a part of the divine self as it is of the human self. The shadow side of reality, then, is intrinsic to all reality, including the divine reality. Only as it is integrated into the whole self, including the divine self, can this duality of reality be recognized, faced, acknowledged, and resolved. The "highest good," so to speak, is not the summum bonum (monopolar goodness which rejects all ambiguity from the inner life of God), but is the integration of good and shadow within the self, both human and divine.

I still cannot determine whether Jung understands his language to be a description of God in distinction from a description of the human psyche. Clearly for him there is no separation of God and psyche, in the sense that if there is a God we know God only through the psyche. In some places Jung speaks of God as being "there" but unknowable as such. The language of the psyche points to "something ineffable," to its "transcendental object," to "the Unspeakable itself." Jung says, "There is something behind these images that transcends consciousness. . . ." He even refers to "the essence of the Unknowable."[16] Regardless of whether God is some other kind of reality than the psyche itself, God is "objective" for Jung at least in the sense that God is an archetype in the psychic collective unconscious that transcends the individual psyche.

At other times, however, Jung seems to say not only that the psyche is the only avenue to God, but that God *is* the psyche. "God is an obvious psychic and non-physical fact. . . . Religious statements without exception have to do with the reality of the psyche and not with the reality of the physis. . . . Religious statements are psychic confessions."[17]

Whether God is "more" than the archetypal psychic collective unconscious remains unclear, then, although for Jung clearly the experience of God (or the archetype of God) is what is important for humans, whether that has another ontological reality or not. At the very least the language points to how deep and unintegrated is the dark side within ourselves.[18] Jung simply seems to be agnostic about the question of whether God is "more" than the psychic collective unconscious. What is important is that "it is only through the psyche that we can establish that God acts upon us, but we are unable to distinguish whether these actions emanate from God or from the unconscious. We cannot tell whether God and the unconscious are two different entities. Both are borderline concepts for transcendental contents."[19]

A variation of this psychological perspective, one that is more explicitly theological than Jung's but yet uses Jung's framework to interpret our theological understanding of God, is Jim Garrison's concept of the "antinomial God." Garrison attempts to provide a theological interpretation of the threat of nuclear annihilation in the twentieth century through a concept of the ambiguous God.[20] Because Garrison insists on interpreting Hiroshima (his metaphor for the threat of nuclear destruction in the modern world) within the requirement that Christians retain the concept of the omnipotent power of God, he is forced, finally, to speak of *The Darkness of God.*

"The central question of this work is why it is that after several thousand million years of life on this planet our species, in our generation, has brought this life to the brink of extinction through thermonuclear war."[21] Contrary to most Christian theology, which interprets Hiroshima wholly as a human event of massive and blasphemous misuse of freedom, Garrison claims that God and humanity both must be perceived as integral to the event of Hiroshima. Hiroshima is ultimately a revelation not only of human freedom and decision but also of God's power and nature. Humans do evil, causing destruction and suffering, but so does God, who instills in us motivation to bring about the apocalypse, all of this to achieve God's higher and finally good purpose.

At the root of the problem, for Garrison, is our inherited theistic notion of God. The doctrines of the summum bonum, according to which God is identified with perfection and is capable only of love, mercy, and goodness, and of the *privatio boni,* according to which evil is deprived of its reality and equated merely with a diminution of the good, are unable to cope realistically with the radical evil of Hiroshima. By adopting a different interpretation of scripture and Jung's notion of the antinomies within God, he proposes a concept of God which, on the one hand, maintains the omnipotent God of classical theism, but, on the other hand, "reveals deeper dimensions of the divine pleroma," which include genuine evil.

Garrison argues on two grounds that classical theism is inadequate. First, scripture teaches that intrinsic evil like intrinsic good comes from God, for God is presented as acting in such a manner as to cause destruction, chaos, suffering, and unhappiness as well as harmony, peace, happiness, and joy. Second, theism is unable to cope realistically with the overwhelming power of evil confronting us in our age. This requires a God of darkness as well as light, a God who is savage and terrible as well as merciful and forgiving. Garrison thus speaks of "intrinsic evil at the hands of God." This ambivalence is in God Godself, not simply in our experience of God.

Garrison continually makes statements about the being and character of God. For example, "God must be understood to be the chief instance of the freedom to commit good and evil,"[22] and "There is something deeper going on within the Godhead itself, something that defies conventional morality or even covenantal promises."[23] The concept of the antinomial character of God is rooted in the biblical ideas of the apocalypse and the wrath of God.[24] Apocalyptic literature understood the all-powerful God to pour forth God's wrath on humanity. There is no range of emotions characteristic of human personality that God does not at certain times express. What human beings and Satan are capable of, God is also able to manifest in even more powerful ways. Although God's destruction stems from a wrath that serves divine love instead of from an infection of sin, God's wrath nevertheless includes forces of darkness that far exceed anything contrived by satanic or human agents. The wrath of God blinds people so that they do not repent and allows God to give full vent to divine wrath in order to affirm God's sovereignty.

The wrath of God seems to be as much a part of the glory of God as is the mercy of God, both equally effective and both equally arising from motivations hidden within the Godhead. What we are doing in the apocalypse of world destruction is based not only on our evil inclinations but also on God's. Thus Hiroshima confronts us simultaneously with new dimensions of human depravity and with deeper dimensions of the shadow side of God.

This interpretation of the darkness of God does not, however, lead Garrison to the conclusion that God is immoral. Nor does he retreat to the usual theistic ploy of claiming that all the destruction wrought by the wrath of God is only apparently evil. What it does force him to do is to reinterpret God as the summum bonum doctrine. The beneficence of God includes the power and the will to work intrinsic evil. Garrison does not doubt that the will of God is beneficent, because God is able finally to integrate the intrinsic good and intrinsic evil God wills into a higher good. But God wills and uses intrinsic evil as well as intrinsic good for God's higher purpose. "The antinomy of God must therefore be seen as complementary aspects within the over-arching beneficence of the will of God."

Historical Visions
of the Darkness God

William Jones sets out to interpret the meaning of black suffering as a religious problem. He concludes that if African-American experience is used as a test case, the theistic concept of God leads to a God who is a white racist. Within the total salvation history of Christian faith, "every alleged act of God's benevolence can easily be interpreted as an instance of His malevolence."[25] His charge of divine racism derives from these themes: Humanity is divided into two groups, an "in" group and an "out" group; there is an imbalance of suffering between these two groups; God is responsible for the imbalance; God's favor or disfavor is correlated with the racial identity of the group; and so God must be a member of the "in" group.

To speak of divine racism, then, is essentially to question God's equal love and concern for all people. The empirical evidence is that God is on the side of some and not others, at least is not for all equally. The inequality of suffering forces one to ask whether there is "a demonic streak in the divine nature."[26] The charge of divine racism, then, is in the final analysis based on a challenge to the claim that God is equally benevolent to all.

Jones, like Cornel West, speaks not only out of the African-American experience, but also out of the empirical-pragmatic tradition in American philosophy. He appeals to the evidence of lived experience. "The quickest and most effective way to execute this attack is to show that events are multievidential;

specifically, the materials and events that have traditionally been interpreted as evidence of divine benevolence can just as easily support the opposite conclusion, of divine malevolence."[27] A malevolent deity is a possible deduction from the evidence of the African-American suffering in America, and it is a short step from a malevolent deity to a white racist deity. In African-American experience, the evidence of malevolence is overwhelming over a four-hundred-year period.

In the case of the African-American suffering, two primary considerations guide the theologian interpreting the "multievidentiality" of suffering. First, the suffering of the innocent can be interpreted as favor, as in the case of Jesus and the cross, suffering is interpreted positively through vindication and exaltation. "Without the exaltation event it is not possible to distinguish between the suffering servant and the rank sinner encountering his deserved punishment."[28] But there is no exaltation-liberation event in black experience to refute the charge of divine disfavor. The absence of such an event seems to confirm that God favors some, especially Jesus in his victory over death, but "the absence of this event substantiates that God is against blacks."[29] The reason God is called a "white racist," then, is that the evidence of history can be interpreted as God's "disfavor" toward African Americans. After four hundred years of suffering there is no resurrection, vindication, exaltation of African-American people as there is among others who have suffered.

The second problem for black experience is not the fact of suffering but its distribution. The depth and the breadth of African-American suffering, four hundred years of unrelieved suffering, can only count as decisive counterevidence against a God who loves all equally. Assuming God's omnigoodness and justice, only two options remain for the African American. Either adopt a theology based on God's benevolence, whereby God becomes a white racist because God bestows God's love on white people and does not bestow it on black people, or opt for atheism.[30] " 'God is a soul brother' and 'God is a white racist' possess equally interpretive probability"[31] in the face of the multievidentiality of the black experience. "There is a profound dilemma confronting blacks when claims about the nature and activity of God are compared with the realities of history."[32]

Jones admits that his argument is polemical; his charge of divine racism can be seen as an *ad absurdum* argument. His concern, however, is not to establish the truth of his charge of divine racism. Rather, "my intent is to demonstrate that the normative frameworks of the black theologians are questionable, because they raise the issue of divine racism, and, once raised, cannot effectively refute the charge with their present theological resources."[33] Jones opts for a "humanocentric theism," which, in concert with "secular" humanism, advocates the functional ultimacy of humanity. "Man must act as if he were the ultimate valuator or the ultimate agent in human history or both. Thus God's responsibility for the crimes and errors of human history is reduced if not effectively eliminated."[34]

Many post-Holocaust Jewish and Christian theologians have found the terrors of modern history to be evidence "beyond a reasonable doubt" against the omnibenevolence of God. If God is the Lord of history, the evidence of history counts against the benevolence of the Lord of history.

Richard Rubenstein, for instance, says, "I am convinced that the problem of God and the death camps is the central problem for Jewish theology in the twentieth century."[35] Rather than accept the pure malevolence implied in the Father-God who is the Lord of Auschwitz, he declares that such a God is dead. Jews have always believed in an omnipotent, beneficent God. God is the ultimate, sovereign, benevolent actor in the historical drama. Every major catastrophe before in Jewish history was interpreted as God's punishment of a sinful Israel. But Rubenstein fails to see how this position can be maintained in the twentieth century without regarding Hitler and the S.S. troops as instruments of God's will. "To see any purpose in the death camps, the traditional believer is forced to regard the most demonic, antihuman explosion in all history as a meaningful expression of God's purposes. The idea is simply too obscene for me to accept."[36]

If one believes God is the omnipotent Lord of history and Israel is God's chosen people, the only possible conclusion is that God willed Hitler to commit six million Jews to slaughter. "I could not possibly believe in such a God nor could I believe in Israel as the chosen people of God after Auschwitz."[37] Like Albert Camus, Rubenstein would rather live in "an absurd, indifferent cosmos in which men suffer and die meaninglessly but still retain a measure of tragic integrity"[38] than to live in a pitiless framework of meaning which deprives us of the consolation that such suffering, though inevitable, is not entirely merited or earned.

> After the experiences of our times, we can neither affirm the myth of the omnipotent God of History nor can we maintain its corollary, the election of Israel. After the death camps, the doctrine of Israel's election is in any event a thoroughly distasteful pill to swallow. Jews do not need these doctrines to remain a religious community.[39]

After Auschwitz we stand in a cold, silent, unfeeling cosmos, unaided by any purposeful power beyond our own resources.

Rubenstein is not left, however, wholly without any sense of the divine. He believes in "the dark of divinity." "I believe in God, the Holy Nothingness known to mystics of all ages, out of which we have come and to which we shall ultimately return."[40] In the end, omnipotent Nothingness is the Lord of all creation. God and nature become one, and "Earth is a Mother, but Earth is a cannibal Mother." To say this is to affirm the demonic side not only in us but in divinity as well. "The tragedies, ironies, and ambiguities of existence cease to reflect historical man's willful rebellion; they become internalized in the self-unfolding of divinity."[41] Death is the true Messiah.

> There is only one Messiah who redeems us from the irony, the travail and the limitations of human existence. Surely he will come. He is the Angel of Death.

Death is the true Messiah and the land of the dead the place of God's true kingdom. Only in death are we redeemed from the vicissitudes of human existence. We enter God's kingdom only when we enter His holy Nothingness.[42]

By affirming the gods of the earth—of life, birth, family, passage, and death—
symbolized and enacted in community rituals, by returning to the religious
community, priestly in form and ritualistic in practice, he accepts and affirms
the tragic sense of life as the only psychologically valid sense of the divine.[43]

John Roth, also, in *A Consuming Fire: Encounters with Elie Wiesel and the
Holocaust*[44] and a series of other essays on theodicy, confronts the "felt needs"
which the realities of history pose for a theodicy that believes in the goodness
of God. "Two are fundamental: a sense that human affairs are far worse than
any good reason can justify or than our powers alone can alter; and, second,
a yearning that refuses to settle for despair that the first feeling generates."[45]

Roth never questions his belief in the sovereignty of God. And he grants
that the omnipotent God uses much of the waste of history as instrumental to
good ends. However, precisely "because the accumulated devastation of history is so vast . . . too much has been lost."[46] In the light of such massive waste,
Roth denies that God cares all that much about history.

If he could bring Jesus back from total lifelessness to life, I believe that God
could have changed the minds of Nazi leaders, thereby preventing Auschwitz.
The reason for my belief has to do with overwhelming power that could be
used for good ends far more than it is. If God wants to be morally defective,
or to claim that he is not even if someone disagrees, or he just wants to be
serenely indifferent to the whole affair, I judge that he can do so.[47]

Responsibility for suffering and evil in history must be shared by us and God
alike. And that responsibility cannot be assigned equitably. God's responsibility lies in the fact that God sets the boundaries, and some of the slaughter could
have been avoided by an omnipotent God who is also good. Religious people must reckon with God as economist who does not wish to be cost effective. The slaughter bench of history shows that God's way of ruling the world
is wasteful. And "this result testifies that such a wasteful God cannot be totally
benevolent. History itself is God's indictment."[48] God knows what God is doing, but that is the problem. The problem for theodicy, in Roth's view, hinges
on the assumption that God holds, but fails to use well enough, the power to
intervene and make history's course less wasteful. Such a God cannot be omnibenevolent.

In order to avoid despair, then, the religious person yields to the spirit of
dissent, which is the appropriate response to the sovereign God who is morally
ambiguous. This sovereign God should be neither ignored nor acquitted, but
put on trial for the massive waste in history. Along with our protest against the
massive evils of history, we must also protest against the sovereign God of history who permits unimaginable waste.[49]

A Soft Defense
of This Perspective

How should we evaluate these grim interpretations of an ambivalent side to God? Is such an idea defensible biblically, experientially, and theologically? Does it have any value in trying to understand our encounter with God and with the suffering and evil of our century?

I want to be clear that the question in this discussion is not whether God's goodness is *identical* to human goodness. There are at least two ways in which clearly it is not. (1) Our minds cannot grasp the fullness of the divine goodness any more than the fullness of the divine being, if for no other reason than that God's goodness is inclusive of an infinite range of goods and ours is of a (very) finite range. Furthermore, the depth of the divine goodness is finally a mystery. Since all our talk about God is based on our experience and on images, metaphors, and analogies drawn from our experience, we cannot know directly what the goodness of God means because God's goodness in its fullness and depth transcends every finite concept of goodness. (2) We do not even have a common idea of human goodness that is widely shared. Because of an incredibly wide range of concepts of "good" among cultures and even within cultures, a common idea of "good" can at most be an idea toward which we strive through mutual discussion. If human goodness cannot be clearly conceived, surely divine goodness cannot be unequivocally defined.

Nor is the issue whether God is the *devil* in disguise, who wills only evil. To claim God is unpredictable, arbitrary, capricious, ambiguous, or injust is not the same as to claim God is evil or acts always for malevolent reasons. Diabolical theories of the divine, which picture the supreme power of the universe as pure malice, are finally indefensible on several grounds. If diabolism were true, the world would be far worse than it is, if there could be any world of value at all. There could be only destruction or sheer chaos. The idea of God as all-good may be difficult to maintain in the face of the suffering of the world, but it is not an absurd idea, and there is enough goodness to negate a diabolical ultimate. The presence of good is at least as problematic for diabolism as theories of absurdity are for any form of theism.[50]

The issue, rather, is whether there is *some* correspondence between our concept of good and God's goodness. If human and divine goodness are equivocal terms, that is, if the difference is not only in degree but in kind, then we must ask ourselves what we are devoting ourselves to and why we should devote ourselves to it as religious people. If, on the other hand, there is some affinity or analogy between divine and human good, then the question of whether God's goodness is more ambiguous than we claim in our idea of omnibenevolence is a meaningful and legitimate question.

How, then, shall we respond to these proposals to think of antinomies within the God who is the source of human good? After resisting the idea for years in thinking about suffering and evil, I have finally come to the conclusion that the evidence from scripture and experience about God and ourselves is more ambiguous with respect to the nature of goodness than traditional theism and modern liberalism have postulated.

With respect to our experience of ourselves, I think one of the reasons we must entertain the concept of divine antinomies is not only because of what it says about God but also what it says about ourselves. The Jungian criticism, and by implication the criticism of Feuerbach, is, I think, insightful, even if it may be in the end inadequate. One of the reasons we have created an image of God as absolute perfection is not that the evidence from scripture and experience leads us to such a concept but because we are unable, or unwilling, to acknowledge the shadowy side of our own nature. Since we cannot come to terms with our own moral ambiguity, we abstract that side of ourselves which we most admire, our goodness, and project it onto our concept of God. At least the God we worship does not possess the antinomies we experience in ourselves. Our concept of the unambiguous God says as much about what we think we admire (and what we want to deny) about ourselves as it says about our experience of God and what much of the scripture says about God. In short, an absolutely perfect God is more an abstraction and a projection onto an idea of God than the human experience of God.

With respect to the biblical picture of God, I do not accept the idea that the God of scripture is evil or demonic, for the reason that I do not think the dominant picture of God in scripture is all that ambiguous, all things considered,[51] and I do not think Christian communities of devotion would have survived with such an ambiguous deity as the object of worship. An ambivalent God is not worthy of the love and loyalty of anyone who is committed to the well-being of the creation.

Nevertheless, I think there is a lot of evidence from scripture to say that "injustice" or "arbitrariness" is a characteristic of the biblical God. That evidence implies, for me, that ideas like summum bonum, all-loving nature, and justice as conceived in theism are not an adequate description of the biblical God.

In Jesus' parables of the vineyard (Matt. 20:1–16) and the prodigal son (Luke 15:11–34), we find two parables in which justice and fairness are not the primary concerns of God at all. It is clear in both parables that although God does not wish to accomplish evil, God's love is "unjust" by the usual definition of justice as fairness in the sense that each person receives his or her due. God's love ignores justice; it goes beyond or even denies the element of fairness that justice seems to imply. Stated positively, God's activity is sheer gratuity, not justice. God is "beyond" justice as promised in the Deuteronomic tradition and demanded by Job. The parable of the vineyard, especially verses 14–15, pictures God as giving equal wages simply because that is what God wants to do, not because it is just by any economic, political, or moral theory of justice (real needs, inalienable rights, human equality, or any other criterion of goodness as justice).

Likewise, in the parable of the son, the father, especially in verse 20, forga
the son without any confession or restitution or promise; the parent's beha
was based on the sheer gratuity of the parent's love. In these parables, (
"unjust." God's mode of operation is not governed by any rational ba

personal needs or legal rights (a juridical or even a moral criterion of goodness). God is very un-American, and could not survive in the American system of legal and moral rights.[52] Indeed, the parable might even be more accurately described as the parable of the prodigal parent.

Even though God may not be as shadowy as Job pictures God to be in the willingness to permit anything to happen to Job to prove something to Satan, God nevertheless gives us something to be "crybabies" about in God's sheer gratuity. Whatever the *love* of God means, it means something other than goodness defined by the establishment and maintenance of justice, human or divine. God sends the rain on the just and the unjust alike. We find God described in much of the scripture as inequitable; one can be as "unjust" in what one accepts as in what one rejects. Indeed, one might argue that insofar as grace and agape dominate the biblical notions of God, God's purposes and actions are *amoral,* that is, they simply operate outside any scheme of law, justice, fairness, and equity.

God's "goodness" is not justice but sheer gratuity. It is greater than, perhaps even indifferent to or even a repudiation of, the justice of needs and rights, obligations and consequences. God may be beyond good and evil, in the sense that God can be said to be "all-loving" in God's sheer gratuity as our theories of fairness, equity, and perfection (or any other theories of the good) are ignored. Although God cannot be called *immoral* in the sense of willing and working for evil (malevolent destruction), God can be said to be *amoral,* or supramoral, or unjust in relation to every theory of justice.

Although I think the theological point this group of theologians is making must be rejected as adequate for a reinterpretation of God in the face of massive suffering and evil, I think they are correct in their insistence that our modern, liberal, bourgeois (and can we even say Deuteronomic and theistic?) ideas of love and justice are not the biblical idea at all. God is love, but love in the Bible is not necessarily what liberal culture values.

God in the Dock

"To you I'm an atheist. To God, I'm the loyal opposition."
(Woody Allen, *Sturdiest Memories*)

These theologies make a contribution to how religious persons might respond to suffering and evil. Even though I do not accept them as adequate doctrines of God, they offer a significant perspective on our grim encounters with God. As the writers of scripture knew, our experience of God is not always soothing and comfortable; at times our encounters with God cause us great discomfort and distress. What they put before us is a reconsideration of the biblical protest against God who is beyond comprehension. Each of these theologians offers a slant ⟶me of our experiences of God in the midst of suffering and evil, and their ⟶y enables a protest against God's role in the midst of that suffering.

In chapter 2, I introduced Walter Brueggemann's claim that the theology of the Old Testament is bipolar. It serves both to legitimate the existing natural and social structure and to embrace the pain caused by it. On the one hand, the Old Testament shares the "common theology" of the ancient Near East. Suffering is to be understood within the framework of justice, law, and retribution. In the Sinai covenant and the Deuteronomic theology, even in the prophets and wisdom literature, the world governed by God has a structure to it. There is an interconnection between actions and their results, between deeds and consequences, and suffering is to be understood within this context as divine retribution and justice.

At the same time, Brueggemann argues, there exists alongside this common theology a protest against its assumptions. A "crisis comes because that theology does not square with Israel's experience of life or Israel's experience of faith, i.e., Israel's discernment of God." There is a restlessness within Israel's faith that moves against the common theology, and this is articulated in Israel's practice of lament.

Moses protests against God, which is surprising since it was he who also articulated the heaviest sanctions in Israel. In Numbers 11:10–15 we read:

> Moses was displeased. So Moses said to the Lord, "Why have you treated your servant so badly? Why have I not found favor in your sight, that you lay the burden of all this people on me? Did I conceive all this people? Did I give birth to them, that you should say to me, 'Carry them in your bosom, as a nurse carries a sucking child,' to the land that you promised on oath to their ancestors? Where am I to get meat to give to all this people? For they come weeping to me and say, 'Give us meat to eat!' I am not able to carry all this people alone, for they are too heavy for me. If this is the way you are going to treat me, put me to death at once—if I have found favor in your sight—and do not let me see my misery."

Moses assaults the throne of God, laments, and prevails.

There are also lament psalms of the Psalter. In Psalm 88, the most dangerous, unresolved, and hopeless of all the psalms, we read:

> You have put me in the depths of the Pit,
>   in the regions dark and deep.
> Your wrath lies heavy upon me,
>   and you overwhelm me with all your waves.
> You have caused my companions to shun me;
>   you have made me a thing of horror to them.
> I am shut in so that I cannot escape;
>   my eye grows dim through sorrow.
> Every day I call on you, O LORD;
>   I spread out my hands to you.
> Do you work wonders for the dead?
>   Do the shades rise up to praise you?
> Is your steadfast love declared in the grave,
>   or your faithfulness in Abaddon?

> Are your wonders known in the darkness,
>   or your saving help in the land of forgetfulness?
> But I, O LORD, cry out to you;
>   in the morning my prayer comes before you.
> O LORD, why do you cast me off?
>   Why do you hide your face from me?
> Wretched and close to death from my youth up,
>   I suffer your terrors; I am desperate.
> Your wrath has swept over me;
>   your dread assaults destroy me.
> They surround me like a flood all day long;
>   from all sides they close in on me.
> You have caused friend and neighbor to shun me;
>   my companions are in darkness.

It is important to note here that the hurt is not that the speaker is shunned, but that God causes the hurt.

Jeremiah continues the lament tradition in Jeremiah 20:7–12, where he calls God his seducer ("you have enticed me," NRSV) and his "dread warrior." This tradition, of course, comes to its culmination in the harsh judgments of Job. Even though Job operates within the common theology of deed and consequence, he moves out of it at places: In Job 9:20, 22–23 he says, "Though I am blameless, he would prove me perverse. . . . It is all one; therefore I say, he destroys both the blameless and the wicked. . . . He mocks at the calamity of the innocent." Notice also in the whirlwind speech in chapter 42, it is Job and not his friends who has spoken what is "right." As Brueggemann says, "The verdict in Job's favor indicates that the obedience received and valued by God is not simply submissiveness and docility, but it is the courage to stand in the face of the Holy One and force the issues in new directions. What is 'right' about Job is not just the final settlement of 42:6, however that is understood, but the whole tradition of speech which refuses to accept the conventions of the accepted order."[53]

Within our own time no one has articulated the biblical tradition of lament, even protest and outrage, more powerfully than Elie Wiesel, especially in his memoir *Night* and his play *The Trial of God*. In *Night* he recalls the Jewish New Year in Auschwitz when ten thousand men had come to pray "Blessed be the Name of the Eternal!"

> Why, but why should I bless Him? In every fiber I rebelled. Because He had thousands of children burned in His pits? Because He kept six crematories working night and day, on Sundays and feast days? Because in His great might He had created Auschwitz, Birkenau, Buna, and so many factories of death? . . . Yes, man is very strong, greater than God. When You were deceived by Adam and Eve, You drove them out of Paradise. When Noah's generation displeased You, You brought down the Flood. When Sodom no

longer found favor in Your eyes, You made the sky rain down fire and sulphur. But these men here, whom You have betrayed, whom You have allowed to be tortured, butchered, gassed, burned, what do they do? They pray to You! They praise Your name! . . . . This day I had ceased to plead. I was no longer capable of lamentation. On the contrary, I felt very strong. I was the accuser, God the accused. My eyes were open and I was alone—terribly alone in a world without God and without man. Without love or mercy. I had ceased to be anything but ashes, yet I felt myself to be stronger than the Almighty, to whom my life had been tied for so long. I stood amid that praying congregation, observing it like a stranger.[54]

In his play, *The Trial of God,* Wiesel's indictment of God is relentless. Wiesel's work is not a denial of God; it is a protest addressed to God. If one could deny God, the question of God's character could be disposed of and would no longer terrorize us. Life might be a threat, but we would know the ground rules: expect nothing, trust no one ultimately, do not hope. But God is not so generous to Wiesel as to be deniable. God must, rather, be called to account. There is a case against God to be pursued relentlessly.[55] Wiesel pursues his case with ironic vigor in his tragic farce. The play is set in Shamgorod, where not long before, on February 25, 1649, a pogrom erupted in the midst of a preparation for the wedding of Hannah, the daughter of Berish, the innkeeper. All Jews except Berish and Hannah were killed. Berish had been tied and forced to watch the rape of his daughter, who was driven mad by the events. Berish, too, had been driven mad, but his madness is a consuming rage, not against the Christians who destroyed the Jews, but against God, who permitted such destruction.

The setting is an evening of the festival Purim, a feast of masks and imbibing. A wandering band of Jewish minstrels comes into the inn to entertain the local Jews, to discover only these two alive. Berish proposes to the band that they perform an impromptu trial, a trial "against the Master of the Universe, against the Supreme Judge." The only stipulation is that he, Berish, be the prosecutor. Although he will serve as prosecutor, and the minstrels the court, there is no defense attorney. An entire act of the play is spent procuring a defense attorney, who turns out to be a stranger named Sam, whom everyone recalls seeing somewhere or other. Sam turns out to be an excellent attorney, urbane, witty, intelligent, and steeped in tradition as he counters every argument of Berish with clever replies.

Sam: "Justice? Whose Justice? Yours?"

Berish: "What kind of question is that? Justice is justice. Mine, yours, his: it's the same everywhere. Is there another?"

Sam: "There is that of God."

Berish: "And it isn't mine? If that is so, then, with your permission—or without it—I reject it, and for good! I don't want a minor, secondary justice, a poor man's justice! I want no part of a justice that escapes me, diminishes me and makes a mockery out of mine! Justice is here for men and women—I therefore want it to be human, or let Him keep it!"[56]

Near the end of the scene, Berish concludes: "I—Berish, Jewish innkeeper at Shamgorod—accuse Him of hostility, cruelty and indifference. Either He dislikes His chosen people or He doesn't care about them—period! But then, why has He chosen us—why not someone else, for a change? Either He knows what's happening to us, or He doesn't wish to know! In both cases He is . . . He is . . . guilty! Yes, Guilty."[57]

Sam asks for evidence instead of anger, and Berish replies that he and Hannah are the facts, the living proof. Sam then shifts his argument to the claim that God must have God's reasons, and Berish must accept those, to which Berish replies: "He annihilated Shamgorod and you want me to be for Him? I can't! If he insists upon going on with His methods, let him—but I won't say Amen. Let Him crush me, I won't say Kaddish. Let him kill me, let him kill us all, I shall shout and should that it's His fault. I'll use my last energy to make my protest known. Whether I live or die, I submit to him no longer."

Although Berish, under pressure from Sam, will not betray his faith and is described by Sam as a defender of God, Berish replies: "I have not opted for God. I'm against His enemies, that's all. . . . I lived as a Jew, and it is as a Jew that I shall die—and it is as a Jew that, with my last breath, I shall shout my protest to God! And because the end is near, I shall shout louder! Because the end is near, I'll tell Him that He's more guilty than ever!"[58]

At the end all is lost. We begin to hear the howling of the mob. Pitifully inadequate defense barricades are erected in the inn. A final gesture is made. Since it is Purim, these survivors will die with the masks on, masks created for the celebration. Then Sam, God's only defender, is begged to intervene with God and "save God's children from further shame and suffering." The judges put on their masks. Sam pulls his out of his pocket and raises it to his face, saying, "So, you took me for a saint, a Just? Me? How could you be that blind? How could you be that stupid? If you only knew, if you only knew."[59] Satan is laughing as he raises his arm to give the signal to the howling mob.

Readers encounter penetrating expressions of faith in the theodicies of protest. They tell us something profound about the enigma of faith.[60] Protest is a strange sort of affirmation. Robert McAfee Brown says, in his review of the play, "Sam is wrong; Berish's act of faith, his willingness to die rather than renounce, does not negate his complaint against God. On the contrary, it strengthens and intensifies it. As one of Wiesel's teachers once said to him, 'Only the Jew knows that he may oppose God as long as he does so in defense of His creation.' "[61]

Exacting Criticisms

Although there are profound insights and resources for faith in theodicies of protest, I think there are severe criticisms one must make about the traditions of a dark side of God. My first criticism can be put in the form of a rhetorical question. Is the God of the Bible as morally ambivalent as some of these theologians claim? Many, if not most, of the biblical examples of an ambiguous God belong to the "common theology" of divine retribution. The grim deeds of God "fit" within a scheme of obligation, disobedience, and punishment, or at least they are understood as part of the overall purposes of God for the nations. This is true of some of the most vengeful acts of God, including Numbers 13, the killing of Nadab and Abihu, the stoning of a young person for blasphemy, the swallowing of rebels against Moses and Aaron, the plague that murdered 14,700 people because some complained about their god's cruelty, the fiery serpents sent to bite and kill when people objected to the taste of manna.

While there may be exceptions to this claim, such as Job and Jeremiah, the majority of the sullen acts of God seem to "fit" within the larger orthodox scheme of justice, retribution, or the divine plan for the nations. These acts are not usually a purely arbitrary unloading of hatred or injustice on the unfortunate. Therefore, the criticism of this kind of God is not a criticism of the grim deeds of an arbitrary God. It is, even more fundamentally, a criticism of the entire Deuteronomic theology of the Bible, in which retribution and vengeance are supposed to make sense. In short, this kind of sullen deity is at the very heart of one of the major strands of biblical religion, the strand attacked by Jeremiah and Job.

Second, I want to ask whether most of these theologians redefine divine goodness as much as they claim to redefine it. They may redefine God as the summum bonum of the Greek philosophical tradition and of medieval theology, but in most cases the final goodness and love of God are still affirmed with confidence if not assurance. Insofar as these theologians end up affirming God, they do not end up with an evil God. None of them substitutes malevolence for love in the concept of God. They do not reverse the claim about a loving God; they simply define love in a more equivocal way than identifying divine benevolence as the summum bonun.

If we take the witness of scripture and the witness of the experience of many Christians seriously in constructing our concept of God, God's goodness and love are surely more ambiguous than a purely philosophical concept of the summum bonum or modern personalistic (can we even say bourgeois?) interpretation of simple goodness and love implies. Perhaps God's "goodness" includes "emotions" of ambivalence, and disgust, and resentment more than we want in our God. Perhaps God's "love" is more aesthetic and less anthropocentric than we humans may desire it to be. Perhaps God's goodness and love "desires" or "intends" more than the personal satisfaction or even fulfillment of human beings considered in isolation from all the rest of creation or as the summit or goal of all creation. An enriched notion of God's goodness and love is called for in Christian theology, but that need does not lead to a concept of an evil God or of evil in God. To say that God's love is larger than, and so a little oblivious to—or at least does not obsess upon—our own satisfactions or purposes as a race or as individuals is not to say that God is intrinsically, inherently, or by nature sullen or evil.

The problem at the center of much of the lament tradition may not be so much the character of God as it is the "cognitive dissonance" between what we experience of God in the real world and what we are taught by our religious and theological tradition we are to believe. The recognition of this gap is not the same thing as the confirmation of a demonic God. Our experience may point to a capriciousness to God's love, or a God of many purposes beyond simply our own satisfaction, or a God of indifference and mercy at the same time. But this experience hardly requires the conclusion that there is a darkness to God that makes omnibenevolence impossible to affirm in the midst of suffering and evil.

Third, even though our idea of God may not be verifiable according to the modern verification principle of positivism, the idea of a loving God is, I think, falsifiable.[62] This claim goes to the very heart of the controversy between many classical theists and other kinds of theists. It is, I think, in principle possible that the counterevidence to a loving God is so compelling that we should conclude there is no such God. Some Jewish and Christian theists, on the other hand, hold that the idea of God is not even in principle possibly falsifiable. Nothing, *literally nothing,* could count as evidence against belief in a just and all-loving God in the theistic sense. In Woody Allen's movie *Crimes and Misdemeanors,* for example, Reuben's father replies to his sister at the table, "If I have to choose between the truth and God, I will choose God." Presumably no kind or amount of evidence, including the Holocaust, could disprove to Reuben's father a loving and just God who wills and accomplishes perfect goodness for all of creation.

It is commonly agreed on by most philosophers and theologians today that no idea of God is or can be verified as true on the basis of empirical evidence from the world. Perhaps one can appeal to evidence that makes such a belief possible, or even plausible. But there is no strict empirical verification for anyone's idea of God. Nevertheless, I think it is possible to *falsify* a concept of God, that is, to appeal to a kind or amount of empirical evidence that would make an idea of God implausible or even unbelievable.

As I will argue in following chapters, I think the mixture of good and evil in our experience makes certain concepts of God possible, plausible, even believable. But the kind and amount of evil in the world can become so counterproductive, so "counterevidential," or the kind of God inferred from the kind and amount of evil in experience so ambiguous, that the evidence overwhelmingly falsifies any concept of God as one who loves and wills good for the world. If the theologians in this chapter are correct about the kind of God that they infer from the evidence of the world, they have not revised the concept of divine goodness; they have falsified the belief in any kind of Judeo-Christian God at all. The conclusion I draw from their discussion is that the nature of God is more ambiguous than simple theistic omnibenevolence offers, but that the evidence the Christians appeal to does not point to a malevolent God at all.

Fourth, is not this perspective on God the nadir of theism, the final acceptance, affirmation, and celebration of the culture of abuse which is spawned or supported by the theistic worship of power? As Susan Thistlethwaite argues, "The worshipful language evoking particularly the power of God over life and death reveals the close relationship between violence and certain understanding of the nature and work of God. . . . This connection between violence and the doctrine of God . . . has existed in understandings of the nature and work of God throughout the history of Christianity."[63]

In my view, the theologies encountered in chapters 4 and 5 confirm my charges against classical theism as a theology of abuse. They are the logical and psychological implications of the view of unilateral, omnipotent power that underlies classical theism when one takes the evidence of experience seriously but refuses to revise the traditional concept of God. Insofar as classical theism is an expression of, or at least deeply shaped by, a unilateral concept of power, the perspective is driven to sacralize a concept of abusing power as somehow good. Such misuse of power is not only acknowledged in these kinds of theology, but is celebrated. We are asked to admire omnipotent power, or at best to protest it if it offends other religious and moral sensibilities, even if it includes indifference or malevolence.

Carl Jung can serve as our example here.[64] Jung's interpretation of Job finally is a justification of evil as necessary to reality itself, or at least the justification of the shadow side as inherent in reality itself. This may be psychologically insightful and helpful in interpreting ourselves. But, as James Williams points out, there is absolutely no distinction between the God of victims and the God of persecutors in Jung's theology.[65] The most important thing to learn about the God of Job is that God is an all-embracing totality who will not, and cannot, stand for and with Job. Growth can take place only through a process of psychic violence. In the end, as is the case with Garrison and Frederick Sontag, anything and everything can be justified by an appeal to the opposites within the divine totality. Williams concludes, "Those for whom desire, rivalry, victimization, and sacrifice can exist only as a kind of expression of Platonic forms within the psyche are, in effect, defending the sacred social order against the consequences of its murders and expulsions."[66]

Fifth, can we worship such a God as is represented in these theodicies? Or, perhaps even more to the point, even if we can, why should we? Why should we be religiously devoted to anything less than the highest good? As John Cobb says, the issue here "is religious or existential before it is philosophical." He continues, "The world as it is in its totality does not make an absolute claim on my loyalty or establish the needed priority in the ordering of my commitments."[67] Neither does omnipotent but malevolent power. Why should we worship anything other than the source of good and well-being? Why should we serve anything that does not enhance human well-being and the well-being of the larger gathering of creatures we call the world?

These are rhetorical questions, implying we should not. The deepest motivation and object of religion is devotion to and service of the good, the well-being of life in all its complexities and ambiguities. Although well-being is larger than human well-being, and human well-being is a much more complex notion than many theodicies and most liberal culture offer, religion should celebrate and serve nothing other than the source of well-being of the creation. Are Christians so enamored with sheer power that they are willing to serve something that is less than wholly good simply because it is all-powerful?

Conclusions and Transition

I believe these theologians, for these reasons, are mistaken in thinking about God as less than omnibenevolent. I do believe that God is ambiguous, that there is a "wildness" to the creative source of good that goes beyond the absolute goodness of classical theism. I also think there is a difference between a kind of "natural piety," which recognizes the depth, complexity, and ambiguity of the divine life, and our "worship and loyalty," which consists of devotion to that aspect of the divine life that works for the well being of the creation. Because human life strives for well-being (here is the argument from chapter 1 again!), we should not serve anything less than the source of good.

I recognize, and indeed affirm, that God is more than a servant of human good; God is the God of all creation and transcends mere human usefulness. To the extent that one understands and experiences God as creator of the entire process of nature, there is a "wildness" and "indifference" and "injustice to human interests" that transcend us. This reality justifies the efforts to describe God we have reviewed in chapters 4 and 5. But the purpose of religion is devotion to and service of the source of good, not the worship of ambiguous power.

There cannot be a radical disparity between divine and human goodness. If Auschwitz and Hiroshima do not qualify as events to which both God and humanity must pronounce an unqualified "No!" or if they can even be conceived as events that can be said by God to be good for divine, cosmic, or human well-being, then what can the distinction between evil and good mean, and what is religion for?

From my point of view, there is far more evidence in our experience against the omnipotence of God than against the goodness of God. To put it bluntly, the evidence about the goodness of God may be ambiguous, but where is there any evidence for the omnipotence of God in its classical meaning? Furthermore, I want to ask these theologians why the concept of omnibenevolence is revisable while the idea of omnipotence is not, especially if experience is relevant in our construction of our idea of God? The same question can be made about divine omnipotence as can be asked about divine omnibenevolence.

> It seems clear to me that if we cannot apply our language to an understanding of God's goodness we should not be able to apply it to God's omnipotence either. Yet the theologians who are making these language claims do not seem to apply the same standards to their understanding of God's

omnipotence. If we cannot, do not, know what infinite goodness would do, we cannot, do not know what infinite power would do either.[68]

Protest theodicies are an appropriate response if one assumes that God either in principle could or in fact does unilaterally cause anything and everything in the world, but for some mysterious reason is malevolent. But there is no empirical evidence for that whatsoever.

Finally, and equally important, I see no religious reason to maintain omnipotence in the classical theistic sense and every religious reason to maintain the omnibenevolence of God. Consequently, I conclude that this particular experiment in thought, grounded though it may be in scripture and experience, is a failure and must be rejected. The next chapters will be an experiment in responding to the problem of evil in a theological way by reconceiving what we mean by power, both human and divine.

6

"I Never Promised You a Rose Garden"

Creation and Tragic Structure

◄ After discussing the rise of modern science during the Renaissance, concentrating on its desire and promise to control nature, Malcolm in *Jurassic Park* claims that the great intellectual justification for science and its assurance of total control have vanished today. In the twentieth century, the vow to control everything through the understanding of natural law was shattered first by Heisenberg's uncertainty principle, then by Godel's theorem that mathematical reason is an arbitrary game.

> And now chaos theory proves that unpredictability is built into our daily lives. It is as mundane as the rainstorm we cannot predict. And so the grand vision of science, hundreds of years old—the dream of total control—has died, in our century. And with it much of the justification, the rationale for science to do what it does. And for us to listen to it. Science has always said that it may not know everything now but it will know, eventually. But now we see that isn't true. It is an idle boast. As foolish, and as misguided, as the child who jumps off a building because he believes he can fly. . . . We are witnessing the end of the scientific era. Science, like other outmoded systems, is destroying itself.[1]

The strength of the theistic tradition for theodicy is that (1) it perceives the extent to which suffering and evil are related to human freedom and its consequences, and (2) it recognizes that the issue of power, divine and human, stands at the center of a Christian interpretation of suffering and evil. The weakness of that tradition, however, is that (1) it drives its insight about the relation of suffering and misused freedom to extreme conclusions and so excludes other important considerations from our interpretation of suffering, and (2) it employs a nonbiblical and indefensible concept of divine power.

From the perspectives of various process theisms and contemporary trinitarianisms, classical theism creates a misrepresentation of the relation of suffering to creation and to God. In the extreme, as I have argued above, it exacerbates the problem of evil finally by justifying all suffering and underwriting an abusive concept of power. Even if classical theism is not driven to these extreme conclusions, however, it still brackets out other considerations that can lead to a more biblical and realistic understanding of suffering and evil. This chapter explores alternative concepts of creation, tragedy, chance, and power as we move toward what I believe to be a more adequate understanding for Christians of the relation of God to human suffering.

Creation and
the Persistence of Evil

Many Christians today have developed a renewed interest in a theology of creation, in part because of the ecological crisis, in part because of our renewed interest in a theology of suffering and evil. Roman Catholic Christians have been embroiled in a controversy over Matthew Fox's "creation theology," and an assortment of Protestant theologians have renewed their consideration of the doctrine of creation after decades of neglect by neoorthodox theologians. Throughout most of the twentieth century in both Europe and North America, Protestant theologians were far more fascinated with sin and redemption than with creation.

Our interpretation of the creation stories in Genesis has a profound impact on how we interpret evil within a Christian framework. How we do an exegesis of the Genesis myths, and what implications we draw from it, deeply influence our understanding of the relation between God and suffering. We have already explored how Augustine interpreted these stories and how his interpretation provided a framework for his theodicy. There are, however, other interpretations possible.

It is clear that classical theism hinges on a *creatio ex nihilo* interpretation of Genesis 1, and that the defenders of theistic theodicies today continue to insist, both on exegetical and religious grounds, on an *ex nihilo* interpretation of the creation stories.[2] Anyone who rejects the traditional *ex nihilo* interpretation of Genesis ends up with a view of the world that denies its created goodness and its absolute dependence on God—so the argument goes. "Can a denial of the *ex nihilo,* interpreted as God's foundational power of originating all that is, be acknowledged as authentically Christian?"[3] The *ex nihilo* doctrine is not only the proper interpretation of scripture; the matter is also an issue of the foundations of religious security. Keith Ward argues, for example, "If I am to put my confidence totally in God, I must believe that absolutely nothing can defeat his purposes. So I must believe that everything is in his power, that nothing can exist without his willing it, in some sense, to be. So this postulate is the foundation of a way of life which embodies total faith."[4]

There are, nevertheless, a number of biblical scholars and theologians who question whether *ex nihilo* is the only or best interpretation of the creation stories in Genesis. For example, Tom Dozeman questions whether such a doctrine is implicit at all in the biblical traditions on creation. "Random quotations of verses from Second Isaiah or Job do not provide a sufficient basis for such a doctrine, especially when the more extended creation texts like Genesis 1 explicitly deny such a conclusion."[5] David Griffin notes that both the King James Version (KJV) and the Revised Standard Version (RSV) translate Genesis 1 as "In the beginning God created the heaven(s) [RSV, "heavens"] and the earth,"[6] although the RSV and New Revised Standard Version (NRSV) have a foot-note which translates the verse as, "When God began to create the heavens and the earth, the earth was without form and void [NRSV, "a formless void"]." Griffin then comments: "The central issue between the two readings is whether creation was *ex nihilo,* i. e., whether God created the world out of absolutely nothing. The traditional reading of Genesis 1:1 does not say that it was but it suggests it more readily than does the alternative reading. And it has been used by traditional theologians to support the doctrine of *creatio ex nihilo.*"[7]

What is at stake in our interpretation (which begins with our translation) of Genesis 1 is the presuppositions about the nature of divine power we are go-ing to employ throughout our entire theology.[8] If the presuppositions of clas-sical theism determine our translation and interpretation of Genesis 1, that is, tell us what Genesis 1 means because that is what it must mean in the light of Christian doctrine, then the problem for theodicy and our answers are set by the first verse of the Bible.

If the power of God and creation must be understood as *creatio ex nihilo* in the theistic sense, then divine power is by definition omnipotent and unilateral, and we are stuck with all the problems we have examined in the preceding chapters. God's power is the only real power there is, and it creates something out of "nothing" (*ouk on* [Gr.], absolute nothingness, absence of anything). If, on the other hand, our text is understood to mean creation out of "nothing" (*me on* [Gr.], no-thing, chaos), then divine power is understood in a more so-cial and relational way. Any power is real only when it exists as a relationship between entities. In this alternative reading, God can still be said to create out of "nothing," but now divine power is understood to create "something" (some ordered or structured "thing") out of "no-thing" (chaos, *me on,* relative noth-ingness, no "thing" in a state of pure chaos). In short, our translation and in-terpretation of Genesis 1 will shape our decision about whether or not we can begin on biblical grounds to reconceive divine power in a theodicy.

In the Genesis story, divine creation is pictured primarily as a process of God's bringing order out of chaos. Something is already there, although it is not yet a "world." The earth is "without form and void," and the Spirit hovers over the face of the dark waters to bring life forms out of preexisting "stuff." Jon Levenson, a Hebrew Bible scholar, argues that *creatio ex nihilo* is an inadequate characteri-zation of creation in a wide range of Old Testament texts.[9] The essence of the idea of creation in the scriptures, he argues, is "mastery" of the given, not cre-ation *ex nihilo.* Creation is the idea of the uncompromised mastery of Yahweh, the God of Israel, over all other gods and even over chaos itself.

Genesis 1, Levenson points out, is not the only Israelite creation story, nor is it the quintessential one. Psalm 82 also is a creation story, and it assumes the mastery of God over chaos. Furthermore, that mastery is not yet complete—

an idea repeated again in Psalm 74. The point of the creation stories in the Bible, then, he argues, is not the production of matter out of nothing but the emergence of a stable community within a benevolent and life-sustaining order. Creation is the defeat by Yahweh of the forces that interrupt that order. Creation means making chaos into relative order.

These forces of chaos were not annihilated in perpetuity in primordial times. After the victory of God, chaos still survives. Evil as chaos is still vital, so the creation remains fragile. In the Flood story, in Psalm 74, and in Isaiah 51, God's ordering is irresistible but it is not constant and inevitable. The waters of chaos survive within the boundaries of creation, as in Psalm 104 and Job 30 and 40. The persistent forces of chaos are circumscribed, but they are not eliminated. In essence, then, creation is the "confinement" of chaos, but not its elimination. The world as creation is not inherently safe (Ps. 74). In summary, Levenson argues:

> I began by defining divine mastery as the critical element in the creation stories of the Hebrew Bible. What emerges in those stories is not the physical universe, but an environment ordered for peaceful human habitation and secure against the onslaughts of chaos and anarchy. . . . YHWH's mastery is often fragile, in continual need of reactivation and reassertion, and at times, as in the laments, painfully distant from ordinary experience, a memory and a hope rather than a current reality. It is, in short, a confession of faith.[10]

By the time we move beyond Psalm 104 to the Priestly cosmogony in Genesis 1:1–2:3, we find a progressive growth of the idea of the sovereignty of God over nature in a culmination of Israel's confession of faith. Although this cosmogony cannot be invoked to support the development of the idea of *creatio ex nihilo* in later Jewish, Christian, and Muslim doctrine, Israel has now come to believe that creation occurred without opposition. Unlike the story in the Enuma Elish, by the time Yahweh creates, Tiamat (or any other form of opposition) has disappeared, and all that remains, apart from God and God's spirit, is dark, inert chaos on which form and order are about to be imposed.

In this Priestly account, the God of Israel has no origin, and God's mastery has no origin. God has always reigned supreme. Creation, however, is the transformation, not the elimination, of the waters of chaos. Although Genesis 1 is not the original, or even final teaching from which all other thought about creation flows, it is one culmination of the Abrahamic faiths. New dimensions are added, however. Finally, for instance, as we noted earlier, in Isaiah 45:5–7, darkness too, no less than light, is the creation of the God of Israel. But in the Priestly story in Genesis 1, creation is not about either the origin or the banishment of evil; creation is about its limitation and ordering.

Monotheism for biblical Israel, then, meant not what it means in the later theistic doctrines of Judaism, Christianity, and Islam. If monotheism refers to anything in the conceptual universe of biblical Israel, it refers to the mastery of Yahweh of the twin worlds of covenant and creation. "In the Hebrew Bible covenant and combat myth are two variant idioms for one ideal—the exclusive enthronement of YHWH and the radical and uncompromising commitment of the House of Israel to carrying out his commands."[11] One cannot argue on biblical grounds that the theological concept of *creatio ex nihilo* and its implications of omnipotent, unilateral power are *the* biblical ideas of creation. If we take the range of biblical ideas of creation seriously in our understanding of divine power and creativity in the midst of chaos and suffering, we have a profound insight into our problem of suffering and evil which is quite different from classical theism.

The Natural Order

If creation is interpreted as God's "mastery" of chaos, as God's Spirit bringing "something" (creatures) out of "nothing" (orderless chaos) by "declaring" (Genesis 1) or "luring" (theistic evolution) or "coaxing" (Nikos Kazantzakis)[12] complex forms out of an existing "primeval soup," the idea of creation implies two affirmations about the world which contribute notions that are exceedingly important for an adequate understanding of suffering and evil within a theological perspective.

First, creation as a world emerging out of no-thing implies a natural orderliness to the world that we can ignore only at our peril in understanding why suffering and evil happen in a world created by God. Efforts to ignore it or to deny it put us in danger and only exacerbate suffering. Although the order of the world cannot be interpreted in this framework as determinism (we cannot change what's already been set by natural law), God nevertheless created and creates a universe of cause and effect, a world we have come to describe as a world of "natural law." Sophisticated interpreters of natural law today know that "natural laws" are not "things" out there that we can find if we look hard enough; natural laws are statistical probabilities of how the world will work in the future given our past experience and our ability to predict degrees of probability. Natural laws are not steel-belted edicts; they are the dependable predictions of how the world will operate under certain conditions.

Second, because the created world is not a fixed, static world but is a world of becoming, of novelty, of change, of development, that is, a world of some degree of freedom, this world order is not the fate of cosmic or scientific determinism. Freedom is not an exception to a world of natural law; it is the element of novelty and unpredictability intrinsic to the ordered world. The implications of the becoming of the created order establish an environment for human experience and interpretation in which suffering, at least in some ways and to some degree, is inevitable or at least unavoidable. I will comment on some further implications of my first point in this section, and of the second point in the next section.

If the world is created by God, either *ex nihilo* by fiat, as theism claims, or by calling a world out of chaos, as the scriptures teach and evolutionary theism and process philosophies claim, then the laws of cause and effect are inherent to the created world. Indeed, talk about the "laws of nature" is a direct correlate of talk about God creating a world, a universe of ordered and interrelated creatures, instead of a multiverse of nothingness (no-things)—if the latter is even a thinkable idea.

If this understanding of creation and natural law is intrinsic to the framework in which Christians think about their created world, then the scientific accounts of pain and suffering are important explanations in any Christian understanding of why human beings suffer the way they do in this kind of world. Why do we suffer? Why did this happen to me? There are "scientific reasons" why bodily pain and mental anguish and social oppressions occur, and if this is the kind of natural world God created and is creating, then scientific explanations are important in any Christian theological understanding of our pain, suffering, anguish, and despair.

I am not arguing here for a materialistic and deterministic view of the world, nor am I arguing for the omnicompetence or infallibility of scientists, technicians, M.Ds and Ph.Ds to explain our world. Nor am I denying any meaning for the notion of miracle within this naturalistic interpretation of the world. But I do contend that if we take the biblical concept of creation into account in trying to understand the grounds and place of suffering in life, and if we do not confine our understanding of suffering and misery to the concept of sin, guilt, and punishment, then the perspectives on the natural order offered by scientific thinkers are significant, even an essential component, in an adequate theological interpretation of human suffering and evil.

The body experiences pain because pain receptors are stimulated by some anomaly inside the body or some violence to the body from outside; the tissues of the body get too hard or too soft because of genetic coding or diet or stress and so close off the blood supply or explode, causing strokes and heart attacks; the immune system of the body is weakened by "defective" genes, diet, stress, radiation, or geographical environment and so succumbs to bacteria and viruses, or causes cells to reproduce at an uncontrollable pace. There are reasons for the pangs of the body and the spirit, and these can be accounted for as much by the kind of world order God created as by any belief that God has decided to punish us for our sins or to educate us for maturity or simply for some mysterious purpose.

We believe we have even become sophisticated in accounting for the more subtle agonizing features of our daily lives through our psychological and sociological theories. Consider how much of our anguish can be accounted for by the Freudian psychoanalytic theory of repression, or the Skinnerian behavioral theory of negative operant reinforcement conditioning, or the Maslowian and Eriksonian humanistic theory of frustrated self-actualization, or Carol Gilligan's explanation of the role of gender in psychological development. Or think of how the various theories of social organization and social change—whether they be Adam Smith's or Karl Marx's conflict theories, or Max Weber's social behaviorism, or Robert Merton's functionalism, or Levi-Strauss's structuralism, or Derrida's and Foucault's poststructural analysis of power, or Kristeva's and Toderov's semiotics of the function of language, or Habermas's and Adorno's post-Marxism—explain how and why some people live in misery and others live in luxury. It is not "irrational" or "accidental" or even "a surprise" that a small segment of our world lives in splendor and the majority live marginally or in abject poverty. There are good geographical, historical, social, economic, racial, and gender reasons for such a disparity of pain, suffering, and evil.

My point is that since the kind of world God created is a world of cause and effect within the natural, social, and inner worlds in which we live, the significance of the scientific accounts of our suffering should not be left in the hands of scientists and medical doctors and professors alone, but are significant resources in the theologian's and pastor's understanding of human suffering as well. Why do we ignore, play down, or even implicitly deny the importance of such factors when we try to offer a *theological* perspective on suffering? We function as if our concept of God the creator has little to do with our understanding of our suffering! If one believes the world is created by God, the facts of the natural world, and the explanations available to interpret those facts, belong as much to the Christian as theologian and pastor as to the philosopher of science or the medical technician. I occasionally wonder how much theological insight we could offer if we simply took the time and effort to understand the natural causes for much of the suffering we endure.

This can be a *very dangerous strategy* if misapplied, for it can become an ideology of repression by the powerful or an ideology of resignation for the victim of much suffering. Such a perspective can be used to say to someone else or to oneself, "Well, that is just the way the world is, so be happy or accept it." One does not have to have an insightful "ideology critique" in order to see how repressive and exploitative such an insight can become if misapplied.

Employed as part of a larger perspective, however, we might draw on this characteristic of creation to reassure ourselves that God did not kill our baby in her crib or trigger a malignancy in my mother's body or force your child to take drugs, or exile a group into slavery in order to punish them for their sins or teach them a lesson. God created a world in which natural processes of cause and effect inexorably lead, under the right circumstances, to crib death, cancer, addiction, and oppression until other processes of healing, reconciliation, grace, and liberation modify, negate, or transform the original set of circumstances into a new creation. The "processes of nature" are not an adequate explanation within a Christian perspective for all the suffering and evil that occurs in our world. But they should be one element within a more comprehensive theological interpretation.

Chance, Good Luck, and Bad Luck

The concept of creation, however, pictures God's world not only as a world of cause and effect. Creation interpreted in this way also implies a world of becoming. Freedom, novelty, change, and chance also characterize this created order. As the writer of Ecclesiastes says, "Again I saw that under the sun the race is not to the swift, nor the battle to the strong, nor bread to the wise, nor riches to the intelligent, nor favor to the skillful; but time and chance happen to them all. For no one can anticipate the time of disaster. Like fish taken in a cruel net, and like birds caught in a snare, so mortals are snared at a time of calamity, when it suddenly falls upon them" (Eccl. 9:11–12). A world of cause and effect is not identical to the Greek concept of fate or the modern notion of determinism, for natural laws are statistical generalization about degrees of probability. The causal order is not an absolute order.

Freedom, in some minimal sense at least, is not confined to the human species. It characterizes all creatures, almost negligible in some creatures or apparent only over vast aeons of time (the duration of stones), strikingly apparent in other creatures (the anticipations and decisions of human beings). In contemporary discussion, this element of creation is evident in the kind of "order of chaos" in nature and in a degree of novelty throughout the creation.[13]

Such a concept of freedom means there is an element of randomness to the world, and that some of what happens to us may be interpreted as "misfortune" as much as it is "injustice" from God, or nature, or neighbor, or governments. Although we have a tendency to seek a single "scapegoat," divine or human, for each disaster that befalls us, it is difficult sometimes to sort out injustice from misfortune. As Martha Nussbaum says, "Matters are rarely so clear. Many cases of human suffering for which we seek to assign blame are due to misfortune, and cannot be imputed to any human [or divine] agency. Many disasters that look like simple misfortune, on the other hand, turn out to contain elements of human injustice."[14]

Within such an understanding of our lives, errors, dead ends, and false trails occur in the evolutionary process, not because God wills them, and not necessarily because God allows them, but because nature has a creativity and randomness—an element of disorder—in its own right.[15] These errors, false trails, and dead ends occur because of chance, because of the unpredictable intersection of individual traits of creatures and environmental stresses. "Accidents" occur because of the creativity of the natural and human worlds. Actualizing possibilities get actualized in ways that are not always predictable in advance.

In a structured world created out of chaos, in which chaos is mastered by God but yet persists, or, as understood in some modern science and philosophy, where chaos or randomness or novelty is characteristic of the natural and social worlds, misfortune or chance or bad luck intertwine with sin and injustice in accounting for why some bad things (as well as some good things) happen to us. Concerning many actual complex events in our lives, it is impossible to decide whether they are better described as injustice or misfortune. Indeed, I suspect many if not most of the complicated events in our lives consist of a complex interweaving of sin, injustice, and bad luck.

In a world of genuine freedom, a perception established on the basis of our actual experience (phenomenology), or divine gift (theism), or unpredictability (quantum science), or some philosophical grounds (idealism), some of what happens to us is merely "bad luck" or "good luck," a chance concurrence of events that could be prevented only in a world where everything was absolutely determined by fate or by God. Although this argument may be unacceptable to some kinds of theistic Christians, I think even most theists, when they face up to the implications of their theistic presuppositions or definitions, believe in some kind of freedom and chance in contrast to divine determinism. Wes Robbins, though himself not a theist, nevertheless speaks for many theists as well as himself.

> My problem with the belief that "God intends the world, that all that is is what it was meant to be," is not that it is unintelligible. I was brought up talking in those terms. I still carry on conversations with friends and family who talk that way. I can talk that way myself in my sleep. So I have no problem whatever making sense of that vocabulary.
>
> I find it unbearable to believe that everything from the Big Bang on through the profligacy of biological evolution, quantum randomness, earthquakes, famines, cancer, the [human immunodeficiency] virus, down to the death of this world in fire or ice is all meant indiscriminately by someone, presumably with the best of intentions. Life's victories are more enjoyable and its defeats more endurable when I believe both to be combinations of the luck of the cosmic draw with whatever changes, for better or for worse, human intelligence manages to introduce into that mix.[16]

There is a chance aspect to all of life, and perhaps, indeed, to all creation. This is not to say there are no causes for everything that happens to us, or even that predictions are unreliable or useless. Chance, from my point of view, does not mean uncaused (though there have been philosophers who have defended the idea of "pure" chance). Nor is a chance event simply an event whose cause is unknown. Rather, a chance event is the concurrence of two independent causal chains of events. If someone sets a bomb to explode an airplane in midair, the plane will crash to the ground and I (likely) will die. Perhaps someone even planted the bomb to blow up the plane in order to kill the person seated next to me. But that does not mean that someone, human or divine, placed me on the plane in order to kill me. I was on the plane because my need to travel swiftly to a specific destination caused me to board that particular flight at that particular time. I was a casualty of the explosion by accident or by chance. Charles Hartshorne argues,

> What happens to us in detail is a matter of how countless agents behave. . . . It follows that the common sense idea of good and bad luck is sound. Not providence but the chance interplay of creaturely decisions assigns the exact form and degree of our fortunes and misfortunes. In spite of Einstein . . . God does throw dice. To have free creatures is to take a chance on what they will do. Life as this philosophy views it is indeed a gamble. It is luck to be born at all, luck to be born of good parents with good brothers and sisters. I reject, as my father did, the idea that one person's good luck is simply God's favor to that person, while the unlucky persons are divinely disfavored. To live is to take chances, and the living God takes chances also.

There is no consistent way to combine freedom with absolute predictability or order. Chance is an inalienable aspect of freedom. X makes decision A, Y makes decision B. What thus happens is a joint occurrence of A and B. Who decided A and B? Clearly not X and not Y? Was it God? Then X and Y only imagined they decided their acts.[17]

This *theological* point (not merely a philosophical one) must not be over-done. The argument does not deny a world created by God, a world of cause and effect, the power of divine purposes and activity, individual or corporate responsibility, miracles in every meaning of the term, or even some form of eschatology. It is rather the claim that within the effort to answer the question, Why did this happen? we must sometimes include the notions of good luck and bad luck. These are appropriate theological notions and not mysterious or impious notions foreign to a Christian interpretation of suffering and evil. They are concepts that have theological meaning.

The concept of evolution and the doctrine of creation, then, converge in Christian theology, for both presuppose that there is a struggle and a danger involved in existence, the struggle both for survival of physical life and for full realization of our potentiality for spirit. Suffering inevitably belongs to the or-der of creation, which is an order of becoming. A pain-free life would be a lifeless life. Although this is hardly an adequate category in trying to explain massive evil or radical suffering, and can also become an ideology of repres-sion and diversion along with many other "explanations," it too is a concept that in proper perspective and proper doses belongs in a comprehensive Christian view of creation and the world of suffering and evil.

The Tragic Element of Creation

We were not put here to have a good time and that's what throws most of us, that sense that we all have an inalienable right to a good time.

(Woody Allen,
"A Conversation with the Real Woody Allen," *Rolling Stone,* 1976)

One of the strengths of classical theism is its correlation of much of our suf-fering with sin and its consequences. However, classical theism is less than ad-equate when it comes to interpreting undeserved suffering. Indeed, such suf-fering is unacknowledged, does not exist, and cannot exist in the theodicies of classical theists. One of the major achievements of contemporary theodicy, such as Wendy Farley's, is that it is much more willing to acknowledge the el-ements of tragedy in some of our suffering. Theodicy must be able to account for the murder of Sethe's daughter, Beloved, in Toni Morrison's *Beloved,* or George's murder of Lennie in John Steinbeck's *Of Mice and Men.* Beloved and Lennie are not guilty of sin; they are not even sacrifices of sinners. They are casualties, even victims, of the tragic structures of society and nature. One might argue that the perpetrators are sinful people, but that claim poses a very complex question about the meaning of sin and responsibility. For the victims, their deaths are intimately tied to the structures of the creation and of society and not to punishment for their sins or the sins of society. In both cases, murder may have been the best or only good acts Sethe or George could have done in an otherwise tragic situation.

When Jesus was born, the birth was good news to Mary. But Jesus' birth was also bad news to all the other mothers in Israel. His birth meant the death of their newborn male babies. Was the death of their babies the punishment for their sin, or for the sin of their forebears? Or was "the slaughter of the innocents" (Matt. 2:16), at least as it was experienced by all the mothers other than Mary, the result of a flawed world in which light is often accompanied by darkness, and great good is often accompanied by massive and undeserved suffering by innocent victims? Was not an indescribable act of divine goodness also accompanied by an indescribable act of violence which had nothing to do with the sin and guilt of the mothers? A world in which good and evil are intertwined within its very fabric can mean that an indescribable act of divine goodness can also be the occasion for an indescribable consequence of radical suffering. This truth is canonized in the Christian tradition when the birth of Jesus is also recognized as the occasion for the slaughter of innocent babies. The one cannot be interpreted independent of the other, as is made clear in Eastern Orthodox tradition, where the "Feast of the Innocents" has become part of the liturgy celebrating Christmas.

I believe tragedy, or at least a tragic element in the creation, should play a significant role in an adequate Christian interpretation of suffering and evil. This concept, to be sure, does not appear as such in scripture. In the West, the archetypal formulation of this concept comes from the Greek tragedies of Aeschylus, Sophocles, and Euripides, and from sixteenth- and seventeenth-century English Elizabethan tragedies. Indeed, Christian theism has had trouble with any such idea because its interpretation of God as creator and redeemer seems to leave no room for a notion of tragedy as something apart from the will of God. The idea of tragedy seemed to impugn the sovereignty of God. Thus, the notion of tragedy in the West has existed outside and alongside Christian theism in the form of drama. I believe an adequate interpretation of creation should bring a notion of tragedy into the Christian interpretation of suffering.

In Greek tragedy the heroine or hero become involved step by step in an intolerable but yet inescapable situation. Aristotle used the term *hamartia* ([Gr.] to err), the notion of the tragic flaw, to describe this circumstance. There is an inherent defect or shortcoming or dilemma within the heroine or hero. This flaw is prompted by will or ignorance or circumstances, by jealousy (Othello), or binding obligations (Antigone), or fatal ignorance (Oedipus), or irresolution (Hamlet). But she or he is confronted in the end by the working of an inexorable set of circumstances that ensures an unhappy outcome, usually out of proportion to the flaw. In much Western tragedy, an element of cosmic collision along with the hero's flaw (often elusive and unwitting), chance, necessity, and other external forces work together to bring about a tragic conclu

Christian theology has not been predisposed toward a concept of tragedy for several reasons. However, in light of the creation as represented in the scriptures, and in light of our experience of the world, I believe Christians should not interpret all suffering as the result of sin and guilt and their consequences. Christians should make room for a notion of a tragic flaw within creation. In the kind of world God creates, tragedy is another one of the components of a world of structure, natural law, novelty, and chance. The reciprocity between law and luck introduces a feature of tragedy into the world. There is room within the divine creativity and will for a "tragic vision."[18]

Some of the suffering of life, and especially the radical, undeserved suffering, is lived as much under the shadow of tragedy and disaster as of sin. Still, tragedy cannot be an adequate theodicy for Christians, lest creation and redemption as primary categories in the Christian vision become problematic and grace become unreal.[19] Clearly one of the most fundamental differences between Stoic and Christian responses to life is the issue of whether the tragic structure of life is answered by resignation or by grace.[20] Nevertheless, a tragic flaw within the creation can be one notion among others in a comprehensive Christian interpretation of suffering and evil.

It is not accidental or incidental, I think, that this intuition in the contemporary discussion has emerged primarily from the experience of feminist theologians. In addition to the hints from Madsen, Plaskow, and others discussed earlier, the concept of tragedy has been significant in the recent writings of Rosemary Radford Ruether. Nature was not originally paradisiacal (benign for us), in Ruether's view, and is not capable of completely fulfilling human hopes for the good, in the sense of conveying a benign regard for individual or communal life. "We humans are the evolutionary growing edge of this imperfectly realized impulse to consciousness and kindness. But this does not separate us from the common fate we share, of organisms that grow and then die."[21] Finitude, she argues, must be separated from sin. Finitude is not our fault, nor is escape from it within our capacities. There are life processes of which we are inescapably a part, and these processes are competitive, destructive, and tragic as well as cooperative, constructive, and comic. "Within the bounds of finitude and mortality, there is certainly much missed plenitude that is outside our control or decision-making; that is tragic, but is not 'sin.'"[22]

Stated in another way, elements of tragedy and elements of sin are intertwined in our world. Relative freedom and the conditions of finitude combine to create events, circumstances, and conditions from which there is no escape. As Marjorie Suchocki puts it, "To reduce the fact of evil to the myriad choices making up the ongoing universe is to overlook the inevitability of conflict when choices necessarily involve exclusion, thus the ambiguity of existence relative to good and evil is real, and the fundamental root of evil in a Whiteheadian understanding must hold both poles together: the subjective pole of choice and the objective pole of finitude are together the root of evil."[23]

One of the most thoughtful discussions of the interrelation of tragedy and presented in Wendy Farley's theodicy. Most Christian theology connects suffering to sin and guilt as the primary clues to the human condition. There is, however, she argues, a dimension to our suffering for which sin and punishment cannot account. She calls it "radical suffering," the kind of suffering present "when the negativity of a situation is experienced as an assault on one's personhood *as such*."[24]

There is for many people a kind of evil that dehumanizes and degrades the human spirit to such an extent that it cannot be traced to punishment, or to aesthetic harmony, or to pedagogy, or to eschatological correction as its justification. "Radical suffering," such as experienced in death camps and child abuse, cannot be understood as something deserved by anyone. "Radical suffering defines the human being as a victim or sufferer, so she (or he) becomes a deformed creature whose *habitus* is suffering. All experience is absorbed into suffering and the sufferer is impaled upon her pain."[25] Such suffering introduces into the problem of evil a surd more terrible than suffering as a consequence for sin. Radical suffering, which simply debases and destroys, must be traced to tragedy rather than the Fall.[26] We live under conditions that can destroy us. With the concept of radical suffering and tragedy, we have moved beyond fault alone to finitude in our account of some suffering and evil.

Radical suffering, then, for Farley, requires a tragic element to complement the ethical component. Tragedy refers to something in the world order, something recalcitrant to human freedom and well-being, that qualifies and even corrupts obligation. "Something in the constitution of the world makes an ethical passion for piety, justice, truth, or compassion self-destructive. The world order itself is implicated as the origin of tragic suffering."[27] Tragedy describes the kind of suffering that is caused, at least in part, by some aspect of creation over which the actor, and especially the victim, has little or no freedom and control. The power of evil to destroy is present in the very structure of the creation.

Relationships can be conflicted, and sometimes necessarily so, as in the relationship between predator and prey. Values, too, can be essentially conflicting. Sidney Hook points out in his description of "the tragic sense of life" in pragmatism that many times there is an inevitable conflict between the good and the good, between good and right, and between right and right. These conflicts go beyond sickness, old age and death, or misused freedom to a structural conflict in the very nature of things.[28]

Furthermore, finitude as such is subject to decay, frustration, hurt, and death. Human beings are necessarily subject to suffering because of the way the world is structured: values conflict and finitude is fragile. Someone is not always guilty of some misdeed or bad intention in some kinds of suffering; suffering in some of its dimensions is an accompaniment of a finite order in which conflicting choices must be made. Some human suffering results from the necessity to choose between intrinsic but conflicting goods, or between equally binding but contradictory obligations.

Some suffering results from the frailty of finitude, such as a fallible memory or the incapacity to see all options or the inevitable ignorance of all the facts or the multitude of creatures pursuing opposing ends. As Farley says, "Creation is tragically structured. . . . Tragedy is the price paid for existence. . . . It is our doom to live under conditions that destroy us."[29] Although the pillars of classical Western theodicy may provide significant and even profound insights into human freedom and guilt as they bear on our suffering, the "tragic vision" also offers insights into how the structures of the creation itself have some bearing on suffering.

One of the most suggestive efforts to bridge the gap between the notions of sin and tragedy as they relate to suffering is suggested in the Minjung concept of "han." Minjung theology comes from Korea and is based on the experience of the common people in Korean history.[30] The primary interpretation of han as it relates to suffering is provided by Andrew Sung Park.[31] In Park's view, han is a complement to sin in helping us understand human suffering. There is both a similarity and a difference between the Western notion of sin and the Eastern notion of han. Han relates evil to sin, but han broadens the concept of sin to include something like an element of tragedy or even fate in the suffering of the oppressed of history. In his view, Christians usually focus on suffering as it is related to sin, that is, on the evil perpetrated by the sinner who is thereby guilty of sin. But Christian theology has seldom focused its discussion of sin and suffering as they are borne by the victim of sin. When that shift is made, the concept of han is available to redress that imbalance for a more comprehensive concept of suffering and evil.

Park does not treat evil as "an ontological or teleological entity." His project focuses on evil as the reality that appears as the result of sin.[32] Han focuses on the consequence of sin in the pain of the victim, whereas sin focuses on the volitional act of the sinner. When one focuses on the former, sin takes on structures beyond the individual will of the sinner; sin becomes han, a kind of tragedy or even fate that is the shadow of sin cast over the victim. The consequences of the injustice of sin shape the inner life and the social world of the victim of sin, a surd of powerlessness and helplessness deep in the life of the sinned against, wounds that scar the world of the oppressed.

Although han is not identical to the idea of original sin in traditional Western theology, it conveys the same sense of the radical interconnectedness of sin, except in han the consequences of sin in the life of the victim are as much in focus as guilt in the life of the sinner. Suffering related to han, therefore, begins to take on some implications of the tragic rupture in the life and world of the victim similar to the tragic flaw in Western literature. As in the Western tradition of tragedy, sin and freedom are interrelated, but for Park the tragic element rests more in the consequences of sin in the life of victims than in any cosmic flaws and structures.

Sin, then, for Park, is an inadequate concept to account for the abysmal depth of human pain and suffering. Sin and han belong together as complex, entangled realities in a Christian interpretation of suffering. When approached from the point of view of the pain of the victim of sin instead of the guilt of the sinner, sin becomes han. It is an experience of deep bitterness and helplessness on the part of the victim. "Han can be defined as the critical wound of the heart generated by unjust psychosomatic repression, as well as by so-cial, political, economic, and cultural repression."[33] Instead of the sinner stand-ing before God as a sinner, han places the suffering of the victims of sin in the context of the tragedy and fate of their lives as victims of sin, struggling against the accumulated frustrated hope and resentful bitterness of han. The victim of han experiences shame instead of blame.

For Park sin and han intertwine in a cyclical relationship. As the "shadow of sin," han points not so much to volitional acts as to "a character trait that has been developed by the infringement of outside forces."[34] Han points to the wounds, unhappy consciousness, oppression, historical determinism, lack of organizing center, and self-sacrifice of the victims of sin. Han is the "propen-sities" or "tendencies" of sin as they work out in the tragic structures of the world. "When the sinful propensities of parents are transmitted to their chil-dren, it is not sin, but rather han which they inherit."[35]

Although Park may be faulted for defining sin in a narrower way than many of the Western doctrines of original sin, tending to confine sin to the willful act of the individual alone, he nevertheless has moved the discussion of the relation of sin and suffering beyond the language of freedom, will, guilt, and punishment to the structures of the world that implicate us in suffering and evil beyond the notion of sin. Although he does not identify these structures of individuals, groups, or even nature as a tragic flaw in the creation itself, he moves beyond sin and guilt as the singular account of the evil in the world to something like a tragic structure in the world. This structure is closely identi-fied with sin, although Park offers no account of a "faulted" creation or tragic "elements" in creation as such apart from the concept of sin. Nevertheless, his interpretation of sin from the point of view of the victim introduces into our account of suffering and evil "structures" or "tendencies" or "propensities" that function like tragedy in the life of the victim and in the social structures of ex-istence. Sin alone cannot account for suffering; han must be correlated with any Christian account of sin in accounting for suffering and evil.

Unilateral and
Relational Power

[Religion] runs through three stages, if it evolves to its final satisfaction. It is the transition from God the void to God the enemy, from God the enemy to God the companion.[36]

The ideas of creation, chance, and tragedy all imply a different concept power than has been characterized as omnipotence. A different concept power can provide the key to a new Christian understanding of God and problems of suffering and evil. From here on through the remainder book I will argue that a relational or social concept of power should the concept of omnipotent power and can tie together the various have discussed so far in this chapter. Such a concept of divine power is far closer to the intuitions of biblical faith and trinitarian doctrine than the concept of omnipotence. It also can account more adequately for the suffering and evil in our experience than traditional doctrine, and it can empower us more realistically to respond to radical suffering with rebellion, promise, and resilient hope.

Power is essential to the world because all things are related to one another through power. There could be no world, because there could be no relationships, without power. Given this assumption, underived, isolated power which exercises unilateral control over another is not the primary meaning of power. Unilateral power is an abstraction (as well as a distortion) of the primary meaning of power. The fundamental power of life, according to Rita Brock, is not isolated, unilateral, dominating power but what she calls "erotic power." Our common understanding of power is "volitional self-assertion," the ability to dominate and to have one's own way, or to directly cause what we want to happen. Erotic power, however, she believes is more basic. It is an ontic category, "the most inclusive principle of human existence."[37]

Erotic power is the power of primal interrelatedness. All other forms of power emerge from the reality of erotic power. "The paradox of personal power is its relational base."[38] The individual can become self-aware and self-accepting only through the relationships that cocreate us. In moving to a non-dualistic, relational understanding of power, where relationship is an ultimate principle of reality, she replaces the concept of dominating power, in which power is a commodity to be struggled for, possessed, increased or lost, and used, with a concept of empowerment through mutual relationships.

Intimate mutual involvement, then, is not a qualification or an abandonment of power and identity. Strength is not the ability to control and hold things external to oneself or to get one's way, the ability to master through individual heroic might. Power, as a primary psychological, social, and ontological concept, is the ability to get along with others and to get things done, the ability to shape each other through the mutual empowerment of a relationship. When erotic power is denied or crushed, it then produces dominance and control. But even the distorted power of control ultimately draws its life from relationships rather than from an isolated self. "All powers, including the most destructive, depend on relationships."[39] Authentic power is neither fusion nor control, but interconnectedness.

Erotic power differs from agape. Unlike agape, which is often defined as "disinterested" or "objective" or, in the case of the divine, "dispassionate" love,[40] erotic love connotes intimacy and mutuality through the subjective engagement of the self in a relationship. Erotic power is the ability to feel our ɔeepest passions in all aspects of our lives. It is the basic yearning for others for self-discovery.

ɔower emerges from erotic power either, in life-giving form, from our acˈledgment of it and our ability to live in that understanding or, in destructive form, from the brokenheartedness that refuses to understand it. The erotic is the basis of being itself as the power of relationship, and all existence comes to be by virtue or connectedness, from the atoms to the cosmos. Erotic power is the fundamental power of existence-as-a-relational-process.[41]

Erotic power, then, is the power to be, to become, to identify with, to connect. The identification of divine love with disinterested, dispassionate love is at best an abstraction, an isolation of one aspect of God's love as God's desire to move toward the creation. At worst it is a demonic distortion of love, a denial of God's desire to connect and be connected with the creation except through some isolated, dispassionate desire unilaterally to impose a one-way relationship of dependence on the creature by a wholly independent God.

Behind Brock's concept of erotic power lies an ontological concept of relational power. Power is coextensive with life itself. To be alive is to exert power in some degree. To be actual means to exercise power. Whenever two people have a relationship, power is present.

From a philosophical point of view, however, power may be conceived in at least two different ways. Although neither form exists in its pure form, and although the distinction is rather simple, the implications of the distinction are thoroughgoing. According to Bernard Loomer, there are two ontological conceptions of power: unilateral power and relational power.

In the patriarchal West our lives and thought have been dominated by the first concept of power. Power has been defined as "the ability to produce an effect." However, Loomer contends, this is a one-sided, abstract, and nonrelational concept of power; it is a truncated view of power and is even demonic in its destructiveness. He refers to this as a unilateral or linear concept of power. "Unilateral power is the ability to produce intended or desired effects in our relationships to nature or to other people. More specifically, unilateral power is the capacity to influence, guide, adjust, manipulate, shape, control, or transform the human or natural environment in order to advance one's power purpose."[42] Such power is one-directional and nonmutual. The focus is on the individual and his or her personal goals and not on the relationship itself, conceived as mutually internal and creative.

With this concept of power, another's gain is my loss. The gain in power by the other is experienced as a loss of my own power and therefore of my status and sense of worth. The idea of being influenced by the other creates insecurity. My relative strength or "size" is determined by the degree to which I am free from the other or the freedom of the other is curtailed by me. Unilateral power presupposes a noncommunal or nonrelational understanding of the self. Not only is this concept of power abstract, Loomer argues; it is also destructive, both for the employer and for the recipient of linear power.

However, "the moral of the principle that power corrupts is not that we should divest ourselves of all power or completely eschew the exercise of power. The total absence of all power is non-existence, and the refusal to exercise the power we possess leads to destruction. The moral is rather that another kind of power is required."[43] The other kind of power that Loomer proposes is relational power. Relational power is "the ability both to produce and to undergo an effect. It is the capacity both to influence others and to be influenced by others. Relational power involves both a giving and a receiving."[44] Real power is the capacity to absorb an influence as much as it is the strength to exert an influence. "The capacity to receive from another or to be influenced by another is truly indicative of power."[45] Put in another way, power *is* a function of the mutuality of internal relatedness. In relational power, the focus is not so much on the members of the relationship as on the relationship itself. One learns not to trust oneself or the other but the relationship itself. The good is an emergent from the relationship.

Behind Loomer's concept of power rests a notion of value, for the problem of defining power is also a question of value. He assumes that the practice of relational power both requires and exemplifies greater "size" or "stature" than that called for by the practice of unilateral power.[46] At its best, receiving is not unresponsive passivity; it is an active openness, and enlarges the experiences and world, "the ranges and depths of complexity and contrast."

What is clear in this reconception of the meaning of power is that we are operating with a social concept of power. In both process-relational and trinitarian perspectives, power is defined as a social concept. Power is socially defined because any and all reality, including the divine reality, is conceived socially. There is a metaphysics of power behind both of these perspectives, just as there is a metaphysics behind classical theism (neo-Platonism). Specifically, there is "the general metaphysical claim that to be anything actual at all, whether the least of such things that can be conceived or the greatest, is to be an instance of process or creative synthesis, and, therefore, the outcome of a free response to the free decisions of others already actual."[47] Nothing whatsoever, not even God, that power than "which no greater can be conceived," can be defined as unilateral power.

If power is social, if power exists only in social relationships, then omnipotent power in the classical meaning of the term is literally a meaningless idea. Omnipotence, in the *ex nihilo* sense of the term and the way in which it is used in classical theism, is conceptual nonsense. "The conclusion seems obvious, then, that the only coherent meaning that 'all-powerful' or 'omnipotent' could have is not all the power there is—since nothing can have that, power being social or divided by the very meaning of the word—but only all the power that any one individual could conceivably have consistently with there being other individuals who as such must themselves also have some power, however minimal."[48]

Although the argument in the above paragraph is strictly definitional, the issue for theodicy goes beyond definition to metaphysics, value, and theology. No theodicy that is strictly conceptual can satisfy us; it must address these three dimensions of the problem as well. The following two chapters on process theology and trinitarianism attempt to do just that, namely, to revise the concept of divine power as metaphysical and theological concepts, and to relate these to our understanding and response to suffering and evil. The metaphysical and theological strands of this revisionary project will constitute the core of the final two chapters.

In concrete life, where real power is relational power and unilateral power is an abstraction, power becomes messy, inextricably related to the ambiguous, contradictory, and baffling (both sinful and tragic) character of concrete existence. This is as true of divine power as it is of finite power, as I will attempt to show in both process theology and trinitarian theology. My purpose is to show how these alternative concepts of power can reshape our understanding of God's power and our understanding of the relation of God to human suffering and evil.

Your God Is Too Big

The notion of God as the "unmoved mover" is derived from Aristotle, at least so far as Western thought is concerned. The notion of God as "eminently real" is a favorite doctrine of Christian theology. The combination of the two into the doctrine of an aboriginal, eminently real, transcendent creator, at whose fiat the world came into being, and whose imposed will it obeys, is the fallacy which has infused tragedy into the histories of Christianity and Mahometanism. When the Western world accepted Christianity, Caesar conquered; the received text of Western theology was edited by his lawyers. The code of Justinian and the theology of Justinian are two volumes expressing one movement of the human spirit. The brief Galilean vision of humanity flickered throughout the ages, uncertainly. In the official formulation of the religion it has assumed the trivial form of the mere attribution to the Jews that they cherished a misconception about their Messiah. But the deeper idolatry, of the fashioning of God in the image of the Egyptian, Persian, and Roman imperial rulers, was retained. The Church gave unto God the attributes which belonged exclusively to Caesar.[49]

In chapters 4 and 5, I considered religious and theological understandings of suffering that are willing to revise the idea of God as an omnibenevolent being and respond by protesting the omnipotent God's seeming malevolence, indifference, or injustice in comparison to our commonly accepted ideas of perfect goodness. I argued that although their response to suffering was biblical and pastoral, their presuppositions about the nature of divine power and character are finally neither persuasive nor tolerable for Christian faith. I turn in chapters 7 and 8 to theologians who refuse to qualify the idea of God's goodness, but are willing to reconsider a different idea of God's power.

Almost all of the theologies we have examined up to this chapter refuse to challenge the concept of God's omnipotence. In his criticism of Frederick Sontag, David Griffin highlights the assumption of the tradition and suggests an alternative. "Yet what has Sontag done except simply accept the traditional concept of divine omnipotence, according to which God has 'full power,' the 'power of ultimate control.' "[50] To Sontag's claim that we must retain the concept of omnipotence because "the tradition has made these affirmations about God's power," Griffin says, "But of course that provides no answer to why he chooses to reaffirm this tradition's affirmations about God's power instead of affirmations about God's total goodness."[51] Revisions of the concept of omnipotence are as discussable as revisions of the notions of real evil and of omnibenevolence. Stated more positively, on the basis of the scriptures, the primary dogmas of the church (Trinity and Christology), and our actual experience of God, ourselves, and the world, we have sound, even compelling, reasons to rethink the meaning of divine power.

Several years ago J. B. Phillips wrote a popular book titled, *Your God Is Too Small*. In reaction to the "puny" and "buddy" God of some popular piety, and in agreement with the Barthian reaction against the liberal God,[52] Phillips argued that God could do more than we think God can do, that indeed there are no limits to God's power. I agree with Phillips's basic claim that our concepts of God can be "too small." If God can only *empathize* with the suffering of the world but can do nothing about it, as we see in some parodies of process theology, God is too small. If God is *identified* with nature, and can do nothing more than what positivists mean by natural law, God is too small. If God is *identified* with human capacities, or human abilities, or human creativity, or human ideals, then God is too small.

But I think the opposite is also true. Our concept of God can also be "too big." It can be driven for reasons of piety or security to the point that God is no longer the God of the Bible, or the triune God, or the God of our actual experience. If God is identified as omnipotent power, as the kind of power that, because of definition, can do "just anything," God is too big. My argument has been that if you work out of the theistic notion of divine omnipotence, "your God is too big." All the theologians we examined up to this chapter shared one assumption: What really makes God God is God's sheer power, God's omnipotent power. That God is "too big."

My argument throughout the remainder of the book is that the most constructive theological resource we have as theologians when rethinking the problem of suffering and evil is a variety of contemporary reconceptions of divine power which are much closer to the biblical, creedal, and experiential evidence than is classical theism. Both process theologies and contemporary trinitarian theologies describe God's power in radically different ways than traditional theism. God's power is God's identification with the suffering of the world, and includes God's vulnerability, God's powerlessness, and God's compassion. God's power is the power of resurrection and transformation, which brings new life out of the suffering and evil of the world. These are the authentic biblical, doctrinal, philosophical, and experiential Christian resources with which we can understand, endure, rebel against, and respond to the suffering and evil of the world.

7

"Thy Compassions,
They Fail Not"
Suffering and Power in Process Theology

> Great is thy faithfulness, O God my Father;
>   there is no shadow of turning with thee;
> thou changest not, thy compassions, they fail not;
>   as thou hast been, thou forever wilt be.[1]

Rabbi Harold Kushner had spent his life as a rabbi trying to help people believe in an all-wise, all-good, and all-powerful God. Then two months after his son Aaron had passed his third birthday, and the day his daughter was born, the pediatrician told his wife in the hospital that Aaron had progeria, "rapid aging," a condition that finally took his life at age fourteen. In his effort to preserve his faith in a good God, he wrote a book, *When Bad Things Happen to Good People,*[2] which became an international best-seller. Above all, Rabbi Kushner refused to blame God for the death of Aaron. Although the traditional answers may contain some grain of truth, he conceded, they all assume that God is the cause of our suffering. In order to escape the offense of such a claim, he offered the explanations of natural causation, randomness, freedom, and the affirmation of the innocence of God. In the end he is candid to admit that his kind of explanation left him with the concept of a limited God.

Rabbi Kushner began by reformulating the question. "Could it be," he asks, "that 'How could God do this to me?' is really the wrong question for us to ask?"[3] The traditional question, as formulated by Job, assumes that God is an Oriental potentate with unchallenged power over the life and property of God's subjects. Kushner, however, gives an unusual twist to his interpretation of the story of Job. In commenting on the second half of the God-speech in chapter 40, for instance, Kushner says, "I take these lines to mean, 'if you think it is so easy to keep the world straight and true, to keep unfair things from happening to people, you try it.' God wants the righteous to live peaceful, happy lives, but sometimes even He can't bring that about. It is too difficult even for God to keep cruelty and chaos from claiming their innocent victims."[4] Such a conclusion did not disturb Kushner. "If God is a God of justice and not of power, then He can still be on our side when bad things happen to us."[5]

Behind Rabbi Kushner's theological interpretation and pastoral counsel lies a reconception of the power of God. His revision begins with the idea that the universe is a universe of natural law. These laws work indiscriminately for all people, good or bad. Natural laws have no way of telling the difference between good people and bad people, and so treat everyone alike. The laws of physics and biology do not make exceptions for nice people. God doesn't change the way the world operates to reward good people and punish bad people.[6]

Furthermore, some things happen for no reason at all. Some chaos in the universe never yielded to God's creative order. Hence, there is still some randomness in the world. Sometimes there is no reason things happen. Frequently the bad things that happen to us are bad luck, not the will of God. "This is perhaps the philosophical idea which is the key to everything else I am suggesting in this book. Can you accept the idea that some things happen for no reason, that there is a randomness in the universe?"[7] When weather patterns shift or drivers steer over the center line or engine bolts sheer on transcontinental flights,

> there is no message in all of that. There is no reason for those particular people to be afflicted rather than others. These events do not reflect God's choices. They happen at random, and randomness is another name for chaos, in those corners of the universe where God's creative light has not yet penetrated. And chaos is evil; not wrong, not malevolent, but evil nonetheless, because by causing tragedies at random, it prevents people from believing in God's goodness.[8]

Finally, Kushner maintains that from the beginning God set Godself the limitation that God will not intervene to take away our freedom, including our freedom to hurt ourselves and others around us. To be human in the image of God "means knowing that some choices are good, and others are bad, and it is our job to know the difference."[9] There is no turning back the evolutionary clock. Freedom of the creature is inaugurated by God's self-limitation, and "God has set Himself the limit that He will not intervene to take away our freedom, including our freedom to hurt ourselves and those around us."[10]

All of this line of argument, Kushner concludes, leads to a view of a limited God. "I believe in God," he says, "but I do not believe the same things about Him I did years ago, when I was growing up or when I was a theological student. I recognize His limitations. He is limited in what He can do by laws of nature and by the evolution of human nature and human moral freedom."[11] God is not helpless, however. While God is not the cause of bad things, God can be in the results of bad things. God can get us in touch with one another to overcome suffering and evil. God offers us courage and strength and perseverance to overcome suffering. God inspires people to help other people who have been hurt by life. But God does not will the bad things that happen to us nor can God unilaterally prevent them.

> I no longer hold God responsible for illnesses, accidents, and natural disasters, because I realize that I gain little and I lose so much when I blame God for those things. I can worship a God who hates suffering but cannot elimi-

nate it, more easily than I can worship a God who chooses to make children suffer and die, for whatever exalted reason.[12]

We do not love God because God protects us from all harm, or because we are afraid of God, but rather because God is the author of beauty and order, the source of strength and courage, "because He is the best part of ourselves and of our world."[13]

Nuancing Kushner's Revision

Harold Kushner's book is an important book for several reasons. First, he takes human suffering as very real, which is more than what some popular books on suffering do that are available today. Second, Kushner makes a significant option in theodicy accessible to a wide readership. Although the theological underpinnings of this view have been available in the United States for at least seventy years, the perspective was sequestered among theologians in the divinity school of the University of Chicago from the early 1920s to the late 1960s and primarily in some other academic theological centers since the 1960s until Kushner's book brought this kind of revised theism to the public. Not since Leslie Weatherhead's sermons preached in London during World War II, published as *The Will of God,*[14] has the general public had available a view that approximates the process view of suffering, evil, and God.

Kushner introduced for popular consideration the concept of the limited God. He refused to conceive of God primarily in terms of omnipotence. Although clearly he did not employ a process theology framework in interpreting his theological ideas (he did not even know about such a theology until a book tour in southern California, where he encountered David Griffin), he offered a view of divine power that approximates at key points the process reconception of divine power. Rabbi Kushner did for laypersons and clergy what process theologians had been doing for decades: offered a new conception of divine power.[15]

Rabbi Kushner's book is not, however, in my opinion, sufficiently nuanced to overcome some fundamental flaws in traditional theodicy that are more adequately addressed by process theology.

First, Kushner's God is still definitely the theistic God. "God *has set Himself the limit* that He will not intervene to take away our freedom. . . . Are you capable of forgiving and loving God even when He has let you down and disappointed you by *permitting* bad luck and sickness and cruelty in His world, and *permitting* some of those things to happen to you (italics added)?"[16] Apparently Kushner's God has set ironclad limitations on divine omnipotence so God cannot any longer unilaterally overcome natural laws, randomness, and human freedom. Yet Kushner is stuck with the basic problem that all theistic forms of the free will defense face when he assumes that, genuine (or even ironclad) as the limitations by God on God, these are nonetheless *self-limitations.* But *nipotent power that is self-limiting can also be in principle self-unlimiting* time and any place. The principle is inconsequential until one consider call "the damn proportionality problem," or what Frederick Sontag and John Roth call "sheer waste." Then we are forced to consider seriously the problem of the moral character of God, which drives Sontag and Roth to "the God of evil" and "the wasteful God," revisions we considered in the chapter on the shadow side of God. But Kushner considers the goodness of God to be a nonnegotiable religious and theological claim.

Ironically, then, this insufficiently nuanced form of revisionary theism leaves us with options of deism, humanism, or dualism. On the one hand, Kushner's God can scarcely do anything. The omnipotent God seems to have established freedom and natural law, but then engages the creation only through (or even *as*) human effort. Kushner comes so close to this view in his description of what God can do that the distinction between divine agency and human activity nearly collapses into humanism. Even if his God does do something, God does it after the event. There seems to be neither the intent nor the power of God in any sense to cause or to prevent or affect what happens through natural law, chance, or human freedom. On the other hand, his distinction, even disjunction, between God and the chaotic element in nature, and between God and natural law, seems to be so thorough that he is threatened by a dualism. In the end, Kushner's God is so limited that his God can scarcely do anything at all.

For example, when we pray, all prayer does is put us in touch with one another. Apparently prayer, and the God prayed to, are not causal agency in creating and transforming the events of suffering in our lives. In an effort to escape the dilemma of omnipotent power, Kushner ends with a powerless God, who either can do nothing, or who does something so indistinguishable from what we do that his position can barely be differentiated from humanism.

Second, the theological issue, especially from a Christian point of view but also I suspect from a Jewish viewpoint, appears in a sentence in his book that gathers electricity like a lightning rod. "I don't know what it means for God to suffer."[17] The theological problem posed by this sentence is not only a christological one, namely, how the cross and resurrection speak to our suffering. The problem, also, is whether Kushner's God is biblical at all. The biblical God of the prophets is the God of "pathos."[18] Douglas Hall, using the Christian language of love instead of the Jewish language of mercy and loving-kindness, puts the issue this way: "What I mean, to put it in the most childish way, is that God's problem is not that God is not able to do certain things. God's problem is that God loves! Love complicates the life of God as it complicates every life."[19]

Kushner's God finally is not the biblical God but, on closer examination, looks more like a sort of religious humanism in which human beings alone respond to suffering and create meaning by supporting one another in a world randomness. His God seems unable to do much of anything. Indeed, in the his God seems to be a rather pathetic onlooker. Speaking equally of clas- theism and Kushner's God, Norman Adams says, "I want no part of such stic] God. But neither do I want a limited God. Western theology is go- ave to do a better job in solving the problem of evil than Kushner has done. Perhaps the good Rabbi is telling us that we are faced with a growing need to revise the inherited models of Jewish and Christian theism."[20]

"And God Repented":
The Biblical God and Process Theology

Process theology provides a new perspective from which to interpret some neglected biblical themes. In chapter 6, I discussed the biblical notion of creation from a process point of view. Now I want to consider the biblical notion that God is affected by and responsive to our suffering, so that God's power and passion in scripture are interpreted in a way quite different from the theistic tradition. Classical theism, with its emphasis on God as absolute, unconditioned, and immutable, finally has had to deny that God in any sense can share reciprocally in our suffering, regardless of the language used in scripture, liturgy, and hymns.

One of the characteristics of the theistic God is *apatheia* (Gr.), from which we get our word apathy. *Apathy* in part means indifference, but in Greek it means something more. *Apatheia* refers to an inability to feel any emotion whatsoever. Stoic philosophers, for instance, believed God must not possess the capacity for feeling; otherwise there could be some other power over God, at least to the degree that someone else could move God to anger or joy or grief, and God would therefore be vulnerable and no longer God.

This is not a groundless and unimportant argument,[21] for if you can make another person joyful or sad, that means that you can influence that person. It also means the other person is vulnerable. You have some power in relation to that person, and the other person cannot be "unconditioned" or "absolute." The logic goes like this: No one can be greater than God; therefore, no one can influence and change God; therefore, in the nature of things, God must be incapable of feeling, which would occasion change in God. Christian theism bought that line of argument. God is *a se,* unmoved, and compassionless (*apatheia*).

But this is not the biblical God at all. Nor is it, for that matter, the God of Jewish and Christian piety. Hosea imagines Yahweh saying,

> How can I give you up, Ephraim?
>> How can I hand you over, O Israel?
> How can I make you like Admah?
>> How can I treat you like Zeboiim?
> My heart recoils within me;
>> my compassion grows warm and tender.
> I will not execute my fierce anger;
>> I will not again destroy Ephraim;
> for I am God and no mortal,
>> the Holy One in your midst,
> and I will not come in wrath.

(Hos. 11:8–9)

Biblical logic is the total reversal of Stoic logic. *Because* I am God, my compassion grows! The biblical idea is expressed in the hymn quoted at the beginning of this chapter, "Great is Thy Faithfulness." It is God's faithfulness, God's unfailing compassion, God's loving-kindness, God's *hesed* that makes God the God of Jews and Christians. That compassion is decisive in what one says about the power of the *passion* of God and the passionate character of the *power* of God.

Terence Fretheim argues that the God of the Old Testament is not the theistic God at all. Theistic exegetes assume that the God of the text must be and so is in absolute control of every situation, sees everything in advance, and is responsive only to God's own will in every situation.[22] There are, however, Fretheim notes, forty explicit references to divine *nicham* (repentance) in Old Testament texts.[23] Although most commentaries interpret these texts within the context of theism, the God of the texts, he argues, does not correspond with traditional theism at all.

The repentance of God in the Old Testament (*nicham*) is not the same as human repentance of sin (*shuv*). Nevertheless, it assumes real change, namely, the capacity to regret, to be sorry, to grieve, to have compassion, to retract, to change one's mind, or to relent. In all cases, the reversal of a direction taken or of a decision made is implied. The text implies not only a reversal but a reversal prompted by one's being moved by the circumstances of the situation in view. This theme, Fretheim argues, is in fact found in a variety of biblical traditions: northern and southern, early and late, including Yahwistic/Elohist; David/Zion; Dueteronomic history; eighth- and seventh-century prophets; exilic and postexilic prophecy; and psalmody.

Divine repentance, then, is a metaphor that commonly functions in later Israel as a key to interpreting the nature of God's activity and power over the years. It stands alongside other themes, such as steadfast love and mercy, to interpret the kind of God whom Israel believed in and worshiped. In sharp contrast to any arbitrariness of divine action, repentance shows the extent to which God's loving and gracious will goes in order to execute God's uncompromising salvific intentions. God's constant availability for repentance stands in the service of God's unchanging divine intention. Neither capricious nor immutable, God undergoes change for the sake of the creation. God's steadfast love and mercy are served by repentance. Although Fretheim does not presuppose nor is he directly engaged in a discussion with process theology, he does say something that sounds very much like Charles Hartshorne. "It would appear that it is essential to speak of both immutability and mutability as essential divine attributes, each in its own sphere."[24]

The language of repentance is an essential component of a much broader language used to speak of God. It has to do with the idea of the divine affectability by the creation. The God who repents is the God who is also provoked to anger, who rejoices over the creation, who responds to the prayers of the people. This is a God who has entered into such a relationship with the world that it is a genuine mutual relationship. It may even be that God has to forsake God's own specific purposes in order to be true to this primary purpose of God.

The same argument is made by Walter Brueggemann, who points to several hints of the efforts of Yahweh to break out beyond the boundary restrictions of the common theology and to articulate a new identity. Specifically, he refers to the Flood story in Genesis 6—8, the story of Sodom and Gomorrah in Genesis 18—19, the poems in Hosea 11 and Jeremiah 30 as examples of God's adaptability to the conditions of the world. Unlike the story of Job, in many Old Testament texts one can argue with God and win.[25]

In commenting on the Flood narrative in Genesis 6, Brueggemann says the story is "not about destructiveness or a lot of water but about the troubled heart of God. Or said in another way, the narrative is not about the anger of God but about the grief of God."[26] The text at the beginning presents a carefully balanced tension between the conventional lawsuit theology (There is wickedness of imagination, evil continually. "I will blot it out") and a new disclosure of the heart of God (The Lord was sorry; it grieved him to the heart. "I am sorry I made them"). At the heart of God things are troubled. Yahweh makes a new resolve and a new promise; a new relation is possible.

Note that the heart of humanity in Genesis 8:21 is as it was in 6:5. The change that makes a future possible is wrought not in the human heart, but in Yahweh's heart, which is filled with sorrow, grief, and regret. The flood is about the inundation of God's person. In all four of the passages Brueggemann interprets, he claims that Yahweh is brought much closer to the hurts that Israel experiences. "Contact with that hurt causes Yahweh to assume a new posture and to recharacterize the future of Israel."[27]

Andrew Park goes on to argue that God's grief for the misery of Israel (Judg. 10:16) and God's crying out like a woman in travail (Isa. 47:6) are carried over into the New Testament. Until humanity is made whole, God will be restless. God cannot be detached from the griefs of humanity. Indeed, the grief of God, Park argues, is carried to the point of showing that God too needs salvation. God's han, the wounded heart of God, needs relationships in order to be resolved. The cross "is not only the symbol of God's intention to save humanity (human perspective), but also the symbol of God's need for salvation (divine perspective)."[28] The cross of Jesus is the symbol of God's crying for salvation because God cannot save Godself. "If salvation is relational, then one cannot save oneself. God needs salvation!"[29]

The Process God and Evil

The Concept of Divine Power Revisited

David Griffin, the process theologian who has written most extensiv[e]
the problem of suffering and evil from a Whiteheadian perspective,[30] sa[ys]
solution dissolves the problem of evil by denying the doctrine of omr[i]

fundamental to it."[31] He rejects the idea of omnipotence on biblical, philosophical, and theological grounds. In Genesis 1, he contends, the preexistent actualities might well have some power of their own which could thwart the divine will, and there might be some eternal principles about the way these actualities can be ordered that limit the sort of situations that are really possible. This, he grants, is a hypothesis, but the *ex nihilo* exegesis is no less a hypothesis than is this one.

The traditional doctrine of omnipotence must be revised on biblical grounds. Power, even in the context of creation, is a relational concept. Power as a social concept means that nothing whatsoever, not even God, can wholly determine something else. Power no longer means the capacity coercively to impose one's will on a totally powerless object; it means the power to affect another free center of power through persuasion. If some concept of omnipotence must be retained, John Cobb claims it means the "optimum persuasive power" in relation to whatever else is, not the capacity unilaterally to impose one's will on another.[32] As Marjorie Suchocki says, supporting Cobb's reconception of omnipotence, "Process theology suggests that the power of hope against despair is not paradoxical at all, but rests with the nature of God as the power for justice. God is the source of the vision and of the reality; there is a locus for justice in the nature of God. The effect of God upon us is the transmission of vision, along with the conviction of its worth and attainability. God is the source of hope. This is the significance of the doctrine of divine omnipotence for us."[33]

The Nature of the Limits of the Divine Power

There are two forms of the notion of limitation on divine power—one, the idea of divine self-limitation (Hick, Kushner, and all other forms of the free will defense); the other, the idea of an essential or ontological limitation of divine power (Griffin and other process views). Some classical theists, though in the history of theology not all, affirm a limitation of divine power, but the limitation is always a *self*-limitation. God freely and voluntarily gives up some of the power God alone possesses, although God can and does sometimes wield that omnipotent power unilaterally even now (as with miracles), and/or will reassert it as divine justice and victory at the end (the eschaton).

The process view, however, is that God is *essentially* limited in God's power. The limitation on God's power is not a result of God's will, but is in the nature of things. This, however, is not the same idea that the theistic free will defenses offer. The theistic concept of self-limitation may claim that the power of creatures is real power, but that power is provisional, wholly derived dependent on, and liable to the infinite power of God, which is the only one or real power there is. Theists may claim that God *does not* exercise omnipotent power (except in the eschaton or on rare occasions in this though miracles, for reasons unknown and unknowable by humans). Or they may claim that God *cannot* exercise that omnipotent power because God is (morally? rationally? or by an odd concept of "self-ontological limitation"?) bound by God's own self-limitation. God says, so to speak, "I can't do that" because "I freely chose not to do that, since I am bound necessarily by my free and perfect decision to limit my power," regardless of how out-of-bounds the choices of human beings get. But in all these free will arguments, the only "really real" power is the one, infinite divine power, and it is conceivable that such power can be in principle the unilateral cause of whatever is.

The problem with the idea of self-limitation is that if God is both omnipotent and eternal, God's power was, is, and will be omnipotent, and so there cannot be eternally genuine or even temporally genuine freedom in any of the creatures that God could not modify or even withdraw or unilaterally override at any time along the line, if God decided for some omniscient reason to do so. Omnipotent power that is self-limited can be, to invent a phrase, "self-unlimited," if the divine will for any reason, known or unknown to us, decides to reassert the divine power.

The theistic concept of self-limitation is employed in the eschatological theodicy of John Hick. Specifically, all's well that ends well, and eschatology assures us ("not as a logical necessity" but as "a contingent but predictable outcome")[34] that God's omnipotent will in the end will bring all of the creation to fulfillment of God's purposes. Thus omnipotent power is the final if not the only real power there is, at least at the end of time. One might observe here that one strength of the idea of an everlasting hell is that it is logically consistent with the idea of genuine human freedom over against a God who is not powerful enough to establish unilaterally God's everlasting love and will for the creation.

The alternative to the concept of theistic self-limitation is the concept of *ontological limitation*. The key to this concept is the claim that there is a limitation on the power of God that is inherent in the structure of the world. Because God and some world (not necessarily this one) are coeternal, and because there are metaphysical principles that apply to any world as such, there is an inherent limitation on the power of God. The principles of limitation may be independent of God in the sense that there are preexisting actualities which have some independent power of their own, or there may be some eternal, uncreated, necessary principles within God (as in the theology of Edgar Brightman and some of the Boston personalist theologians). These are principles independent of God by which any actuality can be, and which determine what is and what is not possible to be. The presupposition (hypothesis) is that God is not the only actuality there is, but that there are nondivine actualities in any world whatsoever.

The import of this notion of divine power for theodicy is that Go[d] *unilaterally* eliminate evil as such or even any particular evil from[...] The reason is not that God is finite or is missing something that[...] God a "real" God, but that God is not the only genuine power[...] world. All actualities, to one degree or other, from God to the[...]

of smoke in the universe, are centers of inherent power simply by virtue of their being. Thus, contrary to the claims of the protest theodicies, God cannot be blamed for a world like ours, for God never is or could be totally responsible for anything that occurs in the world. Suffering and evil, therefore, are not something God can unilaterally prevent or eliminate from the world even if the divine will were omnibenevolent.

What God Does in Process Theology: Creating and Redeeming the World

What can God do if God is not omnipotent in the theistic sense? There is a way within a process framework to say God creates the world out of nothing. If nothing refers to a state of absolute chaos in which there is no-thing but very low-grade actual occasions happening at random, without being ordered into enduring individuals, then process theology affirms creation out of nothing.[35]

In process theology, God creates and redeems the world in every moment of its actuality. God creates the world by initiating every actual occasion through an "initial aim"; God redeems the world by experiencing the world in God's "consequent nature" and transforming the world in God's "primordial nature."[36] God originates or creates the world in the sense that every event in every moment comes to be by God's "willing" or "calling" the event into existence by offering possibilities, which are the means through which God exercises divine guidance of the world. In technical terms, God is the "principle of concretion," and every "actual occasion" (every concrete event or moment of experience out of which the world is made) is inaugurated through the initial aim of God toward the best possible "enjoyment" or "satisfaction" that can be achieved, given the real possibilities in the present. There is no event whatsoever that could be without the immediate, direct, creative activity of God.

The creative power of God can be represented in poetic form as well as in metaphysical language. Formulated in metaphor, God is creator of the world as a composer or a conductor, writing the score a few bars ahead of the orchestra or conducting the orchestra; or as an improviser in a jazz band rather than a performer of the music *ex nihilo*. Nikos Kazantzakis conveys the "lure" of God as creator in this fashion:

> Blowing through heaven and earth, and in our hearts and the heart of every living thing, is a gigantic breath—a great Cry—which we call God. Plant life wished to continue its motionless sleep next to stagnant waters, but the Cry ~aped up within it and violently shook its roots: "Away, let go of the earth, 'k!" Had the tree been able to think and judge, it would have cried, "I want to. What are you urging me to do! You are demanding the im- 'e!" But the Cry, without pity, kept shaking its roots and shouting, 't go of the earth, walk!"
> ~d in this way for thousands of eons; and lo! as a result of desire life escaped the motionless tree and was liberated.
> ~eared—worms—making themselves at home in water and

mud. "We're just fine here," they said. "We have peace and security; we're not budging!"

But the terrible Cry hammered itself pitilessly into their loins. "Leave the mud, stand up, give birth to your betters!"

"We don't want to! We can't!"

"You can't, but I can. Stand up!"

And lo! after thousands of eons, man emerged, trembling on his still unsolid legs.

The human being is a centaur; his equine hoofs are planted in the ground, but his body from breast to head is worked on and tormented by the merciless Cry. He has been fighting, again for thousands of eons, to draw himself, like a sword, out of his animalistic scabbard. He is also fighting—this is his new struggle—to draw himself out of his human scabbard. Man calls in despair, "Where can I go? I have reached the pinnacle, beyond is the abyss." And the Cry answers, "I am beyond. Stand up!" All things are centaurs. If this were not the case, the world would rot into inertness and sterility.[37]

In process theology, however, God not only presents an initial aim for the best possibility for every actual occasion. God *experiences* in God's consequent nature the immediate experience of every actuality, *saves* what is good out of that experience in God's primordial nature, and *lures* the best possible satisfaction in the next actual occasion by presenting a new initial aim. God literally creates and redeems the world from moment to moment. John Cobb describes this process understanding of how God creates in this way:

> The total reality out of which each human occasion arises includes not only the adjacent events in the brain and the past human experiences but also God. Like other events, God influences the becoming occasion by being what he is. He entertains a purpose for the new occasion, differing from that entertained by the previous human experience. He seeks to lure the new occasion beyond the mere repetition of past purposes and past feeling or new combinations among them. God is thus at once the source of novelty and the lure to finer and richer actualization embodying that novelty. Thus God is the One Who Calls us beyond all that we have become to what we might be.[38]

Although God is the supreme actuality, the only actuality infinite in existence, possibility, faithfulness, and goodness, God is never the single, unilateral cause of any event whatsoever that God creates and redeems. Mingling with the initial aim of God in every event is also the causal power of the past in all its complexity, a rich range of graded possibilities, and above all the freedom of the agent to decide what to actualize in the moment of concrete decision. Stated in less philosophical language, God always wills the best possible good to be achieved in every situation we encounter, but cannot unilaterally cause the best to happen. Although God is the *supreme* cause in the sense just described, God is never the *sole* cause. God's power is more the power to persuade, that is, the power to create, to sustain, to lure, and to rebuild, than the power to impose, that is, to control.

This process view of creation is reflected in a contemporary hymn titled "Spirit." The song begins with the chorus:

> Spirit, spirit of gentleness,
> Blow through the wilderness, calling and free,
> Spirit, spirit of restlessness,
> Stir me from placidness,
> Wind, wind on the sea.

The first two stanzas go:

> You moved on the waters,
> You called to the deep,
> Then You coaxed up the mountains
> From the valleys of sleep,
> And over the eons,
> You called to each thing,
> "Awake from your slumbers
> And rise on your wings."

> You swept through the desert,
> You stung with the sand,
> And you gifted your people
> With a law and a land,
> And when they were blinded
> With their idols and lies,
> Then You spoke through Your prophets
> To open their eyes.[39]

The Will of God
in Process Theology

One of the significant contributions of process theology to an understanding of suffering and evil is that it has a very precise notion of the will of God. *God does not will everything that happens, but God has a will in literally everything that happens.* God did not will the death of Susan Smith's babies, but God wills the best possible good to come out of the death of the two children. As Marjorie Suchocki puts it, "In comparison to Leibnitz, then, Whitehead's vision offers not the best of all possible worlds, but the best possible for any world."[40] No moment, no event, no creature, no person could come to be without the will of God (the initial aim) for the best possibility for every event. While God does not will everything that happens, because creatures decide what to do with God's aim or lure, God wills the best possible good given the real possibilities within the context of what has happened and can happen. So process theologians give a very central place to the concept of the will of God in their theodicy. Ironically, process theologians talk about the will of God in *every* situation, righteous or sinful, comic or tragic, lucky or fateful, routine or resplendent, not simply in the perplexing or desperate situations in our lives.

One must say, then, that the will of God is not an overwhelming mystery to process theologians. Indeed, the will of God is specifiable in every situation from a process point of view. God creates, sustains, redeems, and lures the world and all its creatures according to God's purpose to create the best possible good from among the real possibilities in every occasion of experience.

A Process Theology
of Value and Good

But it is the aim of God that is knowable in process theology; the specific content must always be discerned in each situation in the light of God's aim. Just as classical theisms have their theories of good or value (good is a mystery hidden in the divine mind; good is whatever God does; good is what God achieves in the eschaton; good is God's aesthetic enjoyment of the creation; good is what God commands us to do; good is justice or wrath or love or mercy or faithfulness), so process theodicy is also based on a theory of the good or value. No theodicy of any type can avoid some such perspective, implied or explicit. Process theology is very up-front about what theory of God's good guides its theodicy. Its theory of good or value can be made explicit.

God seeks everywhere and always, in every event whatsoever, intrinsic good. Intrinsic goodness is defined as a world of beauty, that is, a world in which there is a balance between intensity of experience and harmony of experience (multiple contrasts intensely felt but mutually compatible).[41] Intrinsic evil, on the other hand, is a lack of balance between these goods, that is, triviality of experience and discord of experience. From a process viewpoint, intrinsic evil is not only suffering but also triviality.

God as creator seeks to create intrinsic good through increased complexity of experience. That is, God seeks to increase the richness of experience of all creatures at all levels of the creation, both high-grade and low-grade creatures. This experience at each possible level of complexity is intrinsically good (not extrinsically good, defined as good only in relation to human interests). Good, then, includes such things as novelty, life, intensity of feeling, consciousness, freedom, and in humans a genuine concern for others.

Given that God seeks to create good and not to avoid evil, and that God is subject to the necessary relation of power and value (to the tragic correlation between the capacity to enjoy and the capacity to suffer), suffering and evil are intrinsic to the creation itself, not an intrusion or a corruption of the creation. Griffin states what is central to the panentheistic understanding of suffering and evil. "My thesis is that this correlation between the capacity to enjoy and the capacity to suffer is a necessary metaphysical correlation, inherent in the nature of things."[42]

If we were to put to Griffin the traditional question, Why did God create us so that we are so susceptible to pain and suffering? he would answer, Because God could not do otherwise without forfeiting those kinds of beings who can experience the kinds of values God seeks to make real. Thus, the world necessarily entails natural evil, because in spite of occasional destructive outbreaks, there is far more value in a world teeming with life than in a dead one.

How God Is Omnibenevolent in Process Theology

The will of God is interpreted within this theory of value. How God creates gets interpreted according to this particular understanding of God's purpose. Within this framework, then, there is always the dilemma of how to know what specific choices fulfill the will of God in this broad sense, but there is no question about the total goodness of God. God is not whimsical, arbitrary, unpredictable, ambiguous, or anything else that might cause one to call into question the perfect goodness of God. Unlike the protest theodicies, there is nothing to question God about or to complain or to protest to God about. One might wince at the tragic conditions of existence or complain about the inevitability of evil because of the structure of the creation, or one might despair at the depth of the creatures' resistance to what God is creating, but one can never doubt the benevolence of God. God always, infallibly, uniformly wills the best possible satisfaction in every situation in the world. As in most forms of classical theism, God's will in panentheism is infallibly good and perfect.

This claim does not mean, however, that God's will is only to avoid evil. Since the quest for greater good is both the reason God creates and how God creates, there is not only a risk but an inevitability of enormous evil as well as of great good. Given the principles within which God works, such as the correlation between the capacity to enjoy and the capacity to suffer, God could avoid evil only by avoiding good as well. God could have avoided all human suffering by refusing to lure this particular animal out of the sea to become human. If God could be indicted at all from a process point of view, the indictment would be for calling this animal out of the ocean, as Kazantzakis imagined, to other possibilities which included great evil as well as great good.

Process theology's limited God, then, is wholly good. Just as Jim Garrison and John Roth never consider qualifying the power of God, process theologians never consider qualifying the goodness of God, for the same religious reasons I elaborated at the end of chapter 5. Vital religion, they believe, is driven by the desire to be in harmony with God, and a malevolent God is not a God one can or should be religiously devoted to. The being classical theists, and especially the protest theologians, call God is not one that process theologians consider worthy of worship. Process thinkers do not believe that possession and exercise of omnipotent power is what inspires our worship as creatures. Worship is not inspired by the adoration of raw power, but by the attraction to the capacity to save the good and to draw greater good out of the conditions of triviality and disharmony that cause suffering. Thus, religious commitments finally require process theologians not to qualify their belief in the total goodness of God.

The Proportionality Problem in Process Theology

This stage of the discussion, of course, brings us back to a fundamental issue between the process theologians and the protest theologians. I call it "the damn proportionality problem," the problem on which almost all theodicies finally falter, since so many of the specific arguments from the various classical theodicies are convincing until they get to this problem. Within the process framework, as in most perspectives, a certain amount of evil is understandable, defensible, inevitable, and even necessary, given the framework. But do we not reach the point at which we must simply say, "They explain too much," and look for an alternative understanding of the nature of evil, or God's goodness, or God's power? Here the process and classical theologians differ significantly from the protest theologians.

The protest theologians claim that "there is too much pointless suffering and waste" in our world to justify anyone, including God, regardless of what assumptions or theory of value one adopts. But the process theologians claim that horrendous as the evil in our world is, it is not so horrendous as to cast doubt on the moral character of that power which makes for a good not our own, that is, the will and power of God to create the good. Griffin puts the matter clearly. We can believe in the goodness of God,

> Unless, of course, the evils that were thereby made possible are so great that the goods that could be achieved are not worth the risk. That is the question that each of us can only answer for ourselves. Those of us who are among the most fortunate people who have ever lived on the face of the earth must of course be aware of our biased perspectives, and must be sensitive to the response that may come from the less fortunate. But, even when trying to take into account my biased perspective, I cannot imagine that I would ever conclude that the evils of life have been so great that it would have been better had life never emerged; or that the evils of human life, as horrendous as they have been (and quite possibly the worst is yet to come!) are such that it would have been better had human life never been created.[43]

Is the Process God Helpless?

Process theologians are sometimes accused of constructing a picture of a helpless God. What, critics ask, can the process God do about the suffering of the world? Is not a limited God ultimately helpless amidst horrendous evil? While God may be "the fellow sufferer who understands" (Whitehead), the One who empathizes and sympathizes with the creatures, God can only star by helplessly sympathetic.

The process God not only identifies with the world through sympatheti perience, however; the process God also works in and with and on the to create and save the world in the way described above. To talk abo as "simply" empathizing with the world, "simply being there with us in our suffering," as if God were an empathetic onlooker helpless to do anything about suffering, is a parody that applies only if one defines divine power as omnipotence. God redeems the suffering of the world in a number of ways: (1) by experiencing in God's consequent nature the good as well as the evil that has been achieved in the world; (2) by transforming in God's primordial nature the events creatures have wrought by selecting from them new possibilities for the future; (3) by seeking richer value by the presentation of new aims in each new situation; and (4) by strengthening the good that is achieved so that the balance between good and evil will be enlarged.

God participates in the suffering of creatures, and through this participation in, affection for, and transformation of the suffering changes the world.[44] God's experience and will contribute something new and effective in literally every event in the world. Not only human beings but also God is the victim of our agelong resistance to God's call to love our neighbors as ourselves. But God is not helpless or hopeless, nor is God's power only the power of empathy and sympathy. Indeed, unlike creaturely power, God is the only infallible power, the only utterly reliable source of hope and help for the transformation of sin and suffering in a world like ours. God is not "finite" or weak or helpless or imperfect, if each of these terms means that God is somehow less than perfect in comparison to some other conceivable deity. God is *perfect* power, or even omnipotent power, if one must retain that term, as long as perfect or omnipotent power means the *maximal power conceivable in a world in which there are other centers of genuine power.*

But then, of course, this claim assumes that "real" power is reciprocal power, the power to create and redeem through transformation rather than to impose unilaterally the autonomous power of one's will on otherwise helpless creatures. What is at stake is what one understands "genuine" creative and transformative power to be, the power that creates and redeems in a world of actual meaning and value.

Process theologians assume genuine power is the power of reciprocity within relationships; trinitarian theologians, as we will see in the concluding chapter, also assume that divine power is the power of the cross and resurrection to transform death, suffering, and evil into the reign of God. Both thoroughly reject theistic unilateral conceptions of power. From process and trinitarian perspectives, unilateral power is an abstraction or a distortion of genuine power, both divine and human.

"The wisdom of the world" (1 Cor. 1:18–31), of course, has always understood genuine power to be unilateral power. The question, then, is whether Caesar or the God of the cross and resurrection is the key to our understanding of power. Most traditional and modern Christians have yet to draw a Christian conclusion that question. The problem of theodicy pushes our backs to the wall on this ion in a way very many find uncomfortable and even intolerable. Some- our deepest suffering, when we are near despair, most of us still long mnipotent power that can unilaterally rescue us or at least reassure us that our suffering is not evil but is disguised good. But neither process nor trinitarian theisms find that kind of God in scripture, tradition, experience, or reason.

Significant Questions
for a Good Theodicy

The important thing, I think, is not to be bitter. If it turns out that there is a God, I don't think He's evil. The worst you can say about Him is that basically He's an underachiever.[45]

Griffin is in effect countering the graffito that "God is an underachiever!" with the assertion that, given his possibilities, God is achieving at grade level.[46]

What are some of the weaknesses and strengths of the process perspective as a theological understanding of suffering and evil? I will begin my evaluation with what some critics consider to be its major liabilities. As I will show in the next chapter, when we come to the trinitarian version of this radical revision of omnipotence, the process framework is not the only possible framework for reconceiving divine power, and process theology is not without its inherent problems and liabilities.

First, to what extent is the process perspective on the world "class dependent" or "class specific"? To what degree does or can this view on evil serve as an ideology for the established middle- and upper-class experience of life in American society? Is it a perspective that encourages persons and groups to believe both that they have had good luck and that they have managed things well enough that they have their own destiny and the destiny of the world in their hands and so do not need apocalyptic solutions? In short, is process theology a bourgeois ideology which serves to create and reinforce the belief that we are free, responsible, capable, and destined to make our own good and evil in a fundamentally supportive environment?

This is a very complex problem. On the one hand, I recall Prathia Hall Winn's sermon in Breyfogel Chapel at United Theological Seminary in which she moved in a subtle but determinate way from the claim that "God has the whole world in God's hands" at the beginning of the sermon to "We have the world in our hands" by the end of the sermon, a viewpoint that was directed to undergird the aspirations and hopes of those who are marginalized by our society but need to believe they are free and able to improve their lives by taking responsibility for good and evil. Such a move, in this case, seemed to be more a "rhetoric of hope" than a repressive middle-class ideology. On the other hand, I recall Tex Sample's Showers Lectures in the same chapel in which he argued that the world of the cultural right experiences the world as so threatened by change and a lack of control over their fate that the primary way they manage their lives with any semblance of security is through the assurance that God providentially provides air canisters to repair tires when one is stranded on the interstate on the way to a church meeting.

The answer to the question of which view is an ideology of repression and which is an ideology of hope quickly becomes very ambiguous. Undoubtedly, many middle-class persons and groups in power employ a view of freedom, responsibility, and decision to justify their oppressions; at the same time, one wonders how the hope of marginalized, oppressed persons and groups is possible without some kind of open, free, novel, and transformative possibility of the world described by process theologians.

If the world in relation of suffering, evil, and good is not something like what the process theologians describe, what hope is there for anyone, unless God unilaterally is going to make everything right and just; but there is no evidence for that anywhere in the world, past or present. Nevertheless, the social location and ideological misuse of the process view of the world with respect to suffering and evil lurks at its edges, if not at its center, as one of its ever-present liabilities.

Second, the religious issue of the worshipfulness of God is decisive in this debate. What makes God worthy of our worship? What traditional ideas of God cannot be reconstructed without God's being no longer worthy of our ultimate loyalty? This fundamental question is faced head-on by nearly all the participants in our discussion, but is perhaps put as bluntly as is possible by James Ross in his review of John Cobb's *God and the World*.

> I would rather spend a lifetime trying to reconcile God's power to bring about, merely by willing it, anything contingent with the reality of evil than to spend two minutes either praying to or worshiping a God who is neither responsible for evil nor capable of having done anything about it. The reality of evil is of no philosophical importance unless we are prepared to consider the existence of a being who was able to do something about it.[47]

This criticism is put less rhetorically and dogmatically by Wolfhart Pannenberg:

> I have a basic hesitation to think of God precisely in the same way as we think of finite things. Maybe that is the most important philosophical point at stake here. If we conceive of God as finite, we have not conceived of God at all. My question concerning the Whiteheadian doctrine of God is whether he has really spoken of God at all. I'm very uncertain about that. I agree with Langdon Gilkey's argument here, that Whitehead has not conceived of God as creator in the sense of the Jewish and Christian traditions. He didn't want to, but of course the Whiteheadian theologians do.[48]

Many people find process theology to be religiously inadequate. That is the most serious charge to be brought against it. If one's religious life is grounded more in confidence in power than in passion, the process God is likely to seem like the comic's underachiever or the theologian's grade-level achiever, not the God of Christian faith. If process theology does not pare away God's power, or does not put God on a leash, it does redefine power to such an extent that many no longer find God worthy of their worship and loyalty. As John Roth puts it, "A God of such weakness, no matter how much he suffers, is rather pathetic. God though he may be, Griffin's God is too small. He inspires little awe, little sense of holiness."[49]

The issue goes to the heart of the nature of the religious life long before it is formulated in theological beliefs. I want to argue that devotion to the faithful and compassionate power of creation and transformation is more religiously attractive and effective than devotion to brute force or hidden omnipotence or even sovereignty. But that is a religious confession, and clearly is not the confession of everyone, and, what I may finally have to recognize and concede, is perhaps not for the vast majority of Christians.

The reasons for such a confession or refusal are not all reducible to gender or temperament. There are sufferers, and they are not all Calvinists, who have been able to endure their suffering only by believing that a perfectly good and omnipotent God did in fact cause or will their baby to die or their adolescent to destroy their life. The world is so chaotic and threatening that only an omnipotent God who somehow causes or permits everything can assure them that there is meaning in whatever happens. There is, finally, no way to settle this controversy by logical argument, or perhaps even by an intuitive appeal to evidence. However, I will argue in the next chapter that Christian faith, primarily on the grounds of its trinitarian liturgies, hymns, and creeds, is so biased toward the power of identification, compassion, and transformation instead of brute power that one is in fact more Christian than the other. Nevertheless, the issue is not all that clear-cut, and much of the tradition of the church, liturgical, creedal, and theological, has been on the side of the theist on this divergence.

Third, at least a few critics are candid enough to admit that this is to a degree a macho issue of power. Perhaps "the most unkindest cut of all" (Brutus's ingratitude to Caesar), at least for any middle-aged male like myself who finds process theology attractive, is made by George Forrell, who applies this analogy to process theologians.

> Some writing by theologians in their early middle-age seems to be characterized by a startling loss of nerve. They have reached their male menopause . . . and the debilitating aspect of this development is their brazen attempt to make this personal debility normative for the entire Christian movement. Why do they have to project their theological impotence on everybody else? . . . Menopause may be a real crisis for a person, but is it hardly the end of human reproduction?[50]

Finally, there is the danger of what Ronald Goetz calls, in a *Christian Century* article, "the rise of a new orthodoxy" among some contemporary theologians. He refers to the dominance of the theme in contemporary theology of the suffering God. Among some true believers it has become just that, and this new orthodoxy has tended to present itself just like every other orthodoxy, namely, as the only possible appropriate and credible set of beliefs for a true Christian (or for any truly humane or rational person).

The charge by some overzealous process theologians that the entire tradition is indubitably wrong and that only process thinkers are reasonable, decent, and "tc" (theologically correct) theologians is, in my opinion, simply wrong. Delwin Brown says, in his review of Barry Whitney's *Evil and the Process God,* that the book's "main purpose is to stimulate a careful consideration of the process viewpoint. It may fail to do so, however, not because it fails as a compelling presentation of Hartshorne and his allies, but because it does not do justice to the complexity of the traditional theism which process thinkers attack."[51]

Process thinkers almost invariably identify the Christian God with philosophical theism, in some ways a medieval and modern construct in its strictest sense. Process critics seldom identify the Christian God with trinitarianism. By doing this they claim that the classical theistic God is static and unaffected by the suffering of the world. But on historical grounds process theologians are simply wrong in identifying the Christian concept of God with theism. The traditional concept of God, not only in liturgy and piety but in dogmatic theology as well, and especially in the creeds, is defined also by trinitarianism, probably as much as it is by philosophical theism.

The trinitarian God is, as I will argue in the next chapter, also related to and affected by the world, as is the process God. One can ask, to be sure (as I will), to what extent in essentialist doctrines of the Trinity the relatedness of God is confined internally to the Godhead and is related only secondarily to the world. And much traditional trinitarian dogma has been interpreted within theistic assumptions and guidelines. Nevertheless, at least some forms of trinitarianism, and especially in the last quarter century throughout the Christian world, entail an essential dynamism and relatedness within their trinitarian concept of God, and most contemporary economic interpretations of the Trinity have even gone so far as to use Luther's language about "the crucified God."

Although much of this book, in one way or another, and to one degree or another, has loosely assumed and been a soft defense of the process approach to our question, I want to conclude this chapter by highlighting two strengths of the technical process theodicies, such as those of Griffin, Hartshorne, Whitney, and others, as they relate to our question.

First, insofar as the development of a full-blown theodicy is a legitimate and important theological task, process theology offers the best full-blown theodicy that it is possible to develop. It is, I believe, the most adequate strict theodicy; that is, it is comprehensive, coherent, and most adequate to Christian scripture, tradition, and our experience of ourselves and our world. Process theodicy is the most compelling of the available technical theodicies in the contemporary theological scene.

Many theologians today, as I discussed in chapter 1, refuse to accept the development of any kind of theodicy. Some do so because theodicy today, they argue, must be replaced by anthropodicy; others, because of the ideological dangers in any kind of theodicy; and still others, because any coherent scheme in the postmodern world is by definition ideological or illusory. A few, however, such as John Hick, John Roth, Stephen Davis, and Frederick Sontag, do offer full-blown theodicies. But I believe process theodicy is the most plausible and compelling of any full-blown theodicy.

Even though I am very skittish about accepting a process theodicy in the strict sense as having reduced the problem of suffering and evil to the "so-called problem of evil,"[52] because I believe every metaphyical system is an imaginative construction of one way one might understand our experience and the world, I still accept it as the best approach, or perspective, or picture of God and the world we have available for our efforts to explore our questions about suffering and evil. One does not have to argue that process theology is the only or the final coherent answer any rational person must believe in order to find it to be the most adequate and the most compelling orientation to the problem in the contemporary world. Many of us, given our understanding of the Christian tradition, our own experience, and our quest for some kind of inclusive perspective on suffering and evil, find process philosophy and theology to be the most plausible in our contemporary context. In my own case, however, I do not want to become a scholastic Whiteheadian theologian, and I believe our actual experience offers too many anomolies to make any system fully adequate. Nevertheless, I find it to be the most useful of all the philosophical frameworks available today.

Second, more specifically, the major contribution of process theology to contemporary theodicy is that it provides a theological framework within which one can literally mean that God is a related, caring, and responding God in the midst of our suffering. When pastors as theologians assure the sufferers in their congregations that "God is the God who understands and responds," they can mean it directly and properly in process theology. There is no waffling or weaseling, no "Well, of course, we know God transcends our suffering, but God has a good reason for permitting this to happen to us," when a pastor preaches and counsels out of a process perspective.

Most classical theisms have denied that any of the language of suffering and piety tells us anything proper about God. Many theological students were convinced by their teachers to believe that all our language about God either is really about ourselves and our experience or at most is only indirectly about God. Religious language is strictly mythological, symbolic, or metaphoric, so if we speak of God as loving us or suffering with us or transforming us, we do not mean to be taken literally or even analogically. Thus, we say, under our breath as reflective religious people or theologians, "Of course, we do not mean this to be taken as really telling us what God is like, but since it makes us feel better, we will use this little pious deception to underwrite our illusions. After all, the real cash value of the language of preaching and pastoral care is its therapeutic value, and religious illusions are more useful than others for most people, especially lay people, so I will keep them alive."

But if the theologian or pastor longs to say (and mean), "When I talk about God as loving, caring, understanding, suffering with us, and transforming our world, I mean that God literally loves us and cares about our suffering, that God really knows what we are feeling because God feels it too, that God faithfully is seeking to redeem our suffering," then process theodicy is a most likely candidate from a theological perspective to fulfill that need.

At the very least, we can see that we need a radically different concept of God today when we encounter the suffering and evil of our time. The need for a more adequate concept of God as the grounds for our understanding and our religious response to suffering has been expressed by Norman Adams in his review of Rabbi Kushner's book.

> Kushner is surely right about the will of God. I, too, am horrified when someone says it must have been the will of God that my own son was killed by a drunken driver. I want no part of such a God. But neither do I want a limited God. Western theology is going to have to do a better job in solving the problem of evil than Kushner has done. Perhaps the good Rabbi is telling us that we are faced with a growing need to revise the inherited models of Jewish and Christian theism.[53]

Whether process theology is the compelling, or even the most adequate or plausible way to talk about the Christian God at the end of the twentieth century is certainly open to debate. But I maintain on the basis of scripture, experience, tradition, and reason that we need a thoroughgoing reconception of our concept of God if we are going to discover a plausible understanding and powerful response to our experience of evil. At the center of that reconception must be a reconception of divine power. On that assertion both process panentheism and trinitarianism agree in offering a theological interpretation and response to our experience of suffering and evil.

8

"God with Us"

The Triune God and Human Suffering

◁ In his memoirs, *Night*, Elie Wiesel recounts an incident in the concentration camp at Buna during the Holocaust. A power station had been blown up, and the Gestapo suspected sabotage. A young child, a servant of one of the overseers, was implicated in the plot, but would not name any of the conspirators. So the S.S. sentenced the child to death, alongside two other prisoners. The three were led in chains to the assembly place and hanged simultaneously. "Where is God? Where is He?" someone standing behind Wiesel asked.

> Then the march past began. The two adults were no longer alive. Their tongues hung swollen, blue-tinged. But the third rope was still moving; being so light, the child was still alive. . . .
>
> For more than half an hour he stayed there, struggling between life and death, dying in slow agony under our eyes. And we had to look him full in the face. He was still alive when I passed in front of him. His tongue was still red, his eyes were not yet glazed.
>
> Behind me, I heard the same man asking:
>
> "Where is God now?"
>
> And I heard a voice within me answer him:
>
> Where is He? Here he is—He is hanging here on this gallows.[1]

What does Wiesel mean in this passage? Does he mean God ceased to exist with the death of this child during the Holocaust? Does he mean that God also suffered the death of the boy on the gallows? Does he mean that God is being blasphemed or mocked by the soldiers and the onlookers? Or is God being held up before the onlookers as judge of the executioners and sustainer of the victim?

This story has been an enigma to me since I first read the book.[2] But this story from modern Jewish experience reminds me of the primary Christian understanding and answer to the problem of the place of God in human suffering. From a Christian perspective, suffering is neither explained nor eliminated by theological explanation; it is entered into and transformed by God. God undergoes our suffering with us in order to transform it from within. The answer to suffering is an Answerer, the God who can triumph over our suffering because God can absorb it and transform it within the divine life.

Immutability or Incarnation:
The Suffering and Transforming God

Perhaps the end of theism had to begin to dawn in order to disclose the existential relevance of a doctrine of the Trinity which must be grounded and explicated anew.[3]

I will state the thesis of my concluding chapter as directly as I can.

1. The twin concepts of the suffering God and the transforming God are the core of any distinctively Christian answer to the problem of evil.

2. The reason this is the most distinctively Christian answer is that it is central to the doctrine of the Trinity. The trinitarian concept of God is more normative for what Christians have to say about God and human suffering than is classical theism. For Christians, Trinity is the definitive liturgical name for God; trinitarian doctrine grows out of the life of Christian worship and reflection. Trinitarian descriptions of God have deeper claims on the life of the Christian than do the intuitions of classical theism, which lie more in Greek philosophy than in Christian worship and practice. The Trinity is a distinctive concept of God.

For Christians this question [about the persistence and power of evil in the world] can be answered affirmatively if the lordship of God is the ministry, crucifixion, and resurrection of Jesus Christ. . . . The crucial point is that a trinitarian understanding of divine providence and the reality of evil is marked not by a pagan notion of God as sheer almightiness but by the power of love at work in the ministry, cross, and resurrection of Jesus. . . . The power of the triune God is not raw omnipotence but the power of suffering, liberating, and reconciling love."[4]

3. The concepts of the relationality of God, and so the suffering and transforming power of God, contrary to what some process theologians claim, is not unique to process concepts of God, but is a common idea shared by trinitarian Christians and process theologians.[5] There are vast differences between theologians who work out of trinitarian dogmatic framework and those who work from a neoclassical philosophical perspective. These theologians differ on methodology, on the sources and norms for their claims, and on their interpretation of the classic loci of Christian thought. But I claim that these differences are, when it comes to the question of God and human suffering, much closer together in their understanding of the power of God and human suffering, than are the triune God and classical theism.

4. Although there is no *one* Christian answer to the problem of suffering and evil, there is a common *disposition* to most Christian views, all along the con-

tinuum from naturalism to trinitarianism, so that one can claim that the suffering and transforming power of God is the distinctively Christian contribution to the problem of theodicy.

The concept of a suffering God is in some respects a problematic, if not repugnant, idea to some Christians. Logically, how can an immutable being undergo the change and jeopardy of finitude? Religiously, how can a mutable deity be God? It is ludicrous, is it not, to think of the infinite God being liable to the conditions of the world? A vulnerable deity is akin to the divine ruler, Hirohito, whose divinity was established in Japan by his descent from the Sun Goddess, but who, because he was subject to finitude, could be demoted from god to mere head of state in 1946, and then to merely another mortal when he later died of intestinal cancer. This is not what a true God is like.

The Stoics believed that because no one could be greater than God, no one could influence God, and therefore God must be incapable of undergoing the experiences of the world. This assumption was taken over by the early Christian theologians as well. Throughout the trinitarian and christological controversies, both the orthodox Christians and the heretics, such as Arius, were in accord on this issue. Athanasius, in his fourth-century *Orations against the Arians,* could not conceive of a God who suffers, at least not in God's deity.

> So, then, let no one be scandalized by the human characteristics [of Christ]. Rather, let people see that the Logos himself is impassible by nature and that he nevertheless has these passions predicated of him in virtue of the flesh he took on, since they are proper to the flesh and the body itself is proper to the Savior. Furthermore, he himself remains as he is—impassible in nature. He takes no hurt from these passions, but on the contrary destroys them and brings them to nothing. And human beings, because their own passions have been transferred to the impassible and abolished, are henceforth becoming impassible and free of them to all eternity. . . . And since it is foreign to God, we do not reckon it to the deity of the Logos but to his humanity, for even though "the Logos became flesh," and even though the flesh became, in the Logos, a bearer of the divine, nevertheless the grace and power come from the Logos. To be sure, he does the works of the Father through the medium of the flesh, but the passions of the flesh are no less evident in him.[6]

This understanding of the divine continued into the development of the doctrine of divine *apatheia* in classical theism.

Even by the third century many Christian theologians had declared as heresy the doctrine of Patripassianism, the belief that God the Father suffered, and later in subsequent christological controversy theopaschitism was also condemned for arguing that God suffered in the death of Jesus Christ. Some contemporary trinitarian theologians continue to hold that God cannot undergo the pain and anguish of the world. Some mean that God the Father could not know pain, and some continue to mean, along with Athanasius, that Jesus Christ in his divine nature did not endure the agony of the cross. Many Christians can say, along with Rabbi Kushner, "Post-biblical Judaism . . . occasionally spoke of a God who suffers. . . . I don't know what it means for God to suffer."[7]

It is significant that many Christians in their innermost core believe that if God is subject to the same anguish we endure, then God cannot resolve our suffering. The issue, for them, is not so much doctrinal debate as it is the religious import of this ancient teaching. Unless something or someone is wholly beyond the travail of the world, they believe, there is no adequate answer to the problem of human suffering. And so God in Godself has to be thought of as impassible and immutable. The only conquest of suffering can be by a "high voltage" God, a God who is in control and can wage a conquest of evil as a power from outside who is invulnerable and above it all, like Saint George slaying the dragon, or Shane restoring law and order, or Rambo reclaiming the country's honor.

But the biblical and theological answer to human suffering is not the conquest from without but rather from within, not the conquest of omnipotence or brute power but the endurance and transformation of suffering love. The Bible, Terrence Fretheim argues, describes three sufferings of God, namely, God rejected, God with us, and God for us.[8] And Marjorie Suchocki argues that the doctrine of the Trinity introduces a dynamic principle into the immutability of the classical theistic God.

> And so it is not sufficient to speak of the classical God as simply the immutable being containing all power, presence, and knowledge; the classical God must be dynamic as well. To account for this, the doctrine of the Trinity answered the tension between immutability and grace, suggesting a divine story that touched human history. . . . In a sense, the doctrine of immutability guaranteed the qualities in God that contrasted with and answered the human problem of evil, and the doctrine of the Trinity guaranteed the ability to apply these qualities to human history.[9]

The suffering of the relational God as a central concept in a distinctively Christian understanding of and response to suffering and evil has become a major theme in recent post-Holocaust, post-Hiroshima theology, among Christians in both the West and the East. Indeed, that theme has become so eminent in Christian theology that by mid-century Daniel Day Williams, in *What Present Day Theologians Are Thinking,* could call it a "structural shift in the Christian mind."[10] The theme was so well established by the 1980s that Ronald Goetz complained in a 1986 issue of *Christian Century* that because of the decline of Christendom, the rise of democratic aspirations, the problem of suffering and evil, and a new scholarly reappraisal of the Bible, the suffering of God has become "the new orthodoxy."[11]

Many examples can be given to show how widespread this "revolution" in the understanding of God has become in recent Christian theology. On the continent, Karl Barth's *Church Dogmatics,* Karl Rahner's *The Trinity,* Eberhard Jungel's *The Doctrine of the Trinity: God's Being Is in Becoming,* Jurgen Moltmann's *The Crucified God,* Wolfhart Pannenberg's *Systematic Theology,* and

Dorothy Soelle's *Suffering* stand out. Among liberation theologians, especially Latin American and feminist, Leonardo Boff's *Trinity and Society,* Elizabeth Johnson's *She Who Is: The Mystery of God in Feminist Theological Discourse,* and Catherine LaCugna's *God with Us: The Trinity and Christian Life* have been significant. Okechukwu Ogbonnaya has contributed to the discussion of social views of God from an African perspective in his *On Communitarian Divinity: An African Interpretation of the Trinity.*

Similarly, the theme has appeared in the theologies of many Asian Christians. From Japan, Jung Lee's *God Suffers for Us* and his *The Trinity in Asian Perspective,* Kazoh Kitamori's *Theology of the Pain of God,* C. S. Song's *The Compassionate God,* and Kosuke Koyama's *Mount Fuji and Mount Sinai,* and from the Korean-American perspective, Andrew Sung Park's *The Wounded Heart of God* all speak of the suffering God. From a North American narrative perspective, we may note William Placher's *Narratives of a Vulnerable God: Christ, Theology, and Scripture,* in addition to Ted Peters's *God as Trinity: Relationality and Temporality in the Divine Life,* Arthur McGill's *Suffering: A Test of Theological Method,* Douglas Hall's *God and Human Suffering,* Gedes McGreggor's *He Who Lets Us Be,* and Paul Schilling's *God and Human Anguish.* Whether or not these books on the triune God as relational constitute "a new orthodoxy," the thoroughness of the reconception of God from a triune point of view can scarcely be doubted.

The Triune God
and Suffering

The power of God is best understood as solidarity. The Trinity is a model of the very being of God as solidarity. It is a perspective on the being of God which is directly counter to the uses of monotheism as a legitimation of the violence of the One against the All.[12]

I will go directly to the heart of the matter. Although the doctrine of the Trinity can be interpreted within a theistic framework, especially around such ideas as immutability, *apatheia,* and omnipotence, the doctrine of the triune God can also be interpreted within a radically different perspective on divine relationality, affectability, and power. When Christology becomes central to the doctrine of God, as it clearly has in trinitarian theology since Karl Barth, then the concepts of divine suffering and divine power among classical theists get radically revised.[13]

The concept of the triune God as it bears on the problem of suffering and evil has much affinity with process theology's criticism of theism and its concept of the relational God. Barbara Zikmund states the claim as directly as it can be stated. "The distinctive contribution of Christianity was not monotheism, but a trinitarian understanding of God which recognized differences in the work of God in history, and also maintained the unity of God."[14] The concept of God, and more particularly the concept of the power of God, is consistently redescribed by the Gospel narratives and by trinitarian doctrine in terms of the life, crucifixion, and resurrection of Jesus Christ. The triune God is the relational God who knows suffering and transformation within God's own life. "The crucial point is that a trinitarian understanding of divine providence and the reality of evil is marked not by a pagan notion of God as sheer almightiness but by the power of love at work in the ministry, cross, and resurrection of Jesus."[15] The kind of power that is characteristic of the triune God is not immutability and raw omnipotence but the power of suffering, liberating, reconciling, and transforming love.

Eberhard Jungel formulates his doctrine of God on the assumption that all talk about God must be trinitarian, not theistic. It must be trinitarian because that is what God has revealed Godself to us to be. This revelation is based not so much on the scanty trinitarian formulas in the New Testament but on the story of Jesus Christ, most especially on the testimony of the cross, for our knowledge of God. The doctrine of the Trinity is shorthand for the significance of the death of Jesus Christ for the being of God. In his first book, *The Doctrine of the Trinity: God's Being is in Becoming,* which is essentially a paraphrase of Karl Barth's exposition of the being of God, Jungel argues that the doctrine of God must begin not with a phenomenology of the divine being, as Charles Hartshorne and Schubert Ogden do,[16] but with God's being as it is revealed to us. The doctrine of the Trinity is an interpretation of God's self-revelation, so is first and foremost the self-interpretation of God. God is what God makes Godself known to be.

Jungel's first book concentrates on the identity of God's being. The doctrine of the Trinity is God's self-revealed knowledge of the oneness and the differentiation of God's being. The Trinity shows that becoming and relatedness instead of being and aseity characterize God.[17] God is three modes of being constituted by their mutual interrelationship. These three modes of being are distinguished within the divine being but are held together by a self-relatedness. Indeed, the modes of divine being are so interrelated that each mode of God's being becomes what it is only together with the other two modes of being. Therefore, "God's being as the being of God the Father, Son, and Holy Spirit is their being in becoming."[18] This relationality is not rooted in ontological necessity but in God's freedom of decision as an event. God wills to be God for us and with us who are not God. God wills to be God for us in relationship. God's being in act becomes manifest to us in the temporal history of Jesus Christ.[19] Consequently, God undergoes the suffering of the opposition to God represented by the suffering of Jesus on the cross.

In his second book, *God as the Mystery of the World: On the Foundation of the Theology of the Crucified One in the Dispute between Theism and Atheism,* Jungel discusses the traditional distinction between the immanent and economic doctrines of the Trinity. Here he accepts Karl Rahner's rule that the immanent Trinity is the economic Trinity and the economic Trinity is the immanent Trinity. Jungel maintains that the immanent and economic doctrines of the Trinity together show that interrelationship exists not only within the divine life but between God and the world. God's relationship with the world outside Godself corresponds with the relationality of the divine life within itself because God in God's being is historical. More specifically, when one understands the way in which Jesus Christ constitutes the divine life, one sees that "here is a correspondence between the inner life of God and God's external relationship to the creation."[20] A separation between the economic and immanent interpretations of the Trinity, then, will not stand. God's being is not only internal relatedness, but because of what constitutes the internal relationship within the divine being (Father, Son, and Holy Spirit), God's being is also God's relation with the world through Jesus Christ. Likewise, the economic doctrine of the Trinity, which considers God's history with humanity through the man Jesus, is also decisive for understanding the immanent doctrine of the Trinity. The economic Trinity speaks of God's history, while the immanent speaks of God's historicity.[21] God's history is God's coming to humanity, while God's historicity is God's being as it comes to humanity. This is the way God is God.

God's being is, therefore, the being of the triune God. The guiding motif for the triune understanding of God is the identification of God with the man Jesus. The crucified man, Jesus of Nazareth, his life and his passion, provides the foundation of faith and knowledge of the triune God. The suffering of Jesus says something not only about Jesus and his relationship to God but also about God's relationship to Jesus.[22] The suffering of Jesus, therefore, leads to statements about the being of God. Jesus' death was not merely an event among humanity but also an event between this man and God, so that Jesus' Godforsakenness is now seen as God's most authentic work. His voice is God's own voice.

In the light of the Easter faith, the cross is no other than faith in the crucified Jesus of Nazareth as God's Son. In the light of the resurrection, God himself was the event that happened on the cross. God identified with Jesus on the cross. To identify with another means the capacity to differentiate oneself. Although this differentiation does not mean or lead to disunity in God, it does mean that the other profoundly defines God's own being. "In this sense, God's identification with the dead Jesus implies a self-differentiation on God's part. The being of this dead man defines God's own being in such a way that one must speak of a differentiation between God and God. But it must immediately be added that it is an act of God himself who effects his identity with the dead Jesus and as its precondition the differentiation of God and God."[23]

This differentiation, though, is not coerced on the being of God. Rather, God defines himself in a free decision when he identified with the dead Jesus. "The kerygma of the Resurrected One proclaims the Crucified One as the self-definition of God."[24] The resurrection is not only a divine action, but is part of the divine being. The divine life has absorbed death into itself. The resurrection is the transformation of death through its reception into the divine life.

The trinitarian interpretation of the suffering and cross of Jesus for the being of God, then, is summarized by Jungel in the following manner:

> For the God who identifies himself with the dead Jesus encounters himself in the death of Jesus in such a way that he participates in Jesus' God-forsakenness. But that is a meaningful assertion only if it is possible to make a real differentiation between God and God. In that God differentiates himself and *thus,* in unity with the crucified Jesus, suffers as God the Son being forsaken by God the Father, he is God the Reconciler. God reconciles the world with himself in that in the death of Jesus he encounters himself as *God the Father* and *God the Son* without becoming disunited in himself. On the contrary, in the encounter of God and God, of the Father and Son, God reveals himself as the one who he is. He is God the Spirit, who lets Father and Son be one in the death of Jesus, in true distinction, in this encounter. The "chain of love" emphasizes God's eternal being in the death of Jesus. Thus God is differentiated in a threefold way in his unity: in the encounter of Father and Son, related to each other as Spirit. But in the fatal encounter, God remains *one* God. For he remains as Father and Son in the Spirit the one "event God."[25]

The most influential advocate of a trinitarian revision of theism and divine power among contemporary theologians in North America has been Jurgen Moltmann. His work focuses primarily, as does Jungel's, on the consequences of a theology of the crucified Christ for "a revolution in the concept of God."[26] We must, he argues, understand the being of God from the death of Jesus Christ. Moltmann seeks to avoid the interpretation of the cross as divine abuse and punishment by moving the cross from soteriology (the punishment of the Son for our sins) to theology (a statement about God in Godself). The cross, Moltmann argues, stands at the heart of the trinitarian being of God.[27] "The fault of earlier Protestant theology was that it did not look at the cross in the context of the relationship of the Son to the Father, but related it directly to mankind as an expiatory death for sin."[28]

Moltmann makes an iconoclastic distinction between a trinitarian theology of the cross and philosophical theism. For theism the nature of divine being is determined by its unity and indivisibility, its lack of beginning and end, its immovability and immutability. Without this kind of God, theists argue, finite being could not find a support against the threatening nothingness of death. Therefore, suffering and death must be excluded from the divine being.

> Death, suffering and mortality must therefore be excluded from the divine being. Christian theology has adopted this concept of God from philosophical theology down to the present day, because in practice down to the present day Christian faith has taken into itself the religious need of finite, threatened and mortal man for security in a higher omnipotence and authority. . . . The God who is the subject of suffering cannot be truly God.[29]

Such a concept of God, however, Moltmann argues, can only give rise to protest atheism, since suffering and death are real experiences of the real world. Atheism, then, is "the twin brother" of philosophical theism, for such a God inevitably becomes "the monotheism of Satan."

Christian faith, however, stands against the theistic concept of God. The doctrine of the Trinity speaks of God in relation to the incarnation and the death of Jesus. God suffered in the suffering of Jesus; God died on the cross of Christ, so that we might live and rise in God's future. God and suffering are not contradictions within a christological perspective, for God's being is in suffering, and the suffering is in God's being itself because God is love.

Moltmann does claim that God is not changeable, but changelessness is a simile. That is, God is not changeable as creatures are changeable. Thus, although God is not changeable in every respect, God is free to change Godself, able to allow Godself to be changed by others of God's own free will by the incarnation in Christ. Furthermore, God does not suffer like creatures; creatures suffer unwillingly, but in Christ God voluntarily opens Godself to the possibility of being affected by another. Suffering, therefore, is not a deficiency in God's being, but God suffers out of the fullness of God's being, that is, out of God's love. Another way to say this is to say that in God's case, this is an active, not a passive suffering.

A trinitarian theology of the cross, then, provides the uniquely Christian concept of God. Trinitarianism marks the Christian concept of God off not only from polytheism and pantheism but also from monotheism. *In trinitarian thought, the death of Jesus says something about the being of God.*

> To understand what happened between Jesus and his God and Father on the cross, it is necessary to talk in trinitarian terms. The Son suffers dying, the Father suffers the death of the Son. The grief of the Father here is just as important as the death of the Son. The Fatherlessness of the Son is matched by the Sonlessness of the Father, and if God has constituted himself as the Father of Jesus Christ, then he also suffers the death of his Fatherhood in the death of the Son. . . . The Son suffers in his love being forsaken by the Father as he dies. The Father suffers in his love the grief of the death of the Son.[30]

All the suffering of the world is encompassed in the affliction of the Son, the grief of the Father, and the comfort of the Spirit.

Moltmann ends, then, with a new concept of God in contrast to classical theism. The doctrine of the Trinity is not only a description of the economy of salvation; it says something about who God is in Godself. The unity and trinity of God belong together. The suffering of the Son says not only something about Jesus and the function of Jesus for us, but also something about the eternal relationship between the Son and the Father. The relationship between the Father and the Son is not static, but is a living relationship within God think that the unity of the dialectical history of Father and Son and Spirit cross on Golgotha, full of tension as it is, can be described so to spea spectively as 'God.'"[32] The cross does not bring an end to the trinit tory in *God* between the Father and the Son in the Spirit, but rath up. The trinitarian identification of God indicates that there is a history and interrelationship within God.

Andrew Park, from a Korean-American perspective, goes a step beyond Jungel and Moltmann when he describes the "wounded heart of God."[33] Divine impassibility and omnipotence are as problematic for him as for Jungel and Moltmann, partly on christological grounds and partly on the grounds of process theology. God suffers not because sin is all-powerful, but because God's love for humanity is too ardent to be apathetic toward suffering humanity. Unlike process theisms, Park argues that no power in the universe makes God vulnerable, but a victim's suffering breaks the heart of God. "To me, God suffers for the Son on the cross not only out of God's love for the Son, but also God's love for humanity."[34] The cross represents God's participation not only in the suffering and death of Jesus, but in the suffering of all victims. Han is that point of contact between God and humanity.

Park, however, goes beyond Jungel and Moltmann to argue that God even needs salvation. God's han, the wounded heart of God, is not only a symbol of God's intent to save humanity but also the symbol of God's need for salvation. The cross is a symbol of God's crying for salvation because God cannot save Godself. "If salvation is relational, then one cannot save oneself. God needs salvation."[35] The destiny of God involves the destiny of humanity. The salvation of humanity is interpenetrated with the salvation of God. "When the cross of Jesus Christ is seen from the perspective of the oppressed, it signifies God's suffering *with them;* seen from the perspective of the oppressors, the cross means God's suffering *because of them.*"[36] When one knows the reality of God only in the midst of experiencing han in the world, the suffering of God sheds new light on the attributes of God. Omnipotence comes to mean "God's vulnerable love shown on the cross and in the death of Jesus is more powerful or persuasive than anything known to us."[37]

Some Differences
among Trinitarians

There are significant differences between trinitarian and process theologians. The doctrine of God as triune is not typically found within the conceptuality of process theology.[38] Also, it is impossible to take the process view of God in Whiteheadian and Hartshornian perspective as a restatement of trinitarian dogma. Instead, one can point out that some of the claims about the triune concept of God are coherent with some of the claims of a process concept of God, st especially in their common criticism of the classical theistic concept of Essentially, the categories of process theology provide one way of understanding God as the active, living, related, suffering, and loving God who is primary causative agency in the world and the chief recipient of what n the world; contemporary immanent and economic interpretations y, like Jungel's and Moltmann's, are other ways to reconstruct the

Christian concept of God, ways rooted more in the liturgical and dogmatic language of the church than either classical or neoclassical ways are located.

What is noteworthy about contemporary discussions about God, however, is the gradual convergence of two theological traditions. Theologians from both sides concur that monotheism, when unqualified or unnuanced, tends to present us with a transcendent supernatural being who is only externally related to the world and so is liable to all the criticisms reviewed earlier in the book. Also, trinitarian theologians talk about God in ways, and even in language, that are much closer to process theology than to classical theism, while some process theologians are increasingly interested in exploring the affinities between process and trinitarian language and relational concepts. Norman Pittenger initiated a reconsideration of convergences twenty years ago when he attempted a preliminary convergence of these two languages.

> The necessity is imposed upon contemporary Christian theologians to say that in his relationship with the creation God is indeed operative in the modes to which I have referred, while in his own existence those modes have some abiding counterpart in the unity of deity. Thus we wish to speak of God as the everlasting creative agency who works anywhere and everywhere, yet without denying the reality of creaturely freedom—hence we point toward God as Parent. We wish also to speak of God as so working that he acts with and besides his creation, by luring it and attracting it toward realizing its possibilities and thereby achieving the fulfillment or satisfaction which is its aim—hence we point toward God as Self-Expressive Word. And we wish finally to speak of God as active in and through his creation in its accepting or "prehending" the lure or attraction which is offered to it, and thereby perfecting and heightening the intensity of its life and achieving fulfillment or satisfaction through a response which is richer and more adequate than the possibilities available through creaturely action alone—hence we point toward God as the Responsive Agency who is the Holy Spirit.[39]

That discussion continues in the conversations between such people as Jungel, Moltmann, and Pannenberg, on the trinitarian side, and Bracken, Suchocki, Cobb, Griffin, Ford, and others, from the process side.[40]

There are similarities and differences between process and trinitarian concepts of God. I have indicated above some of the similarities both in agenda and ideas. There are, however, persisting differences.[41] Process theologians grant that the new trinitarian theologies talk about God as dynamic and relational, but this tends to be a relationship that exists primarily within the Godhead and only secondarily with the creation. Although the ultimate unity of God is communal, relational, and mutual, God is still *a se,* self-sufficient, whose inner self can, in no *essential* way, be related to that which is other than God's self. The problem, from a process point of view, is how a totally self-sufficient and self-contained God, which is only internally social, can have real relationships with anything outside Godself. The trinitarian answer, of course, is that by a free, unilateral decision, God chooses to relate to the world. The issue, though, is whether this is still a purely external relationship (with no effect on the divine being), as in theism, or how the world has any real effect on God (since the relationship is an eternal one between the Father and the Son through the Spirit within the Godhead), as in the revisionary trinitarianism of Jungel and Moltmann.

For process theologians, the relationship between God and the world can be real only if the world is essentially involved within the trinitarian life of God, that is, if God prehends the world in such a way that the world also constitutes the life of the trinitarian God. Strictly economic interpretations of the doctrine of the Trinity succeed in overcoming this debate, but such an interpretation of the Trinity is not a metaphysical doctrine of the triune identity of God, and so leaves the questions unanswered. Trinitarians like Jungel, Moltmann, and Rahner are clear that a separation between the economic and immanent doctrines of the Trinity cannot stand, but the debate remains between process and revisionary trinitarians about the extent to which the latter remain within the theistic set of assumptions about aseity.

There are also significant differences among the current interpreters of the trinitarian concept of God on the questions we have been exploring throughout the book about the nature of God. At least two questions are not settled simply by adopting a trinitarian instead of a process concept of God.

1. There is a divergence between trinitarians who believe God suffers because God is internally related to the world in Christ and so is affected by suffering and knows powerlessness, and those who believe God suffers simply because God in God's trinitarian life knows mutuality and in God's freedom and power wills to emulate that inner relatedness with the world through the incarnation. This difference over "real relations" exists between the process theologians and most trinitarians, but also among some trinitarians as well. In the cases of Jungel and Moltmann, for example, significant as are their differences from classical theism, God's powerlessness (on the cross) is a self-willed powerlessness and reflects the relationship between the Father and the Son and not an internal (constitutive) relationship between God and the world. The world depends on God for its being, but God in no way depends on the world for the divine being.

2. There is a split between those who advocate the traditional immanent or essentialist doctrines of the Trinity and some of the recent strictly economic doctrines of the Trinity. In the former, represented, for example, by Jungel, Moltmann, Rahner, and Arthur McGill, interrelationship and mutuality take place within the Godhead. There is nothing essential in the relationship between God and the world, even though there is talk about interdependence between the two. Talk about mutuality refers to the divine reality in itself; talk about the equality of the Father, Son and Spirit is talk about "intradivine" equality. It is the Trinity locked up in itself in mutuality, so to speak.

In recent economic views of the Trinity, represented by Catherine LaCugna and Barbara Zikmund, talk about the mutuality of the "persons" of the triune God is talk about the work of the divine "persons" in our salvation. The economic view has come to shape much of the contemporary discussion. As Catherine LaCugna says, "The Bible, liturgy and early Christian creeds do not show any predilection to settle questions of God's 'inner' life; they speak only of God's presence in the world through the Son and Spirit."[42] Talk about the Trinity is talk about where the divine "persons" actually exist and are known intimately in our history.

I will not discuss this point in great detail, but I will show how it works itself out in a couple of cases. Moltmann tries to avoid any charge of a finite God, or even Patripassianism, by arguing that the Father and the Son both experience the crucifixion but experience it differently. The Son suffers the agony of God-forsakenness, while the Father suffers the grief of the loss of his Son. But this suffering is experienced by God internally within the Godhead. There is no "threat" in his teaching that God is limited or internally (necessarily) related to the world in God's being in any sense.

There are other trinitarians, however, such as kenotic theologians, who argue that the being of God even as "absolute" or beyond finitude must be reconceived in the light of God's economy, or God's self-giving love. Moving beyond the idea that God gave up or self-limited some of the divine attributes during the incarnational state as the Son, Geddes McGreggor proposes to rethink God's being, including God the Father, in the light of God's work of sacrificial love. This requires a new concept of God which goes beyond even Moltmann's revision of the Trinity. The kenotic theme in Philippians, McGreggor argues, should be used to understand all God's characteristics and actions, not merely God the incarnate second person of the triunity. That is, God is *always* and in *all respects* self-humbling and self-limiting, not simply in the second person.

A God Involved with Suffering

I will not pursue in detail the differences between contemporary theopassionist theologies. What I want to maintain is that, quite apart from the debate about how process theology is to be evaluated in relation to the dogma of the Trinity on its philosophical doctrine of the temporal God, and vice versa, and quite apart from the internal debates among the new immanent and economic trinitarian doctrines of the suffering God, the triune God of the Nicene and Chalcedonian Christian creeds is absorbed in our suffering in ways that are far more thorough and consequential for our thinking about God and human suffering than any form of the classical theistic God has conceived or even entertained.

The same claim can be made about the biblical God. I discussed earlier Terrence Fretheim's exegesis of the theme of the repentance of God, that is, God's grief, compassion, and retraction in the Old Testament, a theme that shows the extent to which the loving and gracious God will go in order to execute God's uncompromising salvific intentions. Walter Brueggemann argued the same point when he showed how God got uneasy at times about the qualities in the common theology that make a god God, and in God's heart, anguished by the disobedience of humans, seeks other options in accomplishing God's purposes.

The point I am making here is that the God who experiences, understands, embraces, and transforms our suffering is not the possession of process theologies. The concept of the suffering and transforming God stands also and equally at the heart of the dogma of the Trinity. This idea of God is investment capital in the bank of the Christian scriptures and orthodox theology when faced with human suffering. However, the idea has been paying very low dividends in our efforts to cover the expenses of theological understanding, pastoral care, and preaching on evil and suffering. I can put my claim bluntly: The concept of the suffering God is intrinsic to the Christian idea of God, for *the Christian God finally is not the God of classical theism but the biblical, trinitarian, and process God.* God is not defined by aseity or impassibility or immutability or omnipotence; God is defined as the triune relational God of suffering and transforming love.

To put my point about the Trinity in the most direct way I can imagine of putting it, by using traditional symbols of the dogma: for Christians, God is not the Father who is usually conceived in classical theistic categories, but God is the Father and the Son and the Holy Spirit. The groaning and travail of the Holy Spirit and the agonizing and endurance of the Son are as *essential to what Christians mean by God* as is the transcendence and reliability of the Father. Such a trinitarian concept redefines what divine transcendence and reliability mean. In trinitarian doctrine, the theistic problem of how to reconcile the omnipotent power of the absolute, unitary, unrelated God to evil and suffering evaporates. Christians who take as normative that their scriptures and their creeds provide the definition of God should never have got themselves into the conceptual bind of theism to begin with. Their God is not the theistic God; their God is the triune, relational God. Robert Jenson, in *The Triune Identity,* provides this summary:

> Trinitarian discourse is Christianity's effort to identify the God who has claimed us. . . . "Father, Son, and Holy Spirit" become the church's name for its God because it packs into one phrase the content and logic of this God's identifying descriptions. . . . Christians bespeak God in a triune coordinate system; they speak to the Father, with the Son, in the Spirit, and only so bespeak God. . . . Only the Trinity as such is God by himself.[43]

Most Christian answers to suffering and anguish have been based on false assumptions about divine immutability and omnipotence. The former is the idea that there is at least one individual who stands outside our suffering, is unthreatened by it, and can rescue us from the outside. The latter is the idea that God does or could from the outside unilaterally use whatever power is necessary to eliminate suffering, but generally chooses not to in favor of some higher purpose.

However, "Not by might, nor by power, but by my spirit, says the Lord of hosts" to Zerubbabel in the vision of Zechariah. The significance of recent developments in biblical exegesis, process theology, and trinitarian theology is that many theologians have begun to question our normal understanding of power which underwrites our inherited concept of God, and this has had the effect of reformulating the Christian understanding of how God conquers the suffering and evil in our world. A trinitarian concept of God requires a revision of our normal assumption that power is brute force, the ability to coerce, and that it is imposed unilaterally from the outside. When power is defined in trinitarian and process terms, where God is no longer an isolated center of raw power out there but is defined by God's relations of love, the power to identify, to persuade, to transform, and to re-create reshapes our understanding of divine power.

God does not look on our suffering from the outside but from within, from the brow and hands of Jesus hanging on the cross. God is "on the gallows" (Wiesel), "the fellow sufferer who understands" (Whitehead), "on the cross" (Luther). What God reveals about Godself in the prison of our suffering and anguish is not the cause, or the character, or the ultimate meaning of that misery. As Kenneth Surin says in his *Theology and the Problem of Evil,* "The God who disengages himself from our afflictions cannot be justified, either by man or himself—the God who is a mere onlooker when confronted with gratuitous suffering is a demon and not a God."[44] God's answer is to enter the travail of life and to conquer the pain, suffering, travail, and evil from within. What God shows in the compassion of God's incarnation is the divine power that accepts, endures, and transforms our anguish. God doesn't provide us with a cosmic perspective on evil. God keeps company with those who suffer, rubs God's nose in it, feels what it is like to have a daughter or son who suffers, and transforms that suffering within the divine life.

I imagine God's economic advisers in their Monday board of directors meeting on the divine economy must have said to God that this kind of economic policy was a bad investment from the very beginning, that God should get out, cut God's losses, take a tax credit, forget it, and return to a solid investment in blue-chip power that all wise deities invest in. Why God chose to follow the foolishness instead of the wisdom of the world and even the wisdom of God's heavenly investment counselors, we do not know with certainty. But for trinitarian and process Christians this is the God we have on our hands, involved with us in the messiness and ambiguities of our lives in a way other than classical theism has taught us.

Unlike dualistic theodicies, which picture God as a fearful commander in chief threatened by an evil empire, the incarnate God does not set up a protective shield around God's vulnerable skies and zap the threatening evil satellites hovering overhead with invisible laser beams. Unlike in monistic theodicies, God is not a positive-thinking huckster who tries to divert our attention away from the grit and grime of life or to anesthetize us to massive suffering by helping us imagine some other more real world out there. Instead, God "emptied himself, taking the form of a slave, being born in human likeness.

And being found in human form, he humbled himself and became obedient to the point of death—even death on a cross" (Phil. 2:7–8).

The Conquest from Within:
Theodicy and Resurrection

It is important to note that Paul does not say in the Corinthian correspondence that Jesus' crucifixion is itself a model of power. He does say that God takes what is weak, "the word of the cross," and through it offers power to those who believe that the crucified Jesus is the Messiah.[45]

I am convinced, as was Paul Tillich, that although there are innumerable theories for understanding the dilemmas of our human lives, there are in the West two primary understandings and responses to human suffering. In *The Courage to Be,* Tillich claims Stoicism "is the only real alternative to Christianity in the Western world."[46] There are, finally, two options, one of resignation and the other of transformation. Even though Christianity, on the basis of its doctrine of creation, shares much in common with the Stoic idea of acceptance,[47] Stoic courage and Christian courage are finally very different. There is, finally, a fundamental difference between cosmic resignation of fate and divine transformation of suffering and evil. Stoic courage to accept and endure one's suffering is based on acceptance of the cosmos as it is, while Christian courage finally rests on confidence in the power of resurrection, re-creation, and transformation. To put the difference bluntly, the Christian vision of the world offers finally the reality of grace in the midst of suffering.

In Christian faith both the cross and the resurrection are intrinsic to the divine life. One cannot have one without the other and have the Christian perspective on human suffering. Thus, the Christian answer to the problem of suffering and evil is not only the identification of God with our suffering. That is but one side of the coin. It includes, also, the power of resurrection, of transformation, of hope in place of despair, of new life in the midst of death. Deep as the roots for such a conception of God's power are, these roots have had a difficult time sprouting and growing in the climate of the theistic assumptions of so much of Christianity.

A recovery of this concept of God is desperately needed by Christians today. As in most human relations, unilateral power is finally of little avail in accomplishing one's intentions. Who, through power tactics, can eliminate the self-destroying habits of a son or daughter who has fallen prey to hard drugs? What nation, through power alone, can ensure world peace? There is no sword that can cut away all forms of danger and distress when relationships are involved. Where persons are concerned, both human and divine, the qualities of empathy, of compassion, and of persuasion are the forms of power that are finally transformative. This is perhaps the deepest claim among all the ideas I have explored throughout this entire discussion. Unilateral power seems to be the ultimate power; if so God must be the ultimate form of that kind of power. But Christians, because of their bias toward a trinitarian instead of a theistic concept of God, believe that persuasive and transforming power is, all things considered, the real power at the heart of things.

Ultimately we will be either transfixed by evil or transformed by grace. When we take evil with full seriousness we are exposed to a reality so entrenched in human life and institutions that it may seem insuperable. Our honesty may invite paralysis. Walter Lowe dramatizes the way in which paralysis can occur in the face of honesty by comparing evil with the cobra. Remarkably, the cobra can devour a rabbit, even though the rabbit is faster. It does so because the moment they make eye contact, the rabbit is paralyzed. Trembling with fear, the victim stands frozen as the snake slowly, rhythmically, closes the distance, and then, at its leisure, strikes. "My point in invoking this image is that we too become paralyzed if we stare at evil too long. We find ourselves imitating it and thus serving it, hypnotized by its power. At such moments it is absolutely crucial that there be some other reality to which we can turn our gaze."[48]

What is the answer to suffering and evil, from the trinitarian point of view, on which we can depend? The answer is Christmas, where God's power hits us with all the force of a hint; the cross, where God's power of identification endures all its pain to the end; Easter, where life in all its travail is transformed into new life through the power of resurrection; and the kingdom of God, where the reign of God in the midst of suffering and evil is accomplished. If the cross and resurrection of Jesus Christ is God's final answer to our travail, then suffering is surmounted by going through it to possibilities of new life, and not around it. The courage that is given to faith in the presence of the crucified and resurrected Christ is the courage of acceptance, endurance, and transformation.

I need to be very clear on this point. Amid all the talk about the suffering God, God's vulnerability, God's compassion, and God's identification with us, the Christian answer is not simply that God looks on with sympathy or even empathy, helpless or powerless in the face of suffering and evil. The Christian answer does not repudiate every idea of divine power. Suffering and evil can be overcome as well as endured. Although acceptance does belong in the Christian lexicon on suffering, the final word is not resignation to inevitability but the grace of resurrection as transformation. Even though Christians have no grounds on which to believe their anguish can either be eluded or eliminated, they do have the promise of the power of the cross and resurrection of Christ. As Henry Nelson Wieman put it, "To enter into the love of God is not to abolish evil but to transmute it and triumph over it."[49]

This means, though, that Christian faith does reject—and thoroughly so— the models of triumph, victory, and conquest which Christian theology has consistently employed in its endeavor to interpret the meaning of the work of God in Christ. The cross and resurrection do not dispense with the idea of power, but they do transform it, radically transform it, for the victory of the cross-resurrection is not a victory from the outside which eliminates evil through a unilateral destruction of it; it is a victory from within which accepts and transforms death in all its forms into the possibility of new life.

If North American Christians are going to respond to suffering from a trinitarian and process point of view, we are going to have to modify our triumphalism or theology of glory with some of Luther's theology of the cross. Our robust theology of glory leads us to believe that God can abolish all our ills if God wants to, like the technician who runs a star-wars defense system that can demolish enemy satellites in the sky from a safe distance. Since God doesn't, we simmer in our juices of despair about why God is not doing this for us, and conclude either that God is not perfectly good, or that God's purposes are beyond our imagination, or, as some conclude, that God has no power at all.

But a theology of the cross is not a theology of impotence. The powerlessness of the cross is the paradigm of God's different mode of power. In the cross, power is the power of identification, participation, endurance, and transformation. The theology of Bethlehem and Golgotha, then, is central to the Christian interpretation and response to human suffering. That is God's way of overcoming the destructive powers of our world.

It is the intention of the doctrine of the incarnation, specifically, and trinitarian doctrine, in more comprehensive form, to claim that the suffering of Jesus is truly the suffering of God in our midst and that the resurrection is God's power of transformation in our midst. We can accept, endure, and transform suffering because God accepts, endures, and transforms suffering into resurrection life.

Karl Barth makes this point from his Calvinist vantage point in *The Humanity of God*. He says of his earlier emphasis on the transcendence of God:

> But did it not appear to escape us by quite a distance that the deity of the living God found its meaning and its power only in the context of His history and of His dialogue with man, and thus in His togetherness with man? . . . Who God is and what He is in His deity He proves and reveals not in a vacuum as a divine being-for-Himself, but precisely and authentically in the fact that He exists, speaks, and acts as the partner of man, though of course as the absolutely superior partner. He who does that is the living God. And the freedom in which he does that is his deity. . . . It is precisely God's deity which, rightly understood, includes his humanity.[50]

Moltmann, from his more Lutheran "theology of the cross," says something similar. "When the crucified Jesus is called 'the image of the invisible God,' the meaning is that this is God, and God is like this. God is not greater than he is in this humiliation. God is not more glorious than he is in this self-surrender. God is not more powerful than he is in this helplessness. God is not more divine than he is in this humanity."[51]

The cross directs our gaze from a lonely, morbid contemplation of our own real anguish, our rabbit-like paralysis in the face of suffering, to the suffering and transforming God in solidarity with us. God undergoes it, accepts it, endures it, and because of that so can we. If we take Bethlehem and Golgotha, the incarnation and the cross, as fundamental to the Christian understanding and response to our suffering, then, just as God accepts the limitations and corruptions of human life, so we can accept our lives in all their sound and fury.

Loneliness, limitations, temptation, and anxiety are part of what it means to be human; chance and bad luck are part of a free and finite world; death is part of the structures of existence. God shows on the cross that these also exist in the very heart of God. They can be accepted, not only because they are part of the created order God has provided, but also because God knows what it is like to be lonely, limited, tempted, anxious, and to die.

But what about premature death? the deaths of hungry children? What about the loneliness of the aged in our youth-oriented culture? of men and women in our prisons? of people without work in our towns and cities? What about the limits experienced by the two-thirds undernourished? the limits felt by women and racial minorities and handicapped? And what about the anxiety that drives an alarming number to suicide? of the fifty-year-olds who are told there is no longer any work for them to do? Are these circumstances to be accepted with joy, knowing that God has also participated in them?

No! The cross does not stand alone in Christian faith. It is one side of a two-sided coin; the other side is the resurrection. God also redeems our suffering. Most Christians do not know how distinctive is this claim among other views. The contrast here between some forms of Judaism and stoicism is striking. Rabbi Richard Rubenstein is utterly clear at this point:

> The Gospel ends beyond tragedy, on a note of hope. Resurrection is the final word. I wish it were so. But I believe my Pharisaic progenitors were essentially correct two thousand years ago when they sadly concluded that the promise of radical novelty in the human condition was a pathetic, though altogether understandable, illusion, that the old world goes on today as it did yesterday and it will tomorrow. Against my deepest yearnings, I am compelled to end with their tragic acceptance rather than the eschatological hope that still pervades my Christian brother after the death of God.[52]

Likewise, there is no resurrection in stoicism. There is no hope that suffering can be transformed into joy or fulfillment; there is only resignation and endurance, for things could not have been otherwise. But for Christians they can be otherwise, because they are otherwise. God raised Jesus from the dead and made him the firstfruits of the new age to come.

Christian faith promises the power of transformation in the face of suffering and evil. If God's mode of conquest is resurrection, creative transformation, we see, then, that there is no possibility that by some fluke God might suddenly decide to suspend God's "powerlessness" and become a Gentile lord who dominates God's creation with violent power. God's vindication of the world's suffering is the world's transformation. God can bring life out of death, hope out of despair, joy out of sorrow. Through the gentle power of re-creation, or transformation, or resurrection, as Charles Wesley said in his hymn, "New life the dead receive."

This does not mean that the Christian promise is that "everything will be all right," for everything has not been, is not, and will not ever be "all right." Suffering is real and can never be expunged; the loss is real and can never be recovered. Everything will not come out "all right," as if the anguish were justified or amounted to nothing in the end. But everything can be resurrected through the power of God in the life of God to become new life. That is not resignation; nor is it denial; nor is it escape. That is conquest from within, a gentle might working to transform suffering into the new creation.

The resurrection from despair to hope, I think, works in the life of the spirit much as it does in the life of nature. I recall an account of Mount Saint Helens given by an airplane pilot as the plane descended into the Portland airport from thirty thousand feet. "For those of you on the right side of the plane," he said, "the snow-covered mountain nearest you is Mount Saint Helens." On May 18, 1980, suddenly, with a force 2,500 times that of the atomic blast at Hiroshima, fire and wind and smoke erupted, bringing down the mountaintop, filling a nearby lake and stream, breaking timber of pine, fir, and hemlock like matchsticks, covering plants and animals with several feet of hot, black ash. In one tick of the clock, a place teeming with life became a valley of dead, dry bones. The ash-covered ground was absolutely sterile and lifeless.

But after a while the volcano produced steam and water, which contained nitrogen and sulphur and provided nutrients for simple organisms. At the same time the wind carried in from hundreds of miles away light, fluffy seeds that quickly took root as they fell into the nutrient-soaked ash. The same wind blew in moths and flies and dragonflies that quickly died from the lack of food, and their tiny bodies provided nutrients for seeds and plants. If there are no other eruptions, in several years Mount Saint Helens will be fully alive again, and eventually will be covered again with tall, thick forest.

The power of the resurrection works like this. It does not eliminate hopelessness and death by slaying the dragon. It works in and through death as a gentle power to re-create new life. And when a final resurrection comes, whatever that means and however that comes, our anguish will not be eliminated or negated but will be transmuted in the life of God. The cross and the resurrection belong together as the two sides of the one Christian response to suffering and evil. They do not negate, they interpret each other.

Easter morning is not a happy ending to an otherwise sad story. The insight of John's Gospel, and of the early church's hymn "God Is Reigning from the Tree," is that Easter is God's writing in vivid sign language that love that is truly compassionate both suffers and is victorious in its suffering. Easter does not contradict Good Friday; Easter vindicates Good Friday. Good Friday—that is how God loves the world, that is how God is victorious over the powers of destruction in the world. God loves the world to the point of sheer passion—through compassion, suffering with, sharing in its anguish.

And hidden within that divine anguish is triumph. It is, as I have stressed over and over, a different kind of triumph than the world in its wisdom knows. "The transformation of Jesus that occurred in resurrection," Marjorie Suchocki says in *God–Christ–Church,* "is no absolute and new beginning. Rather, the transformation is fashioned through the experience of crucifixion. . . . The resurrection power of God does not annihilate the past, it transforms the past."[53]

By presenting the cross as merely the prelude to the resurrection, a day on the way to Easter, or even by separating Good Friday and Easter, as all forms of triumphalism do, we betray our fear of engaging the depth of anguish, both human and divine, and we divulge our lack of comprehension of the way in which God triumphs over suffering. God's victory is through, not over or around, anguish. The victory of God is the victory of suffering love, which transforms death to new life. The pain, sorrow, and alienation of the past are picked up into the life of God, experienced in their fullness, transformed by the divine wisdom, and put back into our lives as new possibilities. In the divine economy compassion and power are correlative terms.

Will this kind of answer satisfy everyone? I doubt it. Our churches are full of people who think of God as a cosmic Caesar who could eliminate their suffering by decree, and so burrow deeper and deeper into self-pity and anger over the question of why God did not prevent the affliction that caused their heartache. The trinitarian God, however, is not a Gentile lord. The Christian God is the God of the cross and resurrection, the God whose power is love and whose might is transformation. Insofar as we are faithful to this tradition, the core of our preaching and counseling will be shaped by a trinitarian and process view of God. There are significant truths from other philosophical and theological perspectives, including theism, but the center holds around the triune identity of God and all that implies about our suffering and transformation.

A Zen tale says something very much like this Christian perspective on our problem. Soyen Shaku walked past a house where he heard much crying because the master of the house lay dead. He entered, being well known in the locality, sat down, and cried with them. Said one of those present, "Master, how can *you* cry? Surely you are beyond such things?" Soyen Shaku answered gently, "It is this which puts me beyond such things."

Liabilities and Assets
in a Trinitarian View of God

1. My most basic question is how thoroughgoing is the revision of the concept of divine power among many of the current trinitarian theologians. Trinitarian answers to the problem of evil still tend to maintain some vestiges of the theistic concepts of power and divine interrelatedness. For all the talk about the relational character of the trinitarian God, the discussion of divine relationships, communion, communication, and interdependence tends to be confined to talk about relationships, communion, communication, and interdependence between the persons within the Godhead. God may be a "so-

ciety" or a "community" or a "family," but the intercommunion takes place inside the Godhead and relationship with the world is external to the eternal divine intercommunion. As Daniel Migliori says, "According to classical trinitarian theology, the three persons of the Trinity have their distinctive identity only in their deepest relationship with each other. They 'indwell' each other; they 'make room' for each other, are incomparably hospitable to each other; or to use still another metaphor, they are united in an exquisite divine dance."[54]

The relationships are intratrinitarian relationships, not internal relationships between God and the world. The history of creation and redemption does not figure prominently in the definition of the triune relationships. As Catherine LaCugna says of Thomas Aquinas, "The structure of the *Summa* shows that Thomas conceives of God first in intradivine terms (God's inner life) and then God's relationship to the creature. . . . The net effect of Thomas's theology is to separate God-Trinity and creature by an ontological chasm that not very easily can be overcome. . . . The combined effect of both Greek and Latin speculative theologies of the Trinity was to depict the Trinity as an intradivine reality, largely cut off from the creature, and self-sufficient."[55] By the medieval period the Trinity has become a monad, internally self-differentiated, but still relating to the creation in much the same way Arius's God had.

It is true that the Cappadocians had predicated relationality at the heart of divine being, and that both contemporary essential and economic interpretations of the Trinity speak of the interrelatedness of God and the world.[56] Nevertheless, there is no inherently reciprocal relationship between God and the world in these forms of trinitarian theology. God in God's being is still unrelated to the world apart from a sovereign, free decision. Thus God still looks very much like the theistic God in terms of the God-world relationship. Although the world depends on God for its being, God does not depend on the world in any sense for God's own being. The relationships finally go only one way. If any relationship or communication or reciprocity exists between God and the world, it is a special, free, and unilateral decision the eternal, omnipotent, aseity God makes in order to establish a derivative relationship with the creation.

When one thinks about interdependence in that sense, one is still thinking out of the theistic concept of being and power. In short, there is nothing intrinsic to a trinitarian concept of God that reconceives power as a social concept outside the Godhead. After God has made a free and unilateral decision to become incarnate in Christ, and thereby to identify with the world in all its messiness, one has the grounds for a nontheistic concept of omnipotence, as all the trinitarians discussed above offer. But the assumption of the framework at the very beginning is the theistic notion of God's aseity, being, and power.[57]

Thus contemporary trinitarian theologians are frequently left with the dilemma that their assumptions are theistic with respect to the nature of the being and power of God while their language about God's relation to the world is nontheistic. While Arthur McGill, for example, redefines power in the life of God as self-giving power, he still assumes the theistic concept of God. "Therefore, should God will that certain creatures dry and shrivel up, losing their vigor and life, he does not attain this by acting upon them positively with violent force, for 'force is no attribute of God.' He simply *withdraws* his action from them."[58] For all his talk about a new conception of divine power defined by the cross and resurrection, his God sounds annoyingly like the theistic God.

Furthermore, even Moltmann, the major spokesperson for the revised trinitarianism of the last two decades, says of the crucified God,

> In the passion of the Son, the Father himself suffers the pains of abandonment. In the death of the Son, death comes upon God himself, and the Father suffers the death of his Son in his love for forsaken man. Consequently, what happened on the cross must be understood as an event between God and the Son of God. In the action of the Father in delivering up his Son to suffering and to a godless death, God is acting in himself. He is acting in himself in this manner of suffering and dying in order to open up in himself life and freedom for sinners. Creation, new creation and resurrection are external works of God against chaos, nothingness and death. The suffering and dying of Jesus, understood as the suffering and dying of the Son of God, on the other hand, are works of God towards himself and therefore at the same time passions of God. God overcomes himself, God passes judgment on himself, God takes the judgment on the sin of man upon himself. He assigns to himself the fate that men should by rights endure. The cross of Jesus, understood as the cross of the Son of God, therefore reveals a change in God, a stasis within the Godhead: "God is other." And this event in God is the event on the cross. It takes on Christian form in the simple formula which contradicts all possible metaphysical and historical ideas of God: God is love.[59]

A related, though somewhat different, point is made by Ted Peters when he points to the dilemma trinitarians face when they talk simultaneously about the divine unity and the divine relationality. When Jungel argues, for example, on his principle of correspondence that what is true for the economic trinity must be true for the immanent trinity, he talks about the divine relationships with the unity of God as a single "person." Within such a concept of person, however, "personalness is necessarily dependent upon someone else to whom one relates. One cannot be personal all by oneself. The question is, Is God personal?"[60] If the idea of person is tied to relationality, as many contemporary trinitarians want to do, then God in the divine unity, the divine "substance," would be one person. But then to whom is the divine person related? If God as a single person is defined by God's relationships, then God as personal requires more than one "person," and that leads to a notion something like Griffin's idea of a metaphysical necessity of something eternally other than God; otherwise one has no correspondence between the internal relational being of the personal God and God's relation to the world. Trinitarians face a dilemma: "to identify the personhood of God with the divine substance would deny the principle of correspondence, but to identify the personhood of God with the three *personae* would deny the divine unity."[61]

Decisive as trinitarian language can be in shaping the Christian perspective on suffering and evil, I do not think it alone is adequate. There are other insights and other doctrines of God that can inform Christian life and thought also. When it comes to the distinctly Christian contribution to theodicy, I believe that contribution can include both trinitarian doctrine and other doctrines of God as well. Consequently, my argument is that both trinitarian doctrine and process philosophical theology can contribute elements to an adequate Christian understanding and response to suffering and evil.

2. Trinitarian theology can be used to underwrite an interpretation of redemption that justifies suffering and evil instead of the transforming of it. The fact of the cross was the deepest scandal in the earliest church. If Jesus was the Messiah, how could he die an ignominious death on a cross? The early church devoted considerable effort to a radical reinterpretation of messiahship and the meaning of a crucifixion on a cross in order to reduce the disgrace. Likewise, the church's classical interpretation of the cross as redemption has become equally a scandal for many Christians today. If Jesus was the subject of his Father's demands for justice, and if God can be represented as a divine child abuser by requiring that his Son be put to death in order to pay for the sins of others, can victims of abuse today interpret the cross and the character of God in any other way than an ultimate justification for abuse? If Christians are to emulate God and God's actions, are we not told by our faith to welcome suffering and abuse as virtuous victims and to worship an abusive God? Or do we require a reinterpretation of the cross today as a symbol of how God was involved in the suffering of the cross?[62]

3. Although it is possible to interpret the cross as divine abuse and as self-immolating sacrifice, there have been and are other ways of interpreting the cross as redemptive. If the relationship between Jesus and God is understood as mutual identification instead of obedient self-sacrifice, and if God's involvement in the cross is understood as God's identification with the pain and suffering of the world to the point of taking that pain and suffering on God-self in an act of total self-identification that leads to resurrection or transformation, instead of as abusive demands for self-immolation, then the cross may be understood as redemption through mutual identification and transformation instead of through punishment and payment.

John Macquarrie offers such an interpretation of the cross. He, too, understands the life and ministry and death of Jesus to be characterized by obedience and absolute self-giving, a life and death that result in reconciliation between God and humanity. However, some ways of interpreting that life and death as reconciliation are more adequate than others. One model that he rejects is the notion of substitutionary atonement, the idea that Christ was punished by the Father for the sins of all people and in the place of all people. Macquarrie calls this model "sub-Christian" and claims it "has to be rejected because of an affront which it offers to reason and conscience."[63]

He interprets the cross, rather, as a paradigm of the extent to which God goes to identify with the evil, sin, and suffering of the world. The self-giving of Christ is continuous with the self-giving of God, and the whole work of atonement is God's work. "The self-giving of Christ, understood as the new sacrifice in which priest and victim are one and the same, brings God's constant self-giving for his creation right into the creation. Here that absolute self-giving, which is of the essence of God, has appeared in history in the work of Jesus Christ, and this is a work on behalf of man, a work of grace."[64] The cross, then, brings into human history the reconciling activity of God in a new and decisive manner, and shows the extent to which God goes to identify with the pain, sorrow, and suffering of the world in order to redeem it.

Whether or not this solves all the problems of the cross as a justification of suffering and abuse is a primary issue represented in much womanist and feminist theology. Although there are other understandings of the work of God in Christ on the cross than the ancient, medieval, or contemporary interpretations of the substitution model—namely, the classic or ransom model and the moral exemplar model—the substitutionary model has been the dominant one in liturgy, hymnody, and theology of the West and has been used to justify suffering as redemptive. Macquarrie's reinterpretation at least attempts to eliminate any abusive features from an interpretation of the cross as redemptive, and thereby eliminate any ideological support for Christians to hypothesize divine abuse from a demanding God or to accept abuse as victims, and Macquarrie's interpretation still emphasizes the self-giving character of God and sustains the claim that this kind of self-giving as identification with the world is redemptive. The power of the cross and resurrection, in his perspective, however, is the power of transformation.

Some may still criticize this as an ideology of suffering, for in the psychology of abuse the victim frequently identifies with the abuser (although, as I understand it, it is identification with the dominating power of the abuser that occurs). Even if a distinctively Christian understanding of the relationship between self-giving love and redemption are interpreted, for instance, by Christine Smith as death and cross as locus and moment of their own defeat and resurrection as victory over death and the cross,[65] I think, nevertheless, we must be very careful to formulate an understanding of the cross as the power of transformation which can create a redeeming instead of oppressive consequence in the lives of those who have suffered most from an ideology of the cross.

It seems to me that the distinctively Christian answer to the problem of suffering and evil is precisely its understanding of the divine power as the identification and transformation of God in the world, especially as that is understood in the cross and resurrection of Jesus Christ. When one takes a trinitarian, and even more specifically, a Christocentric focus on the problem of suffering and evil, the cross and the resurrection become the primary Christian approach to our question. Trinitarianism is not a complete theodicy. It does not offer an answer to the larger speculative questions of the origin and character of evil, such as theism and process theology do. It does not answer every question that can be asked about the causes of human suffering and how Christians can respond to and answer these questions. What it offers, instead, is a distinctive perspective, namely, a narrative and a theological formulation about who God is, what God is like, and how God deals with the pain, sin, sorrow, and suffering of the world. Even though Christians have to be very careful in how they state this claim in order not to be misunderstood, or not inadvertently to provide an ideology that undercuts the very redemption the interpretation claims to offer, this claim stands as the distinctively Christian perspective on the question of evil and suffering.

4. For all these criticisms, however, I conclude with the claim that the process theologies and the trinitarian theologies speak together with one voice in opposition to the theistic answer to the problem of suffering and evil. Their common strategy is to affirm a notion of divine power that is more biblical, is more true to our experience, and is more coherent with the centrality of the cross and resurrection than is theism. Within such a strategy, God "answers" our problem of pain, sorrow, and suffering through God's own suffering and transformation of the world. In contrast to the omnipotent God who wills everything that happens in our lives, they speak together of the suffering and transforming God whose will and power are the redemption of the suffering and evil of the world. To be sure, they come to this shared conclusion from different philosophical and theological points of view. Process theologians think that broader philosophical speculations based on the primary intuitions and claims of the Christian witness lead to this revision of the divine power in human suffering. Trinitarian theologians think of the Christian answer more in terms of the language of Christian liturgy and dogma, which also leads their theology to a radically different view of the redeeming power of God in the face of suffering than much of the tradition offers.

With one voice, then, they speak of a new Christian perspective on the problem of evil. God does not cause our suffering, God does not will our suffering. God identifies with our suffering and works faithfully, everlastingly, and infallibly to transform our suffering into the highest possible good or into life lived within the realm of God's resurrection. This is the distinctively Christian answer to the problem of evil.

In their larger, more comprehensive views on evil, especially if they venture to develop a more comprehensive theodicy, Christians may share some of the insights of Stoics, atheists, Buddhists, deconstructionists, and a wide range of other philosophical perspectives in the West. But their view of God, of the nature of God's power and agency, and of God's relation to the world is the key, the core, the center, the definitive Christian insight or perspective on our question.

At the level of primary vision, Christians should be in dialogue with other visions to see what they can learn about other views of suffering and evil. But the "bias" they bring to the discussion is their distinctive view of divine power and grace. Above all, within their own communities, this vision of God should guide their preaching, teaching, pastoral care, and political life. The questions they ask, the answers they discover, and the life they live in a world full of so much pain, suffering, sin, injustice, and death will be underwritten, shaped, and enacted within their distinctive vision of the suffering and transforming God.

Notes

Notes for Chapter 1

The title of this chapter is based on Gordon Lightfoot's song "The Wreck of the Edmund Fitzgerald," in which he asks where has the love of God gone, as the wives and children of the crewmen aboard a giant ore carrier, which sank in Whitefish Bay in Lake Superior in November 1975, wait to hear the fate of their loved ones. From the album *Summertime Dream*, 1976.

1. William Styron, *Sophie's Choice* (New York: Bantam Books, 1979), 625. The movie version of the story, starring Meryl Streep as Sophie, was directed, produced, and written by Alan Pakula in 1982. For discussion of this novel within the context of Holocaust literature, see Richard Rubenstein and John Roth, *Approaches to Auschwitz: The Holocaust and Its Legacy* (Atlanta: John Knox Press, 1987), 279–83. For a compelling account of the tragedy and suffering of racism in the United States, see the story of Sethe in Toni Morrison, *Beloved* (New York: Penguin Books, 1987).

2. *New York Times Magazine* (July 4, 1995).

3. Larzer Ziff, review of the novel *Sophie's Choice, Commonweal* (May 11, 1979): 278.

4. Nancy Frankenberry, *Religion and Radical Empiricism* (Albany, N.Y.: SUNY Press, 1987), 84. "Before we undertake the comparatively high-level discriminations of the world by means of the senses or linguistic forms, the subject is aware of itself and others as causally efficacious powers mutually interacting with a world of qualitative values where memories of the past and anticipations of the future are felt as given."

5. William Dean, *American Religious Empiricism* (Albany, N.Y.: SUNY Press, 1986), 36.

6. The quote is from the German idealist Malwida von Meysenburg, quoted in William James, *The Varieties of Religious Experience* (New York: Mentor Books, 1958), 304.

7. See, for example, Schubert Ogden's argument on "the strange witness of unbelief," in *The Reality of God* (New York: Harper & Row, 1966), especially chaps. 1 and 4.

8. Philip Ziegler, *The Black Death* (New York: Harper Torchbooks, 1969) chap. 14. *The Encyclopaedia Britannica*, 15th ed. (1985), vol. 9, 493, e~ mates that two-thirds to three-fourths died in various parts of Europe, ~

25,000,000, or one-fourth of the total population, dying during the Black Death. Albert Camus, in *The Plague* (New York: Modern Library, 1948), has Dr. Rieux recalling that he read somewhere of some thirty or so great plagues known in history accounting for nearly a hundred million deaths (p. 35).

9. James Crenshaw, ed., *Theodicy in the Old Testament* (Philadelphia: Fortress Press, 1983), 2; Peter Berger, *The Sacred Canopy: Elements of a Sociological Theory of Religion* (Garden City, N.Y.: Doubleday & Co., 1967), 58.

10. Berger, *Sacred Canopy,* 3.

11. Ibid., 29.

12. Clifford Geertz, "Religion as a Cultural System," in *The Religious Situation,* ed. Donald R. Cutler (Boston: Beacon Press, 1968), 643.

13. Ibid., 661.

14. Daniel Migliori, *Faith Seeking Understanding: An Introduction to Christian Theology* (Grand Rapids: Wm. B. Eerdmans Publishing Co., 1991), 99.

15. Ivan, in Fyodor Dostoevsky, *The Brothers Karamazov* (New York: Bantam, 1970), 294.

16. Frances Young, *Face to Face: A Narrative Essay in the Theology of Suffering* (Edinburgh: T. & T. Clark, 1990), 26.

17. Ibid., 51.

18. Ibid., 67.

19. Albert Camus, *The Plague* (New York: Modern Library, 1948), 35.

20. Eva Fleischner, ed., *Auschwitz: Beginning of a New Era?* (New York: KTAV Publishing House, 1977), 34.

21. *Time* (June 10, 1991).

22. That dream still is alive in some of our cultural heroes and is imbibed at least at a certain level by large numbers of people in our society. See Garry Wills, *Reagan's America* (New York: Penguin Books, 1988), esp. chap. 41, "Original Sinlessness."

23. Isaiah Berlin, *The Crooked Timber of Humanity: Chapters in the History of Ideas,* quoted in *The Christian Science Monitor* (August 26, 1991): 13.

24. See Ernest Becker, *The Denial of Death* (New York: Free Press, 1973), and *The Structure of Evil* (New York: Free Press, 1968).

25. David Thomson, ed., *The New Cambridge Modern History,* vol. 12, "The Era of Violence, 1898–1945," ed. 1960, 1st ed.

26. Gil Elliot, *Twentieth Century Book of the Dead* (New York: Charles Scribner's Sons, 1972), 1. See also Edith Wyschogrod, *Hegel, Heidegger, and Man-Made Mass Death* (New Haven, Conn.: Yale University Press, 1985), in which she describes "the kingdoms of death" and the "logic of mass death" in the modern world.

27. Robert McNamara, interview, *Good Morning America,* ABC, November 24, 1995.

28. Richard Rubenstein and John Roth, *Approaches to Auschwitz: The Holocaust and Its Legacy* (Atlanta: John Knox Press, 1987).

29. This cancer is not confined to our four-hundred-year history with Africa. Executive Order 9066, February 19, 1942, put nearly 120,000 Japanese citizens and alien residents (nearly two-thirds were American born) in ten concentration camps (the term used by Roosevelt) for two-and-a-half years as potential spies and sabo-urs. As Asians they were barred from citizenship, thus leaving them defenseless. Richard Drinnon, *Keeper of the Concentration Camps: Dillon S. Myer and*

American Racism (Berkeley, Calif.: University of California, 1987), and Arthur Zich, "Japanese Americans: Home at Last," *National Geographic* (April 1986).

30. *Time,* "Letters to the Editor" (June 17, 1991).

31. *Time* (June 10, 1991).

32. *Time* (July 1, 1991), 4.

33. Peter Berger, *The Sacred Canopy,* 23.

34. Schubert Ogden, *The Reality of God* (New York: Harper & Row, 1966), chap. 8.

35. Berger, *Sacred Canopy,* 51.

36. Becker, *The Denial of Death.* See also Arthur McGill, *Death and Life: An American Theology* (Philadelphia: Fortress, 1987).

37. Ibid., 13, 15.

38. Becker, *Denial of Death,* chap. 2.

39. Crenshaw, "The Shift from Theodicy to Anthropodicy," in Crenshaw, ed., *Theodicy in the Old Testament,* 4.

40. Ibid.

41. Kenneth Mitchell and Herbert Anderson, *All Our Losses, All Our Griefs: Resources for Pastoral Care* (Philadelphia: Westminster Press, 1983).

42. John Hick, *Evil and the God of Love,* revised ed. (New York: Harper & Row, 1978), chaps. 14, 15.

43. Jeffrey Russell, *Mephistopheles: The Devil in the Modern World* (Ithaca: Cornell University Press, 1986), 17.

44. Ibid., 23.

45. See, for example, the recent work of Ron Rosenbaum on Hitler, "Explaining Hitler," *New Yorker* 71 (May 1, 1995): 50–70; and of Arthur McGill on popular culture, *Death and Life;* and of Russell's various works on the devil.

46. James Poling, *The Abuse of Power: A Theological Problem* (Nashville: Abingdon Press, 1991), 11, 128, 146.

47. Rebecca Chopp, *The Praxis of Suffering: An Interpretation of Liberation and Political Theologies* (Maryknoll, N.Y.: Orbis Books, 1986), 1–3.

48. Wendy Farley, *Tragic Vision and Divine Compassion: A Contemporary Theodicy* (Louisville, Ky.: Westminster/John Knox Press, 1990). She defines "radical suffering" as "suffering that has the power to dehumanize and degrade human beings (for example, child abuse or death camps) and that cannot be traced to punishment or desert" (12). See also pp. 21, 53–54, 64.

49. Carl Goldberg, *Speaking with the Devil: A Dialogue with Evil* (New York: Viking Penguin, 1996), 3–5.

50. "By evil we mean that which thwarts continuously and seriously the potential goodness of creation, destroying alike its intelligibility and meaning and making life as we experience it so threatening, so full of sorrow, suffering, and apparent pointlessness" (Langdon Gilkey, *Maker of Heaven and Earth: A Study of the Christian Doctrine of Creation* [Garden City, N.Y.: Doubleday & Co., 1958], 178).

51. This argument has been made by William Jones in *Is God a White Racist?* (New York: Anchor Press, 1973), and is made by Doughboy [Ice Cube] while sitting in a car with his friends in *Boyz N the Hood.*

52. Rem Edwards, *Reason and Religion: An Introduction to the Philosophy of Religion* (New York: Harcourt Brace Jovanovich, 1972), 30. (Italics added.)

53. David Griffin, *God, Power, and Evil: A Process Theodicy* (Philadelphia: Westminster Press, 1976), 9.

54. For a discussion of the social context of theodicy, see James Livingston, *Modern Christian Thought: From the Enlightenment to Vatican II* (New York: Macmillan & Co., 1971), 5–6.

55. Nel Noddings, *Women and Evil* (Berkeley, Calif.: University of California Press, 1989), 1.

56. Ibid., 130.

57. Jones, *Is God a White Racist?*

58. Kathleen Sands, *Escape from Paradise: Evil and Tragedy in Feminist Theology* (Minneapolis: Fortress Press, 1994), 85, 90, 96, 101, 138–39.

59. Farley, *Tragic Vision,* 12–13, 23–29, 40–41, 59–65.

60. Emile Townes, ed., *A Troubling in My Soul: Womanist Perspectives on Evil and Suffering* (Maryknoll, N.Y.: Orbis Books, 1993), 15, 48, 85–86, 109, 118, 151, 161, 200, 220. Several authors in this volume even refer explicitly to Jones's book on the racist God, pp. 22, 85, 160, 209–10.

61. Edwards, *Reason and Religion,* 30. (Italics added.)

62. Three contemporary examples of efforts at strict theodicy are Alvin Plantinga, *God, Freedom and Evil* (New York: Harper & Row, 1974); Michael Peterson, *Evil and the Christian God* (Grand Rapids: Baker Book House, 1982); and Stephen Davis, *Encountering Evil: Live Options in Theodicy* (Atlanta: John Knox Press, 1981).

63. Farley, *Tragic Vision,* 69.

64. Kenneth Surin, "Theodicy," *Harvard Theological Review* 76 (1983): 225–47. See also *Theology and the Problem of Evil* (Oxford: Basil Blackwell Publisher, 1986).

65. Terrence Tilley, "The Use and Abuse of Theodicy," *Horizons* 11 (1984): 304–19. See also, *The Evils of Theodicy* (Washington, D.C.: Georgetown University Press, 1991).

66. Stanley Hauerwas, *Naming the Silences: God, Medicine, and the Problem of Suffering* (Grand Rapids: Wm. B. Eerdmans Publishing Co., 1990), chap. 2.

67. Ibid., 41.

68. Ibid., 78–79.

69. Ibid., 35.

70. An example of this interpretation of Christianity is offered by P. T. Forsyth in his description of the cross as a means of atonement: "The cross is not a theological theme, nor a forensic device, but the crisis of the moral universe on a scale far greater than earthly war. It is the theodicy of the whole God dealing with the whole soul of the whole world in holy love, righteous judgement and redeeming grace" (*Justification of God* [1916], quoted by Alister McGrath, *Christian Theology: An Introduction* [Oxford: Basil Blackwell Publisher, 1994], 353).

Notes for Chapter 2

The title of this chapter is based on a Ray Stevens song.

1. Joni Eareckson, *Joni* (Grand Rapids: Zondervan Publishing House, 1976).

2. Dave Dravecky, *Comeback* (Grand Rapids: Zondervan Publishing House, 1990).

3. Dave Dravecky and Jan Dravecky, *When You Can't Come Back* (Grand Rapids: Zondervan Publishing House, 1992), 42.

4. Ibid., 142.

5. When I refer to "classical theists," I refer to such theologians in the West as Augustine, *The City of God,* Books 11 and 12; Anselm, *Prosologium* and *Monologium;* Thomas Aquinas, *Summa Theologiae* 1 (God: The Divine Unity), qq.1–26; John Calvin, *Institutes of the Christian Religion,* Book 1, "The Knowledge of God the Creator," chaps. 5, 10–14; René Descartes; Gottfried Leibniz; Immanuel Kant; Friedrich von Hügel; Frederick Schleiermacher, *The Christian Faith,* part 1, sect. 2, and "The Power of Prayer in Relation to Outward Circumstances," in *Selected Sermons of Schleiermacher* (New York: Funk & Wagnalls, n.d.), 38–51; Carl Henry, *God, Revelation, and Authority,* vol. 1 (Waco, Tex.: Word, 1976); James Montgomery Boice, *The Sovereign God* (Downers Grove, Ill.: InterVarsity, 1978), chaps. 9–10.

6. John Hick, "The Judeo Christian Concept of God," in *Philosophy of Religion,* 2d ed. (Englewood Cliffs, N.J.: Prentice-Hall, 1973), 4–14; J. I. Packer, "What Do You Mean When You Say God?" *Christianity Today* (September 10, 1986): 27–31; Rem Edwards, *Reason and Religion: An Introduction to the Philosophy of Religion* (Harcourt Brace Jovanovich, 1972), chap. 7; Boice, *The Sovereign God,* part 3.

7. Elizabeth Johnson, *She Who Is: The Mystery of God in Feminist Theological Discourse* (New York: Crossroad, 1993), 19.

8. Richard Swinburne, *The Coherence of Theism* (Oxford: Clarendon Press, 1977), 2.

9. Packer, "What Do You Mean?" 28.

10. J. L. Crenshaw, "Theodicy," *Interpreter's Dictionary of the Bible, Supplementary Volume,* ed. Keith R. Crim et al. (Nashville: Abingdon Press, 1976), 895.

11. J. Christiaan Beker, *Suffering and Hope: The Biblical Vision and Human Predicament* (Grand Rapids: Wm. B. Eerdmans Publishing Co., 1994), 60.

12. John Hayes, *Introduction to the Bible* (Philadelphia: Westminster Press, 1971), 231–232.

13. Walter Brueggemann, *Old Testament Theology: Essays on Structure, Theme, and Text* (Minneapolis: Fortress Press, 1992), chaps. 1 and 2. These two chapters originally were published as "A Shape for Old Testament Theology, I: Structure Legitimation; and II: Embrace of Pain," *Catholic Biblical Quarterly* 47, 1 and 3 (January and July, 1985): 28–46, 395–415.

14. Brueggemann, *Old Testament Theology,* 15.

15. Ibid. I will pick up the other half of Brueggemann's thesis, the sharp critique of the common theology, in chap. 4.

16. Frederick Schleiermacher, *The Christian Faith* I (New York: Harper Torchbooks, 1963), 200–203, 211 ff.

17. John Hick, *Evil and the God of Love,* rev. ed. (New York: Harper & Row, 1978), chaps. 3–4.

18. Augustine, *Confessions* 7.16.104. See also *On Nature and Grace* 22.534, and *Enchiridion* 11.662. See also *City of God* 11.17, and 12.3.

19. Augustine, *Confessions* 7.4–6, and *City of God* 11.22.

20. Augustine, *On the Spirit and the Letter,* 461; *On Nature and Grace,* 523, and *City of God,* Book 13.

21. Augustine, *On Grace and Free Will,* 767. See also Aquinas, q.22, a.2.

22. Augustine, *City of God* 14.11.255.

23. See Arthur O. Lovejoy, *The Great Chain of Being* (New York: Harper & Brothers, 1936), chap. 7, for a brilliant discussion on this Enlightenment principle, or almost any current literature on pluralism, multiculturalism, and transcultural studies. "Those of more liberal persuasion accept pluralism as a positive aspect of human reality. They affirm diversity, pluraformity and difference as deeply positive human values. Like Jesse Jackson they prefer a rainbow community. For Gayraud Wilmore diversity, for all the exasperating tensions and problems it creates, is an asset. He calls it 'a gift of God to be treasured rather than despised'" (Norman Thomas, "Teaching Religions in a Global Seminary," unpublished, 7).

24. For a similar perception in the context of feminist and womanist discussions of God the Father, see Susan Thistlethwaite, *Sex, Race, and God: Christian Feminism in Black and White* (New York: Crossroad, 1991), 114–17, 121.

25. Cheryl A. Kirk-Duggan, "African-American Spirituals: Confronting and Exorcising Evil through Song," in *A Troubling in My Soul: Womanist Perspectives on Evil and Suffering,* ed. Emile Townes (Maryknoll, N.Y.: Orbis Books, 1993), 161, 165. (Italics in original.)

26. *Luther's Works,* N. Pelikan and H. T. Lehman, eds. (St. Louis: Concordia Publishing House, 1955–76), vol. 33, 189.

27. Calvin, *Institutes of the Christian Religion,* 1.17.218.

28. Ibid., 3.23.948.

29. Ibid., 1.16.2,3,4.

30. Edwards, *Reason and Religion,* 178.

31. Thomas Oden, *The Living God* (San Francisco: Harper & Row, 1987), vol. 1, 75.

32. Calvin, *Institutes,* vol. 2, 956.

33. Calvin, *Commentary on Genesis,* chap. 3, v. 1.

34. The Westminster Confession of Faith, *Book of Confessions* (Louisville, Ky.: Office of the General Assembly, Presbyterian Church [U.S.A.], 1991), 8:6.014, .016, .017.

35. Ibid., 8:6.014.

36. The Constitution of the Presbyterian Church (U.S.A.), Part I, *Book of Confessions* (New York: Office of the General Assembly, 1983), 6.191–6.192.

37. Thomas Aquinas, *Summa Theologica,* Question 22, Article 2, 232–33. Calvin, in one point, makes the same argument, distinguishing between principle and secondary cause. See quote and endnote above.

38. Oden, *Living God,* 80.

39. See, for example, Thomas Dozeman, "The Genesis of Covenant and the Loss of Divine Freedom," United Theological Seminary *Journal of Theology* (1989): 70–77.

40. For a discussion of this difference, see Langdon Gilkey, *Reaping the Whirlwind: A Christian Interpretation of History* (New York: Seabury Press, 1976), chap. 7, esp. 167–170.

41. The Heidelberg Catechism, *Book of Confessions,* 4.027.

42. Leslie Weatherhead, *Time for God* (Nashville: Abingdon Press, 1967), 98–99.

43. Anselm, *Cur Deus Homo,* 1.xvii.

44. Calvin, *Institutes* 1.16.201.

45. Michael Peterson, *Evil and the Christian God* (Grand Rapids: Baker Book House, 1982), 55.

46. Alvin Plantinga, *God, Freedom, and Evil* (New York: Harper Torchbooks, 1974), 64.

47. Stephen Davis, ed., *Encountering Evil: Live Options in Theodicy* (Atlanta: John Knox Press, 1981), 72.

48. Quoted in Ron Rosenbaum, "Staring into the Heart of the Heart of Darkness," *New York Times Magazine* (June 4, 1995): 58.

49. Calvin, *Institutes,* Book 1, chap. 17, 218.

50. H. L. Mencken, *American Mercury* (1929).

51. I do not mean to single out Plantinga for this criticism. Any theodicy in the strict sense of the term falters with this strategy. See, for example, John Hick's Irenean theodicy, in which he too, on the very last page of his book, retreats, finally, to a possibility argument (*Evil and the God of Love,* 386).

52. John Hick, in Davis, *Encountering Evil,* 87.

Notes for Chapter 3

1. Albert Camus, *The Plague* (New York: Modern Library, 1948), 87.

2. Ibid., 87–88.

3. Ibid., 89.

4. Most modern Christians are distressed by the claim that God causes all that happens, and will do whatever they must do to deny this implication of their theistic beliefs. "Prominent in the theology of the last two hundred years is the rejection of the notion that God is the direct author and effector of all events, outward and inward, large and small, significant and insignificant. What the divine rule may entail is the subject of endless debates; but that it does not entail a divine 'causation' or 'determination' of all events is almost universally agreed upon. . . . As we have noted, this tradition of autonomy, enlarged into a central credo of the Enlightenment, traces itself at least back to Job. . . . The strict identification of what happens in nature with the will of God and so with the moral will of God is largely denied" (Langdon Gilkey, "Power, Order, Justice, and Redemption," in *The Voice from the Whirlwind: Interpreting the Book of Job,* ed. Leo Perdue and Clark Gilpin [Nashville: Abingdon Press, 1992], 166–67).

5. Langdon Gilkey, *Reaping the Whirlwind: A Christian Interpretation of History* (New York: Seabury Press, 1976), 168.

6. Lucius Garvin, *A Modern Introduction to Ethics* (Boston: Houghton Mifflin Co., 1953), 450.

7. For a discussion of suffering as judgment in the biblical and theological tradition, see S. Paul Schilling, *God and Human Anguish* (Nashville: Abingdon Press, 1977), chap. 6.

8. Joel Freeman, *God Is Not Fair: Coming to Terms with Life's Raw Deals* (San Bernardino, Calif.: Here's Life Publications, 1978), chap. 4.

9. Ibid., 58.

10. Ibid., 33.

11. Ibid., 59, 62.

12. Another version of this argument is that "we need what we get." Suffering is the *distributive justice* of God directed toward our sin. It has to do with apportioning among individuals whatever goods, privileges, burdens, or restrictions are consistent with the production of the best possible society or with the kingdom of God (Garvin, 451). Suffering is divine punishment, but this punishment seems to be less sadistic. Punishment as distributive justice is oriented toward the future. It is God's corrective justice given for the purpose of remedial training. Such punishment is thought to be good if it works as either a deterrence or a reform in the life of the sufferer. Suffering is God's punishment *in order that* God's purposes of well-being for the individual, for the community, or for the next life may be achieved, not *because of* a past evil deed.

13. Christiaan Beker, *Suffering and Hope: The Biblical Vision and the Human Predicament* (Grand Rapids: Wm. B. Eerdmans Publishing Co., 1987), 45.

14. Ibid., 48.

15. John Telford, ed. *The Letters of the Rev. John Wesley, A.M.,* vol. 5 (London: Epworth Press, 1931), 252.

16. John Hick, *Evil and the God of Love* (New York: Harper & Row, 1978), part 4; and Stephen Davis, ed., *Encountering Evil: Live Options in Theodicy* (Atlanta: John Knox Press, 1981), chap. 2.

17. Beker, *Suffering and Hope,* 97.

18. Ibid., 102.

19. Corrie ten Boom, *The Hiding Place* (Old Tappan, N.J.: Fleming H. Revell Co., 1971), 150, 195.

20. See Richard Veith, *Holy Power, Human Pain* (Bloomington, Ind.: Meyer Stone, 1988).

21. See Marjorie Suchocki's book on original sin from a process philosophy and theology perspective, *The Fall to Violence: Original Sin in Relational Theology* (New York: Contiuuum, 1994). A summary can be found in her essay "Original Sin Revisited," School of Theology at Claremont *Occasional Paper* 1/3 (September 1991): 1–8.

22. Wendy Farley, *Tragic Vision and Divine Compassion: A Contemporary Theodicy* (Louisville, Ky.: Westminster/John Knox Press, 1990), 64.

23. Beker, *Suffering and Hope,* 101.

24. Howard Huston, student paper, Sept. 10, 1991, 2.

25. Joanne Carlson Brown and Rebecca Parker, "For God So Loved the World," in *Christianity, Patriarchy, and Abuse: A Feminist Critique,* ed. Joanne Carlson Brown and Carole Bohn (New York: Pilgrim Press, 1990), 18.

26. Rita Brock, *Journeys by Heart: A Christology of Erotic Power* (New York: Crossroad, 1988), 56.

27. Ibid. Mary Daly discusses this same point under her notion of "the scapegoat syndrome," in *Beyond God the Father* (Boston: Beacon Press, 1973), chap. 3, esp. 75ff.

28. Brown and Parker, "For God So Loved the World," 2.

29. Ibid., 3.

30. Quoted in Mary Daly, *Beyond God the Father,* 13.

31. David Griffin, *God, Power, and Evil: A Process Theodicy* (Philadelphia: Westster Press, 1976), 21–23, 84–86, 252–54.

32. C. S. Lewis, *The Problem of Pain* (New York: Simon & Schuster, 1996; originally published 1962), 33.

33. Stephen Mitchell, *The Book of Job*, transl. Stephen Mitchell (New York: Harper & Row, 1979), xxiii. (Italics original.)

34. Hick, *Evil and the God of Love,* 370.

35. Ibid.

36. John Hick, "Critique of Stephen Davis," in *Encountering Evil,* 86.

37. Ibid., 87.

38. David Griffin, "Critique of Stephen Davis," in *Encountering Evil,* 87–88. John Roth makes a similar argument when he claims that logical possibility does not equal soundness. "Critique of Stephen Davis," in *Encountering Evil,* 90.

39. David Griffin, *Evil Revisited: Responses and Reconsiderations* (Albany, N.Y.: SUNY Press, 1991), 47.

40. See, for example, S. G. F. Brandon, "Idea of God from Prehistory to the Middle Ages," and James Collins, "Idea of God, 1400–1800," and especially Langdon Gilkey, "Idea of God since 1800," in *Dictionary of the History of Ideas,* ed. Philip Wiener (New York: Charles Scribner's Sons, 1973), vol. 2, 331–66.

Notes for Chapter 4

1. William Blake, "The Tiger," in *The Works of William Blake* (Hertfordshire: Wordsworth Poetry Library, 1994), 71–72.

2. *Roger Ebert's Movie Home Companion,* 1989 ed. (Kansas City, Mo.: Andrews & McMeel), 7–8.

3. Nicholas Wolterstorff, *Lament for a Son* (Grand Rapids: Wm. B. Eerdmans Publishing Co., 1987), 67.

4. I must admit to the reader that I found the conclusions of this viewpoint to be so offensive on religious, theological, and moral grounds and so counter to my own experience and intuitions that I taught my course in theodicy three times before I would include this material in the syllabus. However, I finally was forced to include it for three reasons: (1) The experience of a "dark side" of God is one of the important themes of scripture and of many religious persons' lives; (2) I was overwhelmed by the amount of material published in the last few years that reflects this viewpoint in one form or another; (3) I am sufficiently convinced by some of the psychological interpretations of this viewpoint, especially Jung's, that I think this viewpoint has to be encountered seriously and accepted somewhere in any theodicy. I personally find the insights in these two chapters (4 and 5) to be an even worse solution to our encounter with evil than classical theism is. It is, from my viewpoint, the nadir of theism. Nevertheless, there is an intuition or insight that I think is present in this kind of theism that is an important element in any theodicy. My way of dealing with these insights is to formulate a concept of the "ambiguity" of God as it is expressed in some feminist theologies and in the naturalistic theism of Bernard Loomer and Bernard Meland. Nevertheless, this form of theism must be considered here because it expresses the beliefs and the experiences of many Jews and Christians as outlined in chapters 4 and 5.

5. See, also, the contrasting reasons given for David's census-taking sin in numbering his people as reported in 2 Sam. 14:1, 10 and the account in 1 Chron. 21:1.

6. Walter Wink, *Unmasking the Powers: The Invisible Forces That Determine Human Existence* (Philadelphia: Fortress Press, 1986), 175.

7. Robert Carroll, *Jeremiah: A Commentary* (Philadelphia: Westminster Press, 1986), 398.

8. Professors Kathleen Farmer and Thomas Dozeman consider this psalm (along with the Jeremiah passage) to be classical expressions in scripture of clinical depression. What justifies its inclusion in the canon, they argue, is not that it conveys traditional Jewish and Christian forms of faith, but that even though it comes from the deepest of depression, it is addressed to God.

9. Walter Brueggemann, "Psalms of Disorientation," *The Message of the Psalms* (Minneapolis: Augsburg Publishing House, 1984), 79.

10. Ibid., 80.

11. Jay McDaniel, *Of God and Pelicans: A Theology of Reverence for Life* (Louisville, Ky.: Westminster/John Knox Press, 1989), 150.

12. Norman Habel, "In Defense of God the Sage," in *The Voice from the Whirlwind,* ed. Leo Perdue and Clark Gilpin (Nashville: Abingdon Press, 1992), 29.

13. Tryggve Mettinger, "The God of Job: Avenger, Tyrant, or Victor?" in Perdue and Gilpin, *The Voice from the Whirlwind,* 42.

14. Raymund Schwager, *Must There Be Scapegoats?* (San Francisco: Harper & Row, 1987), 47–67.

15. James Poling, *The Abuse of Power: A Theological Problem* (Nashville: Abingdon Press, 1991), 166. See chap. 8, esp. 155–66.

16. G. Stanley Kane, "The Concept of Divine Goodness and the Problem of Evil," *Religious Studies* (March 1975): 49.

17. Richard Veith, in *Holy Power, Human Pain* (Bloomington, Ind.: Meyer Stone, 1988), comes close to implying such an idea in his description of "despotic" ideas of God, although even he does not mean this in the strict sense. He defines "despotism" as divine indifference or injustice or maliciousness. He leaves one with the impression that such a God wills only "evil," though I know of no Christian theologian who leaves one with the impression that God wills only evil or is a devil. "God the despot" implies, rather, that God's goodness is an ambiguous goodness, that is, that divine love includes within it qualities of indifference, injustice, and maliciousness.

18. A student in my theodicy class refers to "what may be described as God's inhumanity to humanity—dare I say God's indivinity to humanity?" Janis Adams, student paper, September 14, 1993.

19. Marie M. Fortune, *Sexual Violence: The Unmentionable Sin* (New York: Pilgrim Press, 1983).

20. Ibid, 194.

21. Ibid., 202.

22. Robert McClelland, *God Our Loving Enemy* (Nashville: Abingdon Press, 1982), 11; cf. pp. 14, 17–19, 32–33, 37–38, 54, 58, 76–80, 100, 116.

23. Belden Lane, "A Hidden and Playful God," *Christian Century* (September 30, 1987): 812–13.

24. Belden Lane, "God Plays Rough for Love's Sake," *Christian Century* (October 14, 1987): 879–81.

25. C. S. Lewis, *A Grief Observed* (New York: Bantam Books, 1961).

26. C. S. Lewis, *The Problem of Pain* (New York: Collier Books, 1962; originally published 1940).

27. Belden Lane, "Fierce Landscapes and the Indifference of God," *Christian Century* (October 11, 1989): 907–10.

28. Judith Plaskow, "Facing the Ambiguity of God," *Tikkun* 6 (September–October, 1991): 70, 96.

29. Ibid., 70.

30. Ibid.

31. Susan Thistlethwaite, *Sex, Race, and God: Christian Feminism in Black and White* (New York: Crossroad, 1991), 63.

32. Rosemary Radford Ruether, "Female Symbols, Values, and Context," *Christianity and Crisis* (January 12, 1987): 463.

33. Ibid., 464–65.

34. Catherine Madsen, "If God Is God She Is Not Nice," *Journal of Feminist Studies in Religion* 5 (Spring 1989): 103–5. See also critical responses from Starhawk, Emily Culpepper, Arthur Waskow, Anne Klein, Karen Baker-Fletcher in the same issue, 105–17.

35. Ibid., 104.

36. Ibid.

37. Kathleen Farmer, "How Long, O Lord? Praying in Anger and Pain," unpublished paper, 5.

38. Ibid., 11.

39. Ibid., 7.

40. David Blumenthal, *Facing the Abusing God: A Theology of Protest* (Louisville, Ky.: Westminster/John Knox Press, 1993), 107. See also 94, 143, 164, 166, 170, 178. 185–86, 224, and chap. 17.

41. Belden Lane, "Dragons of the Ordinary: The Discomfort of Common Grace," *Christian Century* (August 21–28, 1991): 772.

42. Ibid.

43. Mary D. Pellauer, "Love and Abuse," *Christian Century* (November 11, 1987): 1014.

Notes for Chapter 5

The title of this chapter is from Isa. 45:7.

1. Tennessee Williams, *Suddenly Last Summer* (New Directions Publications, 1958), 19–20, 22. For a theological comment on this play, see Gordon Kaufman, *Systematic Theology: An Historicist Perspective* (New York: Charles Scribner's Sons, 1968), 310–11.

2. Mark Twain, "Letter VII," *Letters from the Earth* (New York: Fawcett World Library, 1963), 34.

3. Carl Jung, *Answer to Job* (Princeton, N.J.: Princeton University Press, 1958), x.

4. Ibid., 91.

5. Ibid., 57. See also p. 66.

6. Nel Noddings points out how, ironically, in the book of Revelation "the new God seems very like Yahweh, exacting terrible and irrevocable vengeance" (*Women and Evil* [Berkeley, Calif.: University of California Press, 1989], 26).

7. Jung, *Answer to Job,* 16.

8. Ibid., 7, 57.

9. Ibid., 20.

10. Ibid., 28.

11. Ibid., 91, 93.

12. Ibid., 42.

13. Ibid., 56, also p. 48.

14. Ibid., 43.

15. Ibid., 39.

16. Ibid., xii, xiii.

17. Ibid., 102, xii.

18. James Poling, *The Abuse of Power: A Theological Problem* (Nashville: Abingdon Press, 1991), 72–73.

19. Jung, *Answer to Job,* 106.

20. Jim Garrison, *The Darkness of God: Theology after Hiroshima* (Grand Rapids: Wm. B. Eerdmans Publishing Co., 1982).

21. Ibid., 122.

22. Ibid., 53.

23. Ibid., 109.

24. Garrison also finds evidence for the antinomial character of God in Harsthorne's concept of the "bipolarity" of God. But his interpretation of bipolarity so misrepresents Harsthorne's idea, by equating it with the antinomies of good and evil in Jung's theology, that I have omitted it from this discussion.

25. William R. Jones, *Is God a White Racist?* (Garden City, N.Y.: Doubleday & Co., 1973), xix.

26. Ibid., 6.

27. Ibid., 7.

28. Ibid., 19.

29. Ibid., 30.

30. Ibid., 33.

31. Ibid., 66.

32. John Roth, "Free at Last? The Pragmatism and Predicament of Black Religious Experience," *American Journal of Theology & Philosophy* 1 (January 1980): 33.

33. Jones, *Is God a White Racist?* 68.

34. Ibid., xxii.

35. Richard Rubenstein, *After Auschwitz: Radical Theology and Contemporary Judaism* (Indianapolis: Bobbs-Merrill Co., 1966), 223.

36. Ibid., 153.

37. Ibid., 46; also pp. 52–56.

38. Ibid., 67.

39. Ibid., 69.

40. Ibid., 154.

41. Ibid., 140.

42. Ibid., 198.

43. The literature questioning the goodness of God based on the evidence of history can also be found in Elie Wiesel, *Night* (New York: Avon Books, 1969) and

The Trial of God; David Blumenthal, *Facing the Abusive God: A Theology of Protest* (Louisville, Ky.: Westminster/John Knox Press, 1993); and John Roth's and Frederick Sontag's works on theodicy.

44. John Roth, *A Consuming Fire: Encounters with Elie Wiesel and the Holocaust* (Atlanta: John Knox Press, 1979).

45. John Roth, "A Theodicy of Protest," in *Encountering Evil: Live Options in Theodicy,* ed. Stephen Davis (Atlanta: John Knox Press, 1981), 20.

46. Ibid., 7–8.

47. Ibid., 33.

48. Ibid., 11.

49. For a theology of "the God of evil," see Frederick Sontag, *God, Why Did You Do That?* (Philadelphia: Westminster Press, 1970); *The God of Evil: An Argument from the Existence of the Devil* (New York: Harper & Row, 1970); *What God Can Do* (Nashville: Abingdon Press, 1979); and "Anthropodicy and the Return of God," in Davis, ed., *Encountering Evil: Live Options in Theodicy,* 137–66.

50. See Don Crosby, *The Specter of the Absurd: Sources and Criticisms of Modern Nihilism* (Albany, N.Y.: SUNY Press, 1988).

51. See, for example, Terence Fretheim's idea of "story and generalization" with respect to the biblical idea of God in *The Suffering of God: An Old Testament Perspective* (Philadelphia: Fortress Press, 1984), 24–29.

52. "Busybodies and Crybabies: What's Happening to the American Character?" *Time* (August 12, 1991): 14–22.

53. Walter Brueggemann, "A Shape for Old Testament Theology, II: Embrace of Pain," *Catholic Biblical Quarterly* 47 (1985): 405.

54. Wiesel, *Night,* 78–79.

55. See Robert M. Brown, "Elie Wiesel's Case Against God," *Christian Century* (January 30, 1980): 109–112.

56. Elie Wiesel, *The Trial of God* (New York: Schocken Books, 1986), 123.

57. Ibid., 125.

58. Ibid., 158.

59. Ibid., 161.

60. In addition to Wiesel, the reader may want to read Blumenthal, *Facing the Abusive God,* chap. 17, and pp. 155, 164, 178–80, 185–89, 200, 225, 235, 240, 242, 247.

61. Brown, "Elie Wiesel's Case," 112.

62. The most powerful expression of this argument in contemporary philosophy of religion is *New Essays in Philosophical Theology,* ed. Anthony Flew and Alasdair MacIntyre (London: SCM Press, 1955), chap. 6, esp. 96–99.

63. Susan Thistlethwaite, " 'I Am Become Death': God in the Nuclear Age," *Lift Every Voice: Constructing Christian Theologies from the Underside* (San Francisco: HarperCollins, 1990), 96.

64. See the criticism of Jung in James Williams, *The Bible, Violence and the Sacred: Liberation from the Myth of Sanctioned Violence* (San Francisco: Harper-Collins, 1991), 178–84. A sympathetic view of Jung and the problem of evil can be found in John Sanford, *Evil: The Shadow Side of Reality* (New York: Crossroads, 1987), esp. chap. 9.

65. Williams, *The Bible, Violence and the Sacred,* 179.

66. Ibid., 184.

67. John Cobb, "Response to Loomer," *American Journal of Theology & Philosophy* (January and May, 1987): 52.

68. Julie Carmean, "Divine Goodness Redefined," class paper, October 31, 1989, 1–2.

Notes for Chapter 6

The title of this chapter is from Joe Smith, *I Beg Your Pardon, I Never Promised You a Rose Garden,* recorded by Lynn Anderson (Sulphur, Louisiana: Lowery Music Publisher, 1971).

1. Michael Crichton, *Jurassic Park* (New York: Ballantine Books, 1990), 313.

2. As one example, see Philip Hefner, "Is Theodicy a Question of Power?" *Journal of Religion* (January 1979): 90–91.

3. Philip Hefner, "The Problem of Evil: Picking Up the Pieces," *Dialog* 25 (Spring 1986): 89.

4. These quotation are taken from Tom Dozeman, review of Keith Ward, *Divine Action* (San Francisco: Harper San Francisco, 1991) in his review in *American Journal of Theology & Philosophy* 14 (May 1993): 207–8.

5. Ibid., 209.

6. The NRSV translates the passage as, "In the beginning when God created the heavens and the earth, the earth was a formless void and darkness covered the face of the deep, while a wind from God swept over the face of the waters."

7. David Griffin, "Creation out of Chaos and the Problem of Evil," *Encountering Evil: Live Options in Theodicy,* ed. Stephen Davis (John Knox Press, 1981), 101. One of the most significant criticisms of the process interpretation and rejection of *ex nihilo* is proposed by Robert Neville, *Creativity and God: A Challenge to Process Theology* (New York: Seabury Press, 1980).

8. For a process-relational interpretation of creation, see Bernard Loomer, "A Process-Relational Conception of Creation," in *Cry of the Environment: Rebuilding the Christian Creation Tradition,* ed. Philip Joranson and Ken Butigan (Santa Fe, N.Mex.: Bear & Co., 1984), 321–28; and Bernard Meland, "A Creative God at Work," *Seeds of Redemption* (New York: Macmillan Co., 1947), chap. 4.

9. Jon Levenson, *Creation and the Persistence of Chaos: The Jewish Drama of Divine Omnipotence* (San Francisco: Harper & Row, 1988). For comment on Griffin's and Levenson's interpretation of creation out of chaos, see Norman Habel, "In Defense of God the Sage," in *The Voice from the Whirlwind: Interpreting the Book of Job,* ed. Leo Perdue and Clark Gilpin (Nashville: Abingdon Press, 1992), 35.

10. Ibid., 47.

11. Ibid., 135.

12. Nikos Kazantzakis, *Report to Greco,* quoted in John Cobb, *God and the World* (Philadelphia: Westminster Press, 1969), 53.

13. See, for example, Eliot Porter and James Gleick, *Nature's Chaos* (New York: Viking Penguin, 1990), and John Briggs, *Fractals: Patterns of Chaos; Discovering a New Aesthetic of Art, Science, and Nature* (New York: Simon & Schuster, 1992).

14. Martha Nussbaum, "The Misfortune Teller," *New Republic* (November 26, 1990): 30.

15. Jay McDaniel, *Of God and Pelicans: A Theology of Reverence for Life* (Louisville, Ky.: Westminster/John Knox Press, 1989), 35.

16. J. Wesley Robbins, "Neo-Pragmatism and the Philosophy of Experience," *American Journal of Theology & Philosophy* (May 1993): 187.

17. Charles Hartshorne, "Understanding Freedom and Suffering," *Catalyst Tape,* vol. 12, no. 9.

18. Douglas John Hall agrees, at least to a degree, with my argument here. Although the biblical view of the radical reality of human suffering is not identical to the Greek, Shakespearean, or Ibsenite view of tragedy, so that "the last word is not a word about the fatal or futile nature of human existence but about the enduring logos which lends to history, for all its apparent vanity and absurdity, a permanent worth and meaning," and therefore, the tragic dimension is "not the ultimate one" in the biblical story, he nevertheless argues that the tragic dimension "is certainly present there, and profoundly so." Whatever the relation between Athens and Jerusalem, these two "foundational spiritual traditions of Western civilization" can point to their common understanding of the tragic element in human life and history (*God and Human Suffering* [Minneapolis: Augsburg Publishing House, 1986], 32–33). This theme is also considered by Reinhold Niebuhr in his discussion of the relation of the concepts of irony and tragedy. *Faith and History: A Comparison of Christian and Modern Views of History* (New York: Charles Scribner's Sons, 1951), 9; and *The Irony of American History* (New York: Charels Scribner's Sons, 1952), chap. 8.

19. One of the other problems in making tragedy a comprehensive idea in the Christian perspective is that it can be used to convince more and more people about the inevitability of suffering, thereby giving a priori victory to the annihilators. On the other hand, to continue on blithely behind the rhetoric of an outmoded optimism in our modern American culture is tantamount to endorsing the repressive and abusive infrastructures of our culture. See Hall, *God and Human Suffering,* 47.

20. Paul Tillich, *The Courage to Be* (New Haven, Conn.: Yale University Press, 1952), chap. 1. "[Collectivist courage] is similar to the Stoic courage to be; and it is in the last analysis Stoicism that underlies that attitude. It is true today as it was in later antiquity that the Stoic attitude, even if appearing in a collectivist form, is the only serious alternative to Christianity" (101).

21. Rosemary Radford Ruether, *Gaia and God: An Ecofeminist Theology of Earth Healing* (San Francisco: Harper San Francisco, 1992), 31.

22. Ibid., 141.

23. Marjorie Suchocki, *The End of Evil: Process Eschatology in Historical Context* (Albany, N.Y.: SUNY Press, 1988), 68.

24. Wendy Farley, *Tragic Vision and Divine Compassion: A Contemporary Theodicy* (Louisville, Ky.: Westminster/John Knox Press, 1990), 53.

25. Ibid., 58.

26. Ibid., 12.

27. Ibid., 25–26.

28. Sidney Hook, "Pragmatism and the Tragic Sense of Life," *Contemporary American Philosophy,* 180–85.

29. Farley, *Tragic Vision,* 61, 64.

30. See Ahn Byung-mu, "Jesus and the Minjung in the Gospel of Mark," in *Minjung Theology: People as the Subjects of History* (Maryknoll, N.Y.: Orbis Books, 1983), 138–52.

31. Andrew Sung Park, *The Wounded Heart of God: The Asian Concept of Han and the Christian Doctrine of Sin* (Nashville: Abingdon Press, 1993), and "Theology of Han (the Abyss of Pain)," *Quarterly Review,* (Spring 1989): 48–62.

32. Park, *Wounded Heart of God,* 185.

33. Ibid., 10.

34. Ibid., 76.

35. Ibid., 80.

36. Alfred North Whitehead, *Religion in the Making* (New York: Meridian Books, 1926), 16.

37. Rita Brock, *Journeys by Heart: A Christology of Erotic Power* (New York: Crossroad, 1988), 26.

38. Ibid., 34.

39. Ibid., 39.

40. The standard discussion of this concept in twentieth-century Protestant theology has been Andres Nygren, *Agape and Eros: A Study of the Christian Idea of Love and the History of the Christian Idea of Love* (Philadelphia: Westminster Press, 1953).

41. Brock, *Journeys by Heart,* 41.

42. Bernard Loomer, "Two Kinds of Power," *Criterion* (Winter 1976): 14.

43. Ibid., 18.

44. Ibid., 20.

45. Ibid.

46. The importance of this value theory in all process-relational theologies and theodicies, including both the process theologians and the naturalistic theologians, should be pointed out here, as so much of their argument depends on this theory of value, in contrast to the theor(ies) of value that underlie most of classical theism.

47. Schubert Ogden, "Evil and Belief in God: The Distinctive Relevance of 'Process Theology,'" *Perkins Journal* (September 1978): 32.

48. Ibid., 33.

49. Alfred North Whitehead, *Process and Reality* (New York: Harper & Brothers, 1929), 519–20.

50. Griffin, in *Encountering Evil,* 153.

51. Ibid., 28.

52. See, for example, Karl Barth, *The Humanity of God* (Richmond: John Knox Press, 1960), 37–38, 41.

Notes for Chapter 7

1. "Great Is Thy Faithfulness," *United Methodist Hymnal* (Nashville: United Methodist Publishing House, 1989), hymn no. 140. Copyright © 1923. Renewal 1951 by Hope Publishing Co., Carol Stream, IL 60188. All rights reserved. Used by permission.

2. Harold Kushner, *When Bad Things Happen to Good People* (New York: Avon

Books, 1981). See also the videotape, *When Bad Things Happen to Good People,* from WTVI Charlotte, distributed by Atlas Video, 1992; and the videotape, *Human Suffering and the Power of God: Rabbi Harold Kushner Interviewed by John Cobb,* distributed by the Center for Process Studies, Claremont, Calif., 1984.

3. Kushner, *When Bad Things Happen to Good People,* 30.

4. Ibid., 43.

5. Ibid., 44.

6. Ibid., chap. 4.

7. Ibid., 46.

8. Ibid., 53.

9. Ibid., 79.

10. Ibid., 81.

11. Ibid., 134.

12. Ibid.

13. Ibid., 146.

14. Leslie Weatherhead, *The Will of God* (Nashville: Abingdon Press, 1944, 1976). Over half a million copies of this book were sold.

15. As Douglas Hall says in his comments on the book, "The basic project in which Rabbi Kushner is involved here is, in my opinion at least, right: representatives of the Judeo-Christian tradition do grave injustice to their sources when they interpret the deity in terms of power." *God and Human Suffering: An Exercise in the Theology of the Cross* (Minneapolis: Augsburg Publishing House, 1986), 155. Also, Langdon Gilkey comments, "This point raises some interesting questions about perhaps the most important contemporary theological interpretation of the problem of evil, namely, that of process theology" ("Power, Order, Justice, and Redemption: Theological Comments on Job," in *The Voice from the Whirlwind: Interpreting the Book of Job,* ed. Leo Perdue and Clark Gilpin [Nashville: Abingdon Press, 1992], 160).

16. Kushner, 81, 148.

17. Ibid., 85.

18. See Abraham Heschel, *The Prophets,* 2 vols. (New York: Harper & Row, 1975, originally 1936); and Douglas Witt, "'And God Repented': Heschel's Theology of Pathos and Our Contemporary Portrait of God," United Theological Seminary *Journal of Theology,* 1987, 67–73.

19. Hall, *God and Human Suffering,* 156.

20. Norman Adams, review of Kushner's book in *Theology Today* 39 (October 1982): 335–36.

21. For instance, Kenneth Surin, in his criticism of process theology for jettisoning the idea of *apatheia,* an essential idea to the classical doctrine of God, says, "It is not entirely clear whether process theologians have a warrant for believing that God's putative inability to suffer emotionally with creaturely beings *necessarily* implies that God is not capable of 'redemptive' involvement with the sufferings of such creatures. Contrary to this belief, it may be possible to affirm that God is 'involved' with the sufferings of creatures *without* having to jettison the 'axiom of apatheia'" ("Process Theology," in *The Modern Theologians: An Introduction to Christian Theology in the Twentieth Century,* ed. David Ford, vol. 2 [Oxford: Basil Blackwell Publisher, 1989], 109).

22. Many of the same arguments are made by Terrence Fretheim in *The Suf-*

fering of God: An Old Testament Perspective (Philadelphia: Fortress Press, 1984).
See also, on the changeability of God, James Crenshaw, *Theodicy in the Old Testament* (Philadelphia: Fortress Press, 1983), 10.

23. Terence Fretheim, "The Repentance of God: A Key to Evaluating Old Testament God-Talk," unpublished, 2.

24. Ibid., 14.

25. See Jon Levenson's point on this, *Creation and the Persistence of Chaos: The Jewish Drama of Divine Omnipotence* (San Francisco: Harper & Row, 1988), chap. 12.

26. Brueggemann, *Old Testament Theology*, 35.

27. Ibid., 42.

28. Andrew Sung Park, *The Wounded Heart of God: The Asian Concept of Han and the Christian Doctrine of Sin* (Nashville, Abingdon Press, 1993), 121.

29. Ibid.

30. His basic texts are: David Griffin, *God, Power, and Evil: A Process Theodicy* (Philadelphia: Westminster Press, 1976), especially part 3; "Creation out of Chaos and the Problem of Evil," in *Encountering Evil: Live Options in Theodicy*, ed. Stephen Davis (Atlanta: John Knox Press, 1981), 101–36; and *Evil Revisited: Responses and Reconsiderations* (Albany, N.Y.: SUNY Press, 1991).

31. Griffin, "Creation out of Chaos and the Problem of Evil," 105.

32. John Cobb, *God and the World* (Philadelphia: Westminster Press, 1969), 90. Charles Hartshorne defines omnipotence as adequate and maximal power. "Adequate cosmic power is power to set conditions which are maximally favorable to desirable decisions on the part of local agents. . . . Instead of saying that God's power is limited, suggesting that it is less than some conceivable power, we should rather say: his power is absolutely maximal, the greatest possible, but even the greatest possible power is still one power among others, is not the only power. God can do everything that a God can do, everything that could be done by 'a being with no possible superior'" (*The Divine Relativity* [New Haven, Conn.: Yale University Press, 1948], 135–38).

33. Marjorie Suchocki, *God–Christ–Church* (New York: Crossroad, 1982), 82–83.

34. Hick, *Evil and the God of Love*, rev. ed. (New York: Harper & Row, 1978), 52.

35. John Cobb and David Griffin, *Process Theology: An Introductory Exposition* (Philadelphia: Westminster Press, 1976), 65–66.

36. For a description of the process view accessible to new students, see Suchocki, *God–Christ–Church*, especially the Appendix; and Norman Pittenger, *Process-Thought and Christian Faith* (New York: Macmillan Co., 1968), Introduction and chap. 1; Cobb and Griffin, *Process Theology: An Introductory Exposition*; and Jay McDaniel, *Of God and Pelicans: A Theology of Reverence for Life* (Louisville, Ky.: Westminster/John Knox Press, 1989), 38, 40.

37. Nikos Kazantzakis, *Report to Greco*, 291–92, quoted in John Cobb, *God and the World*, 53.

38. Cobb, *God and the World*, 82.

39. *The Presbyterian Hymnal* (Louisville, Ky.: Westminster/John Knox Press, 1989), hymn no. 319, copyright © 1978 by James K. Manley.

40. Marjorie Suchocki, *The End of Evil: Process Eschatology in Historical Context* (New York: SUNY Press, 1988), 119.

41. For a more explicit discussion of this, see David Griffin, *God, Power, and Evil,* esp. 282–85.

42. David Griffin, "Creation out of Chaos and the Problem of Evil," 107.

43. Griffin, "Creation out of Chaos," 110.

44. For a criticism of any form of Patripassianism, see Christiaan Beker, *Suffering and Hope: The Biblical Vision and the Human Predicament* (Grand Rapids: Wm. B. Eerdmans Publishing Co., 1987), 96–98.

45. Woody Allen in the movie *Love and Death.*

46. Philip Hefner, "Is Theodicy a Question of Power?" *Journal of Religion* (January 1979): 91.

47. James Ross, *Journal of the American Academy of Religion* (1970), 314–15.

48. Wolfhart Pannenberg, "A Theological Conversation with Wolfhart Pannenberg," *Dialog* 11 (1972): 294.

49. John Roth, "Roth's Critique," in *Encountering Evil: Live Options in Theodicy,* ed. Stephen Davis (Atlanta: John Knox Press, 1981) 121.

50. George Forrell, "Contra Process Eschatology," *Dialog* 15 (Summer 1976): 214.

51. Delwin Brown, review of *Evil and the Process God,* by Barry Whitney, *Journal of the American Academy of Religion* 54 (Fall 1986): 619.

52. Phillip Devenish, "Evil and Theism: An Analytic-Constructive Resolution of the So-Called Problem of Evil," University Microfilms, 1977.

53. Norman Adams, review of *When Bad Things Happen to Good People,* by Harold Kushner, *Theology Today* 39 (October 1982): 336.

Notes for Chapter 8

1. Elie Wiesel, *Night* (New York: Avon Books, 1960), 76.

2. For recent interpretations of this story, see Dorothy Soelle, *Suffering* (Philadelphia: Fortress Press, 1975), 145; Jurgen Moltmann, *The Crucified God: The Cross of Christ as the Foundation and Criticism of Christian Theology* (New York: Harper & Row, 1974), 373–74; Kenneth Surin, "Theodicy," *Harvard Theological Review,* 240–41; and Paul Brand and Philip Yancey, *In His Image,* 279–80.

3. Eberhard Jungel, *God as the Mystery of the World: On the Foundations of the Theology of the Crucified One in the Dispute between Theism and Atheism* (Grand Rapids: Wm. B. Eerdmans Publishing Co., 1983), 371.

4. Daniel Migliori, *Faith Seeking Understanding: An Introduction to Christian Theology* (Grand Rapids: Wm. B. Eerdmans Publishing Co., 1991), 114–16.

5. This thesis is shared also by Ted Peters. "What process theists . . . have in common with the Barthian legacy is exploration of the temporal character of God and process character and relational character of the divine reality. . . . The process school has no patent on such ideas, however. They are now the common property of nearly all participants to the current trinitarian discussion." *God as Trinity: Relationality and Temporality in Divine Life* (Louisville, Ky.: Westminster/John Knox Press, 1993), 122. For a discussion of the idea of the Trinity by process theologians, see Joseph Bracken and Marjorie Suchocki, eds., *Trinity in Process: A Relational Theology of God* (New York: Continuum, 1996).

6. Athanasius, *Orations against the Arians,* Book 3, in *The Christological Con-*

troversy, ed. Richard Norris (Philadelphia: Fortress Press, 1980), 93, 101. See also p. 90. The same argument is made by Nestorius in his "First Sermon against the Theotokos," where he says "that Christ as God is unaffected by change," 26; see also pp. 130 and 137; and by Cyril of Alexandria in his "Second Letter to Nestorius," 133, 134, and 144.

7. Harold Kushner, *When Bad Things Happen to Good People* (New York: Avon Books, 1981), 85.

8. Terrence Fretheim, *The Suffering of God: An Old Testament Perspective* (Philadelphia: Fortress Press, 1984), 123–26, 126–37, and 148.

9. Marjorie Suchocki, "God, Sexism, and Transformation," in *Reconstructing Christian Theology,* ed. Rebecca Chopp and Mark Taylor (Minneapolis: Fortress Press, 1994), 30–31.

10. Daniel Day Williams, *What Present Day Theologians Are Thinking,* rev. and enlarged ed. (New York: Harper & Brothers, 1959).

11. Ronald Goetz, "The Suffering of God: The Rise of a New Orthodoxy," *The Christian Century* (April 16, 1986), 385–89.

12. Susan Thistlethwaite, "I Am Become Death: God in the Nuclear Age," in *Lift Every Voice: Constructing Christian Theologies from the Underside* (New York: HarperCollins, 1990), 106.

13. The debate about theism is not confined to process and trinitarian theologians. Discussion about the extent to which God is to be identified with theism has taken place within at least three different contexts: (1) When scholars in the American Philosophical Association debate the existence or nonexistence of God, the debate usually assumes that it is the theistic God that is under discussion, whereas in the American Academy of Religion, especially in the Philosophy of Religion and Religious Reflection sections, the discussion is seldom about theism but more frequently about any concept of God at all, from religious feminism to theological naturalism to pragmatism to postmodernism. (2) John Cobb points out that in the English-speaking world, belief in God is virtually equivalent with theism, whereas in Germany since Kant very few philosophers or theologians have called themselves theists or taken their bearing from theism ("The Problem of Evil and the Task of Ministry," in *Encountering Evil: Live Options in Theodicy,* ed. Stephen Davis [Atlanta: John Knox Press, 1981], 172). (3) The criticism of theism is a recurring theme in a number of other points of view, such as William Placher, *Narratives of a Vulnerable God: Christ, Theology, and Scripture* (Louisville, Ky.: Westminster/John Knox Press, 1994), and Theodore Jennings, *Beyond Theism: A Grammar of God-Language* (New York: Oxford University Press, 1985), chap. 2.

14. Barbara Zikmund, "The Trinity and Women's Experience," *Christian Century* (April 15, 1987): 355. See also Catherine LaCugna, "The Practical Trinity," *Christian Century* (July 15 and 22, 1992), and *God for Us: The Trinity and Christian Life* (Harper SanFrancisco, 1991), and "The Baptismal Formula, Feminist Objections, and Trinitarian Theology, *Journal of Ecumenical Studies* (Spring 1989), 235–50. See also Patricia Wilson-Kastner, *Faith, Feminism and the Christ* (Philadelphia: Fortress Press, 1983), 131–37, and Susan Thistlethwaite, note 12 above.

15. Migliori, *Faith Seeking Understanding,* 116.

16. Eberhard Jungel, *The Doctrine of the Trinity: God's Being Is in Becoming* (Grand Rapids: Wm. B. Eerdmans Publishing Co., 1976), 100, n.150.

17. See Ted Peters' discussion in *God as Trinity: Relationality and Temporality* 90–91.

18. Jungel, *The Doctrine of the Trinity,* 63.

19. Ibid., 83

20. Peters, 92. "Jungel's assumption and assertion is that because God is self-related, God can be world-related. . . . Evidently, according to Jungel, if God were not self-related, God could not be world-related" (93).

21. Eberhard Jungel, *God as the Mystery of the World,* 346–47.

22. Ibid., 352, 357.

23. Ibid., 363.

24. Ibid., 364.

25. Ibid., 368.

26. Jurgen Moltmann, *The Crucified God: The Cross of Christ as the Foundation and Criticism of Christian Theology* (New York: Harper & Row, 1974), 201.

27. Ibid., 207

28. Ibid., 201.

29. Ibid., 214–15

30. Ibid., 243, 245

31. Ibid., 264–65.

32. Ibid., 247.

33. Andrew Park, *The Wounded Heart of God: The Asian Concept of Han and the Christian Doctrine of Sin* (Nashville: Abingdon Press, 1993), 120–27.

34. Ibid., 121.

35. Ibid.

36. Ibid., 125.

37. Ibid., 127.

38. In addition to the Bracken and Suchocki book noted above, earlier process discussions of the Trinity include Norman Pittenger, *God in Process* (London: SCM Press, 1967); Anthony Kelly, "Trinity and Process: Relevance of the Basic Christian Confession of God," *Theological Studies* (September 1970); Norman Pittenger, "Trinity and Process: Some Comments in Reply," *Theological Studies* (June 1971); Lewis Ford, "Process Trinitarianism," *Journal of the American Academy of Religion* (June 1975); John Cobb, *Christ in a Pluralistic Age* (Philadelphia: Westminster Press, 1975); Norman Pittenger, *The Divine Triunity* (Philadelphia: Pilgrim Press, 1977); Schubert Ogden, "On the Trinity," *Theology* (1980); Joseph Bracken, "Process Philosophy and Trinitarian Theology," *Process Studies* (Summer 1981); Marjorie Suchocki, *God–Christ–Church: A Practical Guide to Process Theology,* new rev. ed. (Crossroad, 1982); Joseph Bracken, *The Triune Symbol: Persons, Process and Community* (Cranbury, N.J.: Associated University, 1991).

39. Pittenger, *The Divine Triunity,* 116. Pittenger proceeds to say, "If th[ ] entails some stretching of the categories of Process Thought, so be it."

40. See Bracken and Suchocki, eds., *Trinity in Process.*

41. See John Cobb, "The Relativization of the Trinity," in Bracken a[ ] *Trinity in Process,* chap. 1.

42. La Cugna, "The Practical Trinity," 680.

43. Robert W. Jenson, *The Triune Identity: God according to the Gospel* (Philadelphia: Fortress Press, 1982), 4, 21, 47, 51.

44. Kenneth Surin, *Theology and the Problem of Evil* (Oxford: Basil Blackwell Publisher, 1986).

45. William Beardslee et al., *Biblical Preaching on the Death of Jesus* (Nashville: Abingdon Press, 1989), 159.

46. Paul Tillich, *The Courage to Be* (New Haven, Conn.: Yale University Press, 1952), 9.

47. Douglas Hall, *God and Human Suffering: An Exercise in the Theology of the Cross* (Minneapolis: Augsburg Press, 1986), chap. 2.

48. Walter Lowe, "Militarism, Evil, and the Reign of God," in *Reconstructing Christian Theology,* ed. Rebecca Chopp and Mark Taylor (Minneapolis: Fortress Press, 1994), 211.

49. Henry Nelson Wieman, *Religious Experience and the Scientific Method* (New York: Macmillan Co., 1926), 108. See also his *The Source of Human Good* (Carbondale, Ill.: Southern Illinois University Press, 1946), 40–45.

50. Karl Barth, *The Humanity of God* (Richmond: John Knox Press, 1960), 45–46.

51. Moltmann, *The Crucified God,* 205.

52. Richard Rubenstein, *After Auschwitz: Radical Theology and Contemporary Judaism* (Indianapolis: Bobbs-Merrill Co., 1966), 264.

53. Marjorie Suchocki, *God–Christ–Church,* 114.

54. Migliori, *Faith Seeking Understanding,* 69–70.

55. Catherine LaCugna, "God in Communion with Us," in *Freeing Theology: The Essentials in Theology in Feminist Perspective* (San Francisco: Harper SanFrancisco, 1993), 90.

56. In addition to the previous discussions, see also Douglas Ottati, "Being Trinitarian: The Shape of Saving Faith," *Christian Century* (November 8, 1995): 1044–47.

57. This point is also made by Thomas Dozeman in a review of Keith Ward's *Divine Action* and Anna Case-Winters's *God's Power: Traditional Understandings and Contemporary Challenges,* in *American Journal of Theology & Philosophy* 14 (May 1993): 210.

58. Arthur McGill, *Suffering: A Test of Theological Method* (Philadelphia: Westminster Press, 1968), 85–86 (italics in original).

59. Moltmann, *The Crucified God,* 192–93.

60. Peters, *God as Trinity,* 94.

61. Ibid., 95.

62. Among many discussions of this problem, see Christine Smith, *Preaching as Weeping, Confession, and Resistance: Radical Responses to Radical Evil* ᶜ ouisville, Ky.: Westminster/John Knox Press, 1992), 12–13, 152–159. See also Rita ⁻k, *Journeys by Heart: A Christology of Erotic Power* (New York: Crossroad, chap. 3; and Delores Williams, *Sisters in the Wilderness: The Challenge of ᵢst God-Talk* (Maryknoll, N.Y.: Orbis Books, 1993), 161–67.

ⁿ Macquarrie, *Principles of Christian Theology* (New York: Charles Scrib-
ʳ 977), 315.

ᵖ0.

Smith, *Preaching as Weeping,* 154–59.

Bibliography

Adams, Marilyn, and Robert Adams, eds. *The Problem of Evil*. Oxford: Oxford University Press, 1990.

Aichele, George. "Slaughter of the Innocents." *Christian Century* (1978):1262–63.

Allen, Diogenes. "The Witness of Nature to God's Existence and Goodness." *Faith and Philosophy* (January 1984):27–43.

Allison, C. FitzSimmons. *Guilt, Anger, and God*. New York: Seabury Press, 1972.

Anders, Timothy. *The Evolution of Evil*. Chicago: Open Court, 1993.

Arendt, Hannah. *Eichmann in Jerusalem: A Report on the Banality of Evil*. Baltimore: Penguin Books, 1963.

Baldwin, Dalton. "Evil and Persuasive Power: A Response to Madden and Hare." *Process Studies* 3 (Winter 1973):259–72.

Ballentine, Samuel. "Prayers for Justice in the Old Testament: Theodicy and Theology." *The Catholic Biblical Quarterly* 61 (October 1989):597–616.

Barnett, Victoria. *For the Soul of the People: Protestant Protest Against Hitler*. Oxford: Oxford University Press, 1993.

Barnhart, J. E. "Persuasive and Coercive Power in Process Metaphysics." *Process Studies* 3 (Fall 1973):153–57.

Bassinger, David, and Randall Bassinger. "Divine Persuasion: Could the Process God Do More?" *Journal of Religion* (1984):332–47.

———. *Divine Power in Process Theism: A Philosophical Critique*. Albany, N.Y.: SUNY Press, 1988.

———. "Human Coercion: A Fly in the Process Ointment." *Process Studies* 15 (Fall 1986):161–71.

———. "Plantinga's 'Free Will Defense' as a Challenge to Orthodox Theism." *American Journal of Theology & Philosophy* 3 (May 1982):35–41.

———. "Divine Omnipotence: Plantinga and Griffin." *Process Studies* 11 (Spring 1981):11–24.

Bayly, Joseph. "The Suffering of Children." *The Spiritual Needs of Children*. Downers Grove, Ill.: InterVarsity Press, 1982.

Beardslee, William et al. *Biblical Preaching on the Death of Jesus*. Nashville: Abingdon Press, 1989.

Becker, Ernest. *The Denial of Death*. New York: Free Press, 1973.

———. *The Structure of Evil*. New York: Free Press, 1968.

Beker, Christiaan. *Suffering and Hope: The Biblical Vision and the Human Predicament*. Grand Rapids: Wm. B. Eerdmans Publishing Co., 1994.

Berger, Peter. "The Problem of Theodicy." Chap. 3 in *The Sacred Canopy: Elements of a Sociological Theory of Religion*. Garden City, N.Y.: Doubleday & Co., 1967.

Berkovitz, Eliezer. *Faith after the Holocaust*. New York: KTAV Publishing House, 1973.

Bertocci, Peter. "Theism." *Encyclopedia of Religion*. Edited by Micea Eliade. New York: MacMillan Publishing Co., 1987.

Blumenthal, David R. *Facing the Abusing God: A Theology of Protest*. Louisville, Ky.: Westminster/John Knox Press, 1993.

Bouchard, Larry. *Tragic Method and Tragic Theology: Evil in Contemporary Drama and Religious Thought*. University Park, Pa.: Pennsylvania State University Press, 1989.

Bracken, Joseph, and Marjorie Suchocki, eds. *Trinity in Process: A Relational Theology of God*. New York: Continuum, 1996.

Brand, Paul, and Philip Yancey. *Pain: The Gift Nobody Wants; Warning: Life Without Pain Could Really Hurt You*. Grand Rapids: Zondervan Publishing House, 1993.

Breslauer, Daniel. "Theodicy and Ethics: Post-Holocaust Reflections." *American Journal of Theology & Philosophy* 8 (September 1987):137–49.

Brown, Jeanne, and Carole Bohn, eds. *Christianity, Patriarchy and Abuse: A Feminist Critique*. New York: Pilgrim Press, 1989.

Brown, Robert M. *Elie Wiesel: Messenger to All Humanity*. South Bend, Ind.: University of Notre Dame Press, 1983.

———. *Religion and Violence*. Philadelphia: Westminster Press, 1987.

———. "Wiesel's Case against God." *Christian Century* (January 30, 1980):109–12.

Brueggemann, Walter. *Old Testament Theology: Essays on Structure, Theme, and Text*. Minneapolis: Fortress Press, 1992.

———. "Psalms of Disorientation." *The Message of the Psalms*. Minneapolis: Augsburg Publishing House, 1984.

Brummer, Vincent. "Can God Do Evil?" "Can Theodicy Console?" In *Speaking of a Personal God: An Essay in Philosophical Theology*. Cambridge: Cambridge University Press, 1992.

Buber, Martin. *Images of Good and Evil*. London: Routledge & Kegan Paul, 1952.

Burgess-Jackson, Keith. "Free Will, Omnipotence, and the Problem of Evil." *American Journal of Theology & Philosophy* 9 (September 1988):175–85.

Burkle, Howard. *God, Suffering and Belief*. Nashville: Abingdon Press, 1977.

Cain, David. "A Way of God's Theodicy: Honesty, Presence, Adventure." *Journal of Pastoral Care* 32 (December 1978):239–50.

Camus, Albert. *The Myth of Sisyphus and Other Essays*. New York: Vintage Books, 1955.

———. *The Plague*. New York: Modern Library, 1948.

Capon, Robert. *The Third Peacock: The Problem of God and Evil*. San Francisco: Harper & Row, 1986.

Cargas, Harry James. *In Conversation with Elie Wiesel*. Ramsey, N.J.: Paulist Newman Press, 1976.

Carmean, Julie. "The Jig of Grace: Sometimes Limping, Sometimes Leaping: A Relational Theodicy for Equipping Saints for Ministry." D. Min. final document, United Theological Seminary, 1996.

Carr, Karen. *The Banalization of Nihilism: Twentieth-Century Responses to Meaninglessness*. Albany, N.Y.: SUNY Press, 1992.

Case-Winters, Anna. *God's Power: Traditional Understandings and Contemporary Challenges*. Louisville, Ky.: Westminster/John Knox Press, 1990.

Casserly, J. V. Langmead. *Evil and Evolutionary Eschatology: Two Essays*. Lewiston, N.Y.: Edwin Mellen, 1990.

Chopp, Rebecca. *Praxis and Suffering: An Interpretation of Liberation and Political Theology*. Maryknoll, N.Y.: Orbis Books, 1986.

Cobb, John. *God and the World*. Philadelphia: Westminster Press, 1969.

———. "The Problem of Evil and the Task of Ministry." In *Encountering Evil: Live Options in Theodicy,* ed. Stephen Davis. Atlanta: John Knox Press, 1981.

Cobb, John, and David Griffin. *Process Theology: An Introductory Exposition*. Philadelphia: Westminster Press, 1976.

Cohn-Sherbok, Dan. *Holocaust Theology*. London: Lamp Press, 1989.

Commins, Gary. "Woody Allen's Theological Imagination." *Theology Today* 54 (1987):235–49.

Cone, James. *A Black Theology of Liberation*. 2d ed. Maryknoll, N.Y.: Orbis Books, 1986.

———. *God of the Oppressed*. New York: Seabury Press, 1975.

———. *The Spirituals and the Blues*. New York: Seabury Press, 1972.

Conway, John. "God and the Germans: Political Witness under Hitler." *Christian Century* (May 19 and 26, 1993):550–53.

Cooper, Burton. *Why, God?* Atlanta: John Knox Press, 1988.

Crenshaw, James. "Popular Questioning of the Justice of God in Ancient Israel." *Zeitschrift fur Die Atttestanmenkicke Wissenschaft* 82 (1970):380–95.

———. "Theodicy." *Interpreter's Dictionary of the Bible*. Supplementary Volume. Nashville: Abingdon Press, 1976, 895–96.

———. *Theodicy in the Old Testament*. Philadelphia: Fortress Press, 1983.

Crosby, Donald. *The Specter of the Absurd: Sources and Criticisms of Modern Nihilism*. Albany, N.Y.: SUNY Press, 1988.

Cunningham, Lawrence. "Pure Evil." *Notre Dame Magazine* 23 (Summer 1994): 42–44.

Dart, John. "Woody Allen, Theologian." *Christian Century* (June 22 and 29, 1977):585–89.

Davidson, Basil. *The African Slave Trade*. Rev. and exp. ed. Boston: Little, Brown & Co., 1980.

Davidson, Joshua. "Salvage." *The Atlantic Monthly* (August 1995):76–88.

Davis, Stephen, ed. *Encountering Evil: Live Options in Theodicy*. Atlanta: John Knox Press, 1981.

———. "God the Mad Scientist: Process Theology on God and Evil." *Themelois* 5 (September 1979):18–23.

Dean, William. "From Integrity to Size." *American Journal of Theology & Philosophy* (January and May, 1987):1–17.

———. "Theology and Boredom." *Religion in Life* 47 (Spring 1979):109–18.

Devenish, Philip. *Evil and Theism: An Analytic-Constructive Resolution of the So-Called Problem of Evil*. Ann Arbor: University Microfilms, 1977.

Dostoevsky, Fyodor. *The Brothers Karamazov*. New York: Bantam Books, 1970.

Douglas, Jane. "Calvin's Use of Metaphorical Language for God: God as Enemy and God as Mother." *Princeton Seminary Bulletin* 8 (1987):19–32.

Drinnon, Richard. *Keepers of Concentration Camps: Dillon S. Myer and American Racism*. Berkeley, Calif.: University of California Press, 1987.

Durham, Ronald. "Evil and God: Has Process Made Good Its Promise?" *Christianity Today* (1978): 10–14.

Eareckson, Joni. *Joni*. Grand Rapids: Zondervan Publishing House, 1976.

Eliot, Gil. *Twentieth Century Book of the Dead*. New York: Charles Scribner's Sons, 1972.

Ellul, Jacques. *Violence: Reflections from a Christian Perspective*. New York: Seabury Press, 1969.

Erisksen, Robert P. *Theologians Under Hitler: Gerhard Kittel, Paul Althaus and Emanuel Hirsch*. New Haven, Conn.: Yale University Press, 1985.

Fackenheim, Emil. *God's Presence in History: Jewish Affirmation and Philosophical Reflections*. New York: Harper & Row, 1972.

———. *To Mend the World: Foundations of Post-Holocaust Jewish Thought*. Bloomington, Ind.: Indiana University Press, 1993.

Farley, Edward. *Good and Evil: Interpreting a Human Condition*. Minneapolis: Fortress Press, 1990.

Farley, Wendy. *Tragic Vision and Divine Compassion: A Contemporary Theodicy*. Louisville, Ky.: Westminster/John Knox Press, 1990.

Fasching, Darrell. *The Ethical Challenge of Auschwitz and Hiroshima: Apocalypse or Utopia?* Albany, N.Y.: SUNY Press, 1993.

————. *Narrative Theology after Auschwitz: From Alienation to Ethics.* Minneapolis: Fortress Press, 1992.

Feinberg, John S. *The Many Faces of Evil: Theological Systems and the Problem of Evil.* Grand Rapids: Zondervan Publishing House, 1994.

Fewell, Donna Nolan, and David Gunn. *Gender, Power, and Promise: The Subject of the Bible's First Story.* Nashville: Abingdon Press, 1993.

Fiddes, Paul. *The Creative Suffering of God.* Oxford: Oxford University Press, 1988.

Fleischner, Eva. *Auschwitz: Beginning of a New Era.* New York: KTAV Publishing House, 1977.

Foley, Daniel Patrick. "Eleven Interpretations of Personal Suffering." *Journal of Religion and Health,* 27 (1988):321–28.

Ford, Lewis. "Divine Persuasion and Coercion." *Encounter* 47 (Summer 1986): 267–73.

————. "Divine Persuasion and the Triumph of the Good." *The Christian Scholar* 50 (Fall 1967):235–50.

Forell, George. "Contra Process Eschatology." *Dialog* 15 (Summer 1976):214–17.

Forstman, Jack. *Christian Faith in Dark Times: Theological Conflicts in the Shadow of Hitler.* Louisville, Ky.: Westminster/John Knox Press, 1992.

Fortune, Marie. *Sexual Violence: The Unmentionable Sin.* New York: Pilgrim Press, 1983.

Fox, Matthew. *Original Blessing: A Primer in Creation Spirituality.* Santa Fe, N. Mex.: Bear and Company, 1983.

Frank, Anne. *The Diary of a Young Girl.* New York: Washington Square Press, 1947.

Frankenberry, Nancy. "Some Problems in Process Theodicy." *Religious Studies* 17 (June 1981):179–97.

Frankl, Victor. *Man's Search for Meaning: An Introduction to Logotherapy.* New York: Washington Square Press, 1963.

Freeman, Joel. *"God Is Not Fair": Coming to Terms with Life's Raw Deals.* San Bernardino, Calif.: Here's Life Publishers, 1990.

Fretheim, Terence. "The Repentance of God: A Key to Evaluating Old Testament God-Talk." Unpublished paper delivered at American Academy of Religion on December 8, 1987.

————. *The Suffering of God: An Old Testament Perspective.* Philadelphia: Fortress Press, 1984.

Friedlander, Saul. *Reflections on Nazism: An Essay on Kitsch and Death.* Bloomington, Ind.: Indiana University Press, 1993.

Frymer-Kensky, Tikva. *In the Wake of the Goddess: Women, Culture, and the Biblical Transformation of Pagan Myth.* New York: Fawcett Books, 1992.

Garrison, Jim. *The Darkness of God: Theology after Hiroshima.* Grand Rapids: Wm. B. Eerdmans Publishing Co., 1982.

Geisler, Norman. *The Roots of Evil.* Grand Rapids: Zondervan Publishing House, 1978.

Gerstenberger, E. S., and W. Schrage. *Suffering.* Nashville: Abingdon Press, 1980.

Gilkey, Langdon. "The Christian Understanding of Suffering." *Buddhist Studies* 5 (1985):49–65.

———. *Maker of Heaven and Earth.* Garden City, N.Y.: Doubleday & Co., 1958.

———. *Reaping the Whirlwind: A Christian Interpretation of History.* New York: Seabury Press, 1978.

———. *Shantung Compound.* New York: Harper & Row, 1965.

Goetz, Ronald. "Cosmic Groanings." *Christian Century* (December 2, 1987):1083–87.

———. Review of Creel's *Divine Impassibility. Christian Century* (October 29, 1986):952–54.

———. "The Suffering God: The Rise of a New Orthodoxy." *Christian Century* (April 16, 1986):385–89.

Gordis, Robert. "The Book of Job." *Thesis Theological Cassettes,* part 1, April (15/3); part 2, September (15/4); part 3, October (15/5); part 4, November (15/6); and part 5, December (15/7), 1984.

Gordon, Ernest. *Through the Valley of the Kwai.* New York: Harper & Row, 1962.

Gorman, Ulf. *A Good God? A Logical and Semantical Analysis of the Problem of Evil.* Stockholm, Sweden: Hakan Ohlssons Forlag, 1977.

Green, Ronald. "Theodicy." *Encyclopedia of Religion.* Edited by Mircea Eliade. New York: Macmillan Publishing Co., 1987.

Green, William. *Moira: Fate, God and Evil in Greek Thought.* New York: Harper & Brothers, 1944.

Griffin, David. "A Comparison of Augustinian and Process Theologies." *Faith and Philosophy* 3 (January 1986):54–67.

———. "Creation ex nihilo, the Divine Modus Operandi, and the Imitatio Dei." *Faith and Creativity: Essays in Honor of Eugene Peters.* Edited by George Nordgulen and George Shields. St. Louis: CBP Press, 1988.

———. *Evil Revisited: Responses and Reconsiderations.* Albany, N.Y.: SUNY Press, 1991.

———. "Exchange with Stephen Davis." *Concepts of the Ultimate.* Edited by Linda Tessier. New York: Macmillan Publishing Co., 1989.

———. *God, Power, and Evil: A Process Theodicy.* Philadelphia: Westminster Press, 1976.

———. "The Holy, Necessary Goodness, and Morality." *Journal of Religious Ethics* 8 (Fall 1980):330–49.

———. "Philosophical Theology and Pastoral Ministry." *Encounter* (Summer 1972):230–44.

————. Review of Marjorie Suchocki's *The End of Evil*. *Process Studies* 18 (Spring 1989):57–63. Suchocki's response, 63–69.

————. "Values, Evil, and Liberation Theology." *Process Philosophy and Social Thought*. Edited by John Cobb and Widick Schroeder. Chicago: Center for the Scientific Study of Religion, 1981.

Gutiérrez, Gustavo. *On Job: God-Talk and the Suffering of the Innocent*. Maryknoll, N.Y.: Orbis Books, 1987.

Hagin, Kenneth. *How You Can Know the Will of God*. Tulsa, Okla.: Kenneth Hagin Ministries, 1983.

Hall, Douglas. *God and Human Suffering*. Minneapolis: Augsburg Publishing House, 1986.

Hallman, Joseph. *The Descent of God: Divine Suffering in History and Theology*. Minneapolis: Fortress Press, 1991.

Harper, Albert. *The Theodicy of Suffering*. San Francisco: Mellen Research University Press, 1990.

Hartshorne, Charles. *The Divine Relativity*. New Haven, Conn.: Yale University Press, 1948.

————. *Man's Vision of God*. Chicago: Willett, Clark & Co., 1941.

————. *Omnipotence and Other Theological Mistakes*. Albany, N.Y.: SUNY Press, 1984.

————. "Understanding Freedom and Suffering." *Catalyst Tapes* 12 (1980). P.O. Box 9085, Waco, Texas 76714.

Hauerwas, Stanley. *Naming the Silences: God, Medicine, and the Problem of Suffering*. Grand Rapids: Wm. B. Eerdmans Publishing Co., 1990.

Hayward, Carter. *The Redemption of God: A Theology of Mutual Relation*. Washington, D.C.: University Press of America, 1982.

Hefner, Philip. "God and Chaos: The Demiurge Versus the Unground." *Zygon* 19 (December 1984):469–86.

————. "Is Theodicy a Question of Power?" *Journal of Religion* 59 (January 1979): 87–93.

————. "The Problem of Evil: Picking Up the Pieces." *Dialog* 25 (Spring 1986): 87–92.

Hick, John. *Evil and the God of Love*. New York: Harper & Row, 1978.

————. *Philosophy of Religion*. 3d ed. Englewood Cliffs, N.J.: Prentice-Hall, 1983.

Hook, Sidney. "Pragmatism and the Tragic Sense of Life." In *Contemporary American Philosophies*. London: George Allen & Unwin, 1970, 169–93.

Howard-Snyder, Daniel, ed. *The Evidential Argument for Evil*. Bloomington, Ind.: Indiana University Press, 1996.

Inbody, Tyron. "How Empirical Is Wieman's Theology?" *Zygon* 22 (March 1987): 49–56.

————. "Radical Empiricism and the Problem of Evil." *American Journal of Theology & Philosophy* (January 1991):35–48.

————. "Religious Empiricism and the Problem of Religious Adequacy." Edited by Michael Shermis. In *The Writings of Larry E. Axel: Studies in Liberal Religious Thought*. Lewiston, N.Y.: Edwin Mellen Press, 1992, 247–60.

Janzen, J. Gerald. *Job*. Interpretation: A Bible Commentary for Teaching and Preaching. Atlanta: John Knox Press, 1985.

Jenson, Robert. *The Triune Identity: God According to the Gospel*. Philadelphia: Fortress Press, 1982.

Jonas, Hans. "The Concept of God after Auschwitz: A Jewish Voice." *Journal of Religion* (January 1987):1–13.

Jones, William. *Is God a White Racist?* Garden City, N.Y.: Anchor Books, 1973.

————. "Theodicy and Methodology in Black Theology: A Critique of Washington, Cone and Cleage." *Harvard Theological Review* 64 (1971):541–57.

Jung, Carl. *Answer to Job*. Princeton, N.J.: Princeton University Press, 1958.

Jungel, Eberhard. *The Doctrine of the Trinity: God's Being Is in Becoming*. Grand Rapids: Wm. B. Eerdmans Publishing Co., 1976.

————. *God as the Mystery of the World: On the Foundation of the Theology of the Crucified One in the Dispute between Theism and Atheism*. Grand Rapids: Wm. B. Eerdmans Publishing Co., 1983.

Kane, G. Stanley. "The Concept of Divine Goodness and the Problem of Evil." *Religious Studies* (March 1975):49–71.

Kaufman, Gordon. *Theology for a Nuclear Age*. Philadelphia: Westminster Press, 1985.

Kekes, John. *Facing Evil*. Princeton, N.J.: Princeton University Press, 1990.

Kitamori, Kazoh. *Theology of the Pain of God*. Richmond: John Knox Press, 1965.

Kriewald, Diedra. *Hallelujah Anyhow! Suffering and the Christian Community of Faith*. Mission Education and Cultivation Program Department for The Women's Division, General Board of Global Ministries, the United Methodist Church, 1986.

Kushner, Harold. *When Bad Things Happen to Good People*. New York: Avon Books, 1981.

Lane, Belden. "A Hidden and Playful God." *Christian Century* (September 30, 1987):812–13; "God Plays Rough for Love's Sake," *Christian Century* (October 14, 1987):879–81; "Fierce Landscapes and the Indifference of God," *Christian Century* (October 11, 1989):907–10; "Dragons of the Ordinary: The Discomfort of Common Grace," *Christian Century* (August 21–28, 1991):772–75.

————. "The Jewish Tradition of Arguing with God." *Journal of Ecumenical Studies* 23 (1986):567–86.

Lee, Bernard. "The Helplessness of God: A Radical Re-appraisal of Divine Omnipotence." *Encounter* 38 (Autumn 1977): 325–36.

Levenson, Jon. *Creation and the Persistence of Evil: The Jewish Drama of Divine Omnipotence*. New York: Harper & Row, 1988.

Lewis, C. S. *A Grief Observed*. New York: Bantam Books, 1961.

———. *The Problem of Pain*. New York: Simon & Schuster, 1996.

Linders, Robert. "Theodicy: Dogma and Experience." *Theology Today* 35 (July 1978):196–201.

Little, Paul. *Affirming the Will of God*. Downers Grove, Ill.: InterVarsity, 1971.

Lommer, Bernard. "The Size of God." *American Journal of Theology & Philosophy*. (January and May, 1987):20–51.

Long, James. *Why Is God Silent when We Need Him the Most? A Journey of Faith into the Articulate Silence of God.* Grand Rapids: Zondervan Publishing House, 1994.

Madden, Edward, and Peter Hare. *Evil and the Concept of God*. Springfield, Ill.: Charles C Thomas, Publisher, 1968.

———. "Evil and Persuasive Power." *Process Studies* 2 (Spring 1972):44–48.

Madsen, Catherine. "If God Is God She Is Not Nice." *Journal of Feminist Studies in Religion* 5 (Spring 1989):103–18.

McCloskey, Pat. *When You Are Angry at God*. Mahwah, N.J.: Paulist Press, 1987.

McGill, Arthur. *Death and Life: An American Theology*. Philadelphia: Fortress Press, 1987.

———. *Suffering: A Test of Theological Method*. Philadelphia: Westminster Press, 1982.

McGinn, Bernard. *Antichrist: Two Thousand Years of the Human Fascination with Evil*. San Francisco: Harper SanFrancisco, 1994.

McGrath, Alister E. *The Making of Modern German Christology*. Grand Rapids: Zondervan Publishing House, 1995.

———. *Suffering and God: Why Me? Why Doesn't God Do Something? Does God Care?* Grand Rapids: Zondervan Publishing House, 1995.

McGreggor, Geddes. *Philosophical Issues in Religious Thought*. Boston: Houghton Mifflin Co., 1973.

McWilliams, Warren. "Divine Suffering in Contemporary Theology." *Scottish Journal of Theology* 33:35–53.

———. "The Passion of God and Moltmann's Christology." *Encounter* 40 (Fall 1979):313–26.

———. *The Passion of God: Divine Suffering in Contemporary Protestant Theology*. Macon, Ga.: Mercer University Press, 1985.

———. "Theodicy According to James Cone." *Journal of Religious Thought* 36 (1979):45–54.

Meland, Bernard. *Fallible Forms and Symbols*. Philadelphia: Fortress Press, 1976.

Meltzer, Milton. *Never to Forget: The Jews of the Holocaust*. New York: Harper-Collins, 1976.

Mesle, Robert. *John Hick's Theodicy: A Process Humanist Critique*. New York: St. Martin's Press, 1991.

———. "The Problem of Genuine Evil: A Critique of John Hick's Theodicy," *Journal of Religion* (1986):412–30.

Migliore, Daniel. *Faith Seeking Understanding*. Grand Rapids: Wm. B. Eerdmans Publishing Co., 1991.

Miller, Randolf Crump. "Process, Evil and God." *American Journal of Theology & Philosophy* 1 (May 1980), 60–70.

Mitchell, Stephen. *The Book of Job*. Translated and with an introduction by Stephen Mitchell. New York: HarperCollins, 1992.

Moltmann, Jurgen. *The Crucified God: The Cross of Christ as the Foundation and Criticism of Christian Theology*. New York: Harper & Row, 1974.

———. *The Trinity and the Kingdom of God: The Doctrine of God*. San Francisco: Harper & Row, 1981.

Morris, David. *The Culture of Pain*. Berkeley, Calif.: University of California Press, 1993.

Morrow, Lance. "Evil." *Time* (June 10, 1991):48–53.

Munson, John. *Evil—Is It Real? A Theological Analysis*. Lewiston, N.Y.: Edwin Mellen Press, 1991.

Murphy, Cullen. "Coming to Grief: The Calibration of Misery."*Atlantic Monthly* (September 1991):20–22.

Noddings, Nel. *Women and Evil*. Berkeley, Calif.: University of California Press, 1989.

Nussbaum, Martha. "The Misfortune Teller." *New Republic* (November 26, 1990): 30–35.

Oates, Wayne, and Charles Oates. *People in Pain: Guidelines for Pastoral Care*. Philadelphia: Westminster Press, 1985.

Ogbonnaya, A. Okechukwu. *On Communitarian Divinity: An African Interpretation of the Trinity*. New York: Paragon House, 1994.

Ogden, Schubert. "Evil and Belief in God: The Distinctive Relevance of Process Theology." *Perkins Journal* (Summer 1978):29–34.

Olson, Roger, Douglas Kelly, Timothy George, and Alister McGrath. "Has God Been Held Hostage by Philosophy? A Forum on Free-Will Theism, a New Paradigm for Understanding God," *Christianity Today* (January 9, 1995):30–34.

Outler, Albert. "God's Providence and the World's Anguish." In *The Mystery of Suffering and Death,* edited by Michael Taylor. Staten Island, New York: Alba House, 1973.

Packer, J. I. "What Do We Mean When We Say God?" *Christianity Today* (September 10, 1986):27–31.

Page, Ruth. *Ambiguity and the Presence of God*. London: SCM Press, 1985.

Park, Andrew Sung. "Theology of Han (Abyss of Pain)." *Quarterly Review* (Spring 1989).

———. *The Wounded Heart of God: The Asian Concept of Han and the Christian Doctrine of Sin*. Nashville: Abingdon Press, 1993.

Peck, Scott. *People of the Lie: The Hope for Healing Human Evil.* New York: Simon & Schuster, 1983.

Perdue, Leo, and Clark Gilpin, eds. *The Voice from the Whirlwind: Interpreting the Book of Job.* Nashville: Abingdon Press, 1992.

———. *Wisdom and Creation: The Theology of Wisdom Literature.* Nashville: Abingdon Press, 1994.

Perkins, Davis. "The Problem of Suffering: Atheistic Protest and Trinitarian Response." *St. Luke's Journal of Theology* 23 (December 1979):14–32.

Perry, Michael. "Taking Satan Seriously." *Expository Times* (January 1990):105–12.

Peters, Ted. *God as Trinity: Relationality and Temporality in the Divine Life.* Louisville, Ky.: Westminster John Knox Press, 1993.

Peterson, Michael. *Evil and the Christian God.* Grand Rapids: Baker Book House, 1982.

———, ed. *The Problem of Evil: Selected Readings.* South Bend, Ind.: Notre Dame University Press, 1992.

Pike, Nelson, ed. *God and Evil.* Englewood Cliffs, N.J.: Prentice-Hall, 1964.

———. "Process Theodicy and the Concept of Power." *Process Studies* 12 (Fall 1982):148–67.

Pittenger, Norman. *Cosmic Love and Human Wrong.* New York: Paulist Press, 1979.

Plantinga, Alvin. *God, Freedom and Evil.* New York: Harper & Row, 1974.

Plantinga, Cornelius. "The Perfect Family: Our Model for Life Together Is Found in the Father, Son, and Holy Spirit." *Christianity Today* (March 4, 1988):24–27.

Plaskow, Judith. "Facing the Ambiguity of God." *Tikkun* 6 (September–October 1991):70, 96.

———. *Sex, Sin, and Grace.* Washington, D.C.: University Press of America, 1980.

Pleins, J. David. *The Psalms: Songs of Tragedy, Hope, and Justice.* Maryknoll, N.Y.: Orbis Books, 1993.

Poling, James. *The Abuse of Power: A Theological Problem.* Nashville: Abingdon Press, 1991.

———. *Deliver Us From Evil: Resisting Racial and Gender Oppression.* Minneapolis: Fortress Press, 1996.

Rahner, Karl. "Why Does God Allow Us to Suffer?" *Theological Investigations* 19. New York: Crossroads, 1983.

Reichenbach, Bruce. *Evil and a Good God.* Fordham Press, 1982.

Richmond, Kent. *A Time to Die: A Handbook for Funeral Sermons.* Nashville: Abingdon Press, 1990.

Ricoeur, Paul. "Evil." *Encyclopedia of Religion.* Edited by Mircea Eliade. New York: Macmillan Publishing Co., 1987.

———. *The Symbolism of Evil.* Boston: Beacon Press, 1967.

Rittner, Carol, and John Roth. *Different Voices: Women and the Holocaust.* New York: Paragon House, 1993.

Robbins, Jerry. "The Negative Theodicy of Elie Wiesel." *Dialog* 26 (Spring 1987): 131–33.

———. "A Pastoral Approach to Evil." *Theology Today* 44 (January 1988):488–95.

Rosenbaum, Ron. "Explaining Hitler." *New Yorker* 71 (May 1, 1995):50–70.

———. "Staring into the Heart of the Heart of Darkness." *New York Times Magazine* (June 4, 1995):36–72.

Roth, John. *A Consuming Fire: Encounters with Elie Wiesel and the Holocaust.* Atlanta: John Knox Press, 1979.

———. "Free at Last? The Pragmatism and Predicament of Black Religious Experience." *American Journal of Theology & Philosophy* 1 (January 1980): 29–36.

Rubenstein, Richard. *After Auschwitz: History, Theology, and Contemporary Judaism.* Indianapolis: Bobbs-Merrill Co., 1969. 2d ed. Baltimore: Johns Hopkins University Press, 1992.

———. *The Cunning of History: The Holocaust and the American Future.* New York: Harper Torchbooks, 1975.

———. "Job and Auschwitz." *Union Seminary Quarterly Review* 25 (Summer 1970):421–437.

Rubenstein, Richard, and John Roth. *Approaches to Auschwitz: The Holocaust and Its Legacy.* Atlanta: John Knox Press, 1987.

Ruether, Rosemary Radford. "Female Symbols, Values, and Context." *Christianity and Crisis* (January 12, 1987):460–64.

———. *Sexism and God-Talk: Toward a Feminist Theology.* Boston: Beacon Press, 1983.

———. *Gaia and God: An Ecofeminist Theology of Earth Healing.* New York: HarperCollins, 1992.

———. "Matthew Fox and Creation Spirituality: Strengths and Weaknesses." *Catholic World* (July–August 1990):169–72.

Russell, Jeffrey. *The Devil: Perceptions of Evil from Antiquity to Primitive Christianity.* Ithaca, N.Y.: Cornell University Press, 1977.

———. *Mephistopheles: The Devil in the Modern World.* Ithaca, N.Y.: Cornell University Press, 1986.

———. *The Prince of Darkness: Radical Evil and the Power of the Good in History.* Ithaca, N.Y.: Cornell University Press, 1988.

———. *Satan: The Early Christian Tradition.* Ithaca, N.Y.: Cornell University Press, 1981.

Ryan, Michael, ed. *Human Responses to the Holocaust: Perpetuators and Victims, Bystanders and Resisters.* New York: Edwin Mellen Press, 1981.

Saiving, Valerie. "The Human Situation: A Feminine View." *Journal of Religion* 40 (April 1960):100–112.

Samuelson, Norbert. *Judaism and the Doctrine of Creation.* Cambridge: Cambridge University Press, 1994.

Sands, Kathleen. *Escape from Paradise: Evil and Tragedy in Feminist Theology.* Minneapolis: Augsburg, 1994.

Sanford, John. *Evil: The Shadow Side of Reality.* New York: Crossroads, 1987.

Schilling, S. Paul. *God and Human Anguish.* Nashville: Abingdon Press, 1977.

———. "God and Suffering in Christian Hymnody." *Religion in Life* (1979):323–36.

Schwager, Raymund. *Must There Be Scapegoats? Violence and Redemption in the Bible.* San Francisco: Harper & Row, 1987.

Schwartz, Hans. *Evil: A Historical and Theological Perspective.* Minneapolis: Fortress Press, 1994.

Schriener, Susan E. *Where Shall Wisdom Be Found? Calvin's Exegesis of Job from Medieval and Modern Perspectives.* Chicago: University of Chicago Press, 1994.

Shaw, Marvin. "The Romantic Love of Evil: Loomer's Proposal of a Reorientation in Religious Naturalism." *American Journal of Theology & Philosophy* 10 (January 1989):33–42.

Simon, Ulrich. *A Theology of Auschwitz: The Christian Faith and the Problem of Evil.* Atlanta: John Knox Press, 1979.

Skrade, Carl. *God and the Grotesque.* Philadelphia: Westminster Press, 1974.

Smedes, Lewis. *Forgive and Forget: Healing the Hurts We Don't Deserve.* New York: Harper & Row, 1984.

Smith, Christine. *Preaching as Weeping, Confession, and Resistance: Radical Responses to Radical Evil.* Louisville, Ky.: Westminster/John Knox Press, 1992.

Soelle, Dorothy. *Suffering.* Philadelphia: Fortress Press, 1975.

Sontag, Frederick. *The God of Evil: An Argument from the Existence of the Devil.* New York: Harper & Row, 1970.

———. *God, Why Did You Do That?* Philadelphia: Westminster Press, 1970.

———. *What God Can Do.* Nashville: Abingdon Press, 1979.

Sontag, Frederick, and John Roth. "Toward a New American Theodicy." *Drew Gateway* 46 (1975–76):56–64.

Sproll, R. C. *God's Will and the Christian: Your Will, God's Will, and How They Relate.* Wheaton, Ill.: Tyndale House, 1984.

Stone, Jerome. *A Minimalist Vision of Transcendence.* Albany, N.Y.: SUNY Press, 1992.

Stuermann, Walter. "God Does Not Play Dice." *Journal of Bible and Religion* 28 (October 1960):399–406.

———. *The Divine Destroyer: A Theology of Good and Evil.* Philadelphia: Fortress Press, 1967.

Styron, William. *Darkness Visible: A Memoir of Madness.* New York: Random House, 1990.

Suchocki, Marjorie. *The End of Evil: Process Eschatology in Historical Context.* Albany, N.Y.: SUNY Press, 1988.

————. *The Fall to Violence: Original Sin in Theological Perspective*. New York: Continuum, 1994.

————. "The Question of Immortality." *Journal of Religion* 57 (July 1977):288–306.

————. "Original Sin Revisited." Occasional paper, no. 3, School of Theology at Claremont, September 1991:1–7.

Surin, Kenneth. "Theodicy?" *Harvard Theological Review* 76 (1983):225–47.

————. *Theology and the Problem of Evil*. Oxford: Basil Blackwell Publisher, 1986.

Sutten, Robert Chester III. *Human Existence and Theodicy: A Comparison of Jesus and Albert Camus*. New York: Peter Lang, 1993.

Swiebocka, Teresa. *Auschwitz: A History in Photographs*. Bloomington, Ind.: Indiana University Press, 1993.

Taylor, Richard. *Good and Evil: A New Direction*. New York: Macmillan Co., 1970.

ten Boom, Corrie. *The Hiding Place*. Old Tappan, N.J.: Fleming H. Revell Co., 1971.

Tennent, F. R. *Sources of the Doctrines of the Fall and Original Sin*. Cambridge: Cambridge University Press, 1903.

"Theodicy and Religious Education: A Symposium." *Religious Education* 84 (Winter 1989).

Thompson, Melvyn. *Cancer and the God of Love*. London: SCM Press, 1976.

Thompson, William. *Evil and the World Order*. New York: Harper & Row, 1976.

Tiger, Lionel. *The Manufacture of Evil: Ethics, Evolution, and the Industrial System*. New York: Harper & Row, 1987.

Tilley, Terence. *The Evils of Theodicy*. Washington, D.C.: Georgetown University Press, 1991.

————. "God and the Silencing of Job." *Modern Theology* 5 (April 1989):257–70.

————. "The Use and Abuse of Theodicy." *Horizons* 11 (1984):304–19.

Tillich, Paul. "The Demonic." In *Interpretation of History*. New York: Charles Scribner's Sons, 1936.

————. *Systematic Theology*. Vol. 2. Chicago: University of Chicago, 1962.

Towner, W. Sibley. *How God Deals with Evil*. Philadelphia: Westminster Press, 1976.

Townes, Emilie, ed. *A Troubling in My Soul: Womanist Perspectives on Sin and Evil*. Maryknoll, N.Y.: Orbis Books, 1993.

Tremmel, William. *Dark Side: The Satan Story*. St. Louis: CBP Press, 1987.

Unamuno, Miguel. *The Tragic Sense of Life*. New York: Dover Publications, 1954.

Urban, Linwood, and Douglas Walton, eds. *Power of God: Omnipotence and Evil*. New York: Oxford University Press, 1978.

Van der Poel, Cornelius. *Growing through Pain and Suffering*. Mystic, Conn.: Twenty-Third Publications, 1995.

Vanauken, Sheldon. *A Severe Mercy, with 18 Letters by C. S. Lewis*. New York: Harper & Row, 1980.

Vanderhaar, Gerard. *Why Good People Do Bad Things*. Mystic, Conn.: Twenty-Third Publications, 1993.

Vardy, Peter. *The Puzzle of Evil*. New York: HarperCollins, 1992.

Veith, Richard. *Holy Power, Human Pain*. Oak Park, Ill.: Meyer-Stone Books, 1988.

Viccio, Stephen. *The Voice from the Whirlwind: The Problem of Evil in the Modern World*. Westminster, Md.: Christian Classics, 1989.

Viney, Donald. "Does Omniscience Imply Foreknowledge: Craig on Hartshorne." *Process Studies* (Spring 1989):32–37.

Walls, Jerry. "Can God Save Anyone He Will?" *Scottish Journal of Theology* (June 1985) 38:155–72.

———. *Hell: The Logic of Damnation*. South Bend, Ind.: University of Notre Dame Press, 1992.

Weatherhead, Leslie. *The Will of God*. Nashville: Abingdon Press, 1944. Reprinted 1972.

Wenham, John. *The Enigma of Evil: Can We Believe in the Goodness of God?* Grand Rapids: Zondervan Publishing House, 1985.

West, Cornel. *Keeping Faith: Philosophy and Race in America*. New York: Routledge & Kegan Paul, 1993.

———. *Race Matters*. Boston: Beacon Press, 1993.

Whale, J. S. *The Christian Answer to the Problem of Evil*. London: SCM Press, 1939.

Whitney, Barry. *Evil and the Process God*. New York: Edwin Mellen Press, 1985.

———. "Process Theodicy." *What Are They Saying about God and Evil?* Mahwah, N.J.: Paulist Press, 1989.

———. "Process Theism: Does a Persuasive God Coerce?" *Southern Journal of Philosophy* 17 (1979):133–41.

———. *Theodicy: An Annotated Bibliography on the Problem of Evil: 1960–1990*. New York: Garland Publishing, 1993.

Wiesel, Elie. *Evil and Exile*. South Bend, Ind.: University of Notre Dame Press, 1990.

———. *Messengers of God: Biblical Portraits and Legends*. New York: Summit Books, 1976.

———. *Night*. New York: Avon Books, 1960.

———. *The Trial of God: A Play in Three Acts*. New York: Schocken, 1986.

Williams, Daniel Day. *The Demonic and the Divine*. Minneapolis: Fortress Press, 1990.

Williams, Delores. *Sisters in the Wilderness: The Challenge of Womanist God-Talk*. Maryknoll, N.Y.: Orbis Books, 1993.

Williams, James. *The Bible, Violence and the Sacred: Liberation from the Myth of Sanctioned Violence*. New York: HarperCollins, 1991.

Williams, N. P. *The Ideas of the Fall and Original Sin*. New York: Longmans, Green & Co., 1927.

Williamson, Clark. *A Guest in the House of Israel: Post-Holocaust Church Theology*. Lousiville, Ky.: Westminster/John Knox Press, 1993.

———. "Process Hermeneutics and Christianity's Post-Holocaust Reinterpretation of Itself." *Process Studies* 12 (Summer 1982):77–100.

———. "Things Do Go Wrong (and Right)." *Journal of Religion,* vol. 63 (1986):44–56.

Willimon, William. *Sighing for Eden: Sin, Evil and the Christian Faith*. Nashville: Abingdon Press, 1985.

Wimmer, John. *No Pain, No Gain: Hope for Those Who Struggle*. New York: Ballantine Books, 1985.

Wink, Walter. *Engaging the Powers: Discernment and Resistance in a World of Domination*. Philadelphia: Fortress Press, 1992.

———. *Naming the Powers: The Language of Power in the New Testament*. Philadelphia: Fortress Press, 1984.

———. *Unmasking the Powers: The Invisible Forces That Determine Human Existence*. Philadelphia: Fortress Press, 1986.

Woelfel, James. *Camus: A Theological Portrait*. Nashville: Abingdon Press, 1975.

———. "The Death of God: A Belated Personal Postscript." *Christian Century* (December 29, 1976):1175–78.

Wolterstorff, Nicholas. *Lament for a Son*. Grand Rapids: Wm. B. Eerdmans Publishing Co., 1987.

Woodruff, Paul, and Harry Wilmer. *Facing Evil: Light at the Core of Darkness*. Chicago: Open Court, 1988.

Wyschogrod, Edith. *Spirit and Ashes: Hegel, Heidegger, and Man-Made Mass Death*. New Haven, Conn.: Yale University Press, 1985.

Young, Frances. *Face to Face: A Narrative Essay in The Theology of Suffering*. Edinburgh: T. & T. Clark, 1990.

Young, Henry. "Black Theology and the Work of William R. Jones," *Religion in Life* 44 (Spring 1975):14–23.

Ziegler, Philip. *The Black Death*. New York: Harper Torchbooks, 1969.

Zucker, Wolfgang. "The Demonic: From Aeschylus to Tillich." *Theology Today* 26 (April 1969):34–50.

Index